Henry Kett

Sermons

Preached Before the University of Oxford, at St. Mary's, in the Year MDCCXC.

Second Edition

Henry Kett

Sermons

Preached Before the University of Oxford, at St. Mary's, in the Year MDCCXC. Second Edition

ISBN/EAN: 9783337087920

Printed in Europe, USA, Canada, Australia, Japan

Cover: Foto ©Lupo / pixelio.de

More available books at **www.hansebooks.com**

SERMONS

PREACHED BEFORE THE

UNIVERSITY OF OXFORD,

AT ST. MARY's,

IN THE YEAR MDCCXC.

AT THE

LECTURE

FOUNDED BY THE LATE

REV. JOHN BAMPTON, M.A.

CANON OF SALISBURY.

BY HENRY KETT, M.A.

FELLOW OF TRINITY COLLEGE.

THE SECOND EDITION,
WITH CORRECTIONS AND ADDITIONS.

LONDON:

PRINTED FOR F. AND C. RIVINGTON, N° 62, ST. PAUL'S
CHURCH-YARD; FLETCHER AND COOKE, OXFORD; AND
MERRIL AND LUNN, CAMBRIDGE.

MDCCXCII.

IMPRIMATUR,

JOHAN. COOKE,

Vice-Can. Oxon.

C. C. C.
May 16, 1791.

TO THE

RIGHT REVEREND

LEWIS BAGOT, LL. D.

LORD BISHOP OF ST. ASAPH.

My Lord,

THE satisfaction, which I feel on being permitted to dedicate the following work to your Lordship, is greatly diminished when I reflect upon its deficiency in every point, which to persons of your refined judgment must appear essential to correct and elegant composition. My sermons, therefore, can have no stronger claim to your patronage, than that, which arises from their connexion with those sacred studies, which amid the most important scenes of active life, you have

ever

DEDICATION.

ever found leisure to cultivate. When you formerly presided over that eminent Society, which owes so large a share of its present reputation and splendour to your salutary institutions, your discourses from the pulpit were admirably calculated, by the energetick seriousness of your delivery, and the judicious selection of your topicks, to confirm the Students of Oxford in the genuine principles of Christianity. Your writings have no less contributed to the same useful and honourable end; since the Trustees of Warburton, as well as the Society for the propagation of the Gospel, have happily afforded you an opportunity of giving similar proofs of your pious labours.

If, my Lord, other reasons were wanting, to induce me to make this publick address, I should notwithstanding think myself justified in sheltering these earliest fruits of my ecclesiastical studies under your protection. I contemplate in your Lordship's character a striking resemblance, both with respect to

firmness

DEDICATION.

firmness of principles, and zeal for the honour of religion, to those primitive Christians, whose conduct I have endeavoured to delineate, and whose virtues furnished the brightest model for the imitation of succeeding ages.

I have the honour to be,

MY LORD,

Your most obedient,

And humble Servant,

HENRY KETT.

Extract from the last Will and Testament of the late Reverend JOHN BAMPTON, *Canon of* SALISBURY.

"I direct and appoint, that the eight Divinity Lecture Sermons shall be preached upon either of the following subjects—to confirm and establish the Christian Faith, and to confute all heretics and schismatics, upon the divine authority of the Holy Scriptures, &c."

SERMON I.

JEREMIAH VI. 16.

Stand ye in the ways and see, and ask for the old paths; where is the good way? and walk therein, and ye shall find rest for your souls.

A Vindication of the writings of the Fathers of the church in general, and a Recommendation of the works of the earliest Fathers in particular. Plan of the ensuing Sermons proposed. The object of them to rectify the misrepresentations of Mr. Gibbon and Dr. Priestley, with respect to the history of the primitive church.

SERMON II.

Mark XVI. 20.

And they went forth and preached every where, the Lord working with them, and confirming the Word, with signs following.

The conduct of the primitive Chriſtians conſidered with reference to the ſix real cauſes of the firſt general eſtabliſhment of Chriſtianity. I. The miraculous powers exercised by the Diſciples and Succeſſors of the apoſtles. II. The Apologies of the firſt Chriſtians. III. The zeal of the firſt Miſſionaries.

SERMON III.

Jeremiah I. 19.

They ſhall fight againſt thee, but they ſhall not prevail againſt thee; for I am with thee, ſaith the Lord, to deliver thee.

IV. The Fortitude of the early Martyrs. The different cauſes to which that fortitude may be attributed, and its immediate influence on the Pagan world.

SERMON IV.

EPHESIANS V. 27.

A glorious Church, not having spot or wrinkle, or any such thing, but holy and without blemish.

V. The Discipline of the primitive church, with respect to its internal regulations, and its opposition to heresy. VI. The Virtues of the first Christians. The combined Effects of the foregoing causes upon private manners and publick institutions among the nations converted to the faith.

SERMON V.

ISAIAH XLIII. 9.

Who among the people can declare this, and shew us former things? Let them bring forth their witnesses, that they may be justified: or let them hear and say, It is truth.

Observations on the character of an Historian in general, applied to the Author of the Decline and Fall of the Roman Empire. Particular review of some striking misrepresentations contained in his fifteenth and sixteenth chapters.

SERMON VI.

JUDE, ver. 3.

Earnestly contend for the Faith which was once delivered unto the Saints.

Remarks on the History of the Early Opinions concerning Christ, and an essay towards a refutation of its leading principles.

SERMON VII.

2 TIMOTHY III. 15.

All Scripture is given by inspiration of God.

Evidences given by the earliest Fathers of the church to the books of the New Testament.

SERMON VIII.

HEBREWS XII. 1.

Wherefore seeing we are compassed about with so great a Cloud of Witnesses, let us lay aside every Weight, and the Sin which doth so easily beset us; and let us run with Patience the Race that is set before us; looking unto Jesus, the Author and Finisher of our Faith.

Recapitulation. Analogy between the primitive church and the church of England. Practical inferences.

JEREMIAH VI. 16.

Stand ye in the ways and see, and ask for the old paths; where is the good way? and walk therein, and ye shall find rest for your souls.

THE Prophet, in the verses preceding the text, represents in a strain of animated and striking description the supine indifference of the Jews, not only to the divine commandments, but to the temporal judgments which had been the immediate consequences of their impiety. Although they had been favoured by the peculiar protection of the Almighty, and convinced of his power and goodness by his frequent interference to shield them from impending danger, and to scatter around them the blessings of prosperity, their disobedience was unchecked by his awful remonstrances, and their stubbornness was ob-

A   durate

SERMON I.

durate and incorrigible. Deluded by errour, and enslaved by sin, they were alike forgetful of the pure precepts of the law, and of the great examples of piety and obedience, which the records of Israel held out to their observation.

The advice of the Prophet was not less adapted to the spiritual wants of the Jews, than calculated to display an intimate acquaintance with the infirmities of human nature. Man is ever averse to that retrospection which carries with it a sense of his own misconduct; and in his eagerness to grasp the pleasures of the present moment, he listens not to the admonitions of past experience. Scorning the salutary ties of prescription, he mistakes novelty for excellence; and reflects not that in proportion as he differs from the wise and the exemplary who have gone before him, he may become profligate in sentiment and degenerate in practise. The pride of opinion weakens his reverence for departed virtue, and abates his curiosity *to ask for the old paths,* which his Predecessors trod, even when the pursuit of their steps would free him from the tyranny of disordered passions, and confirm the principles of his wavering mind.

At

SERMON I.

At a period, diftinguifhed as the prefent is, by an eager fpirit of inveftigation, it cannot be thought improper, in humble conformity with the advice contained in the text, to leave the beaten fields of literary refearch, and to explore thofe paths of Ecclefiaftical Learning, which are too undefervedly neglected. While the greateft diligence is applied to every fubject which is honoured with the name of antiquity; he cannot fairly be expofed to cenfure who recommends to general notice thofe objects of fpeculation, which combine an inquiry into remote times with the furvey of characters fo renowned for piety and virtue, as the Fathers of the Church. If his purfuit can in any degree counteract the violence of licentious opinions, and check the progrefs of Infidelity, it cannot be derided for being frivolous, or condemned for being unprofitable. But if it fhould prove an object of higher confequence, by fixing the attention more fteadily upon the great ftandard of moral and religious duty, which is fet up in the Gofpel of Chrift; it may fairly be efteemed the faithful guide to ufeful knowledge, and the powerful auxiliary to true religion.

Whatever relates to thofe, who have participated with us the common privileges of Chriftianity, and made the beft ufe of its advantages,

vantages, for the enrichment of their understanding, as well as the direction of their conduct; is a subject of curious and profitable inquiry. Their characters and actions command our reverence, and their sentiments fail not to excite our curiosity. We naturally desire to know what sense they annexed to the scriptures; what was their conviction of the divine origin of Christianity; and upon what grounds they embraced the faith themselves, and recommended it to others.

Objections rise in various forms to stop the progress of these researches. As much diligence has been employed in multiplying their number, and augmenting their force: the same diligence may not be wholly unsuccessful in reducing them to their natural size, and in shewing that they are very far from being insurmountable.

The Fathers of the Church then, have been represented as unfavourable to the cultivation of rational and manly piety; because we are told, that in their writings occur the reveries of fanaticism, and the conjectures of visionary refinement.

Now, as the use which ought to be made of their works consists in adhering to whatever is excellent, and disregarding whatever is frivolous; no danger can be incurred by the judicious student, if he should meet with some scattered instances of weak argument and unrestrained imagination. Since there is the widest difference between a blind and implicit reverence for every work which is sanctioned by the name of antiquity, and a selection of those parts of its genuine productions which may be made conducive to solid improvement and moral benefit. Such a line of discrimination is universally marked out in all departments of literature and science to make them produce the desired ends. To reject the expositions of the fathers, when they reject the obvious and rational interpretation of scripture, is a valuable and unerring rule, and an effectual security against being misled. The failings of a few, in a few instances, ought not to involve the works of all in indiscriminate and uncandid condemnation. To abandon them because some proofs of visionary refinement are to be found, is equally unreasonable and unjust, as to censure the study of the Hebrew language, on account of the forced constructions of Hutchinson; or to relinquish the researches of natural philosophy, on perusing the fanciful theories of Cartesius.

SERMON I.

Moralists observe that due remarks on the pernicious tendency of vitious indulgence may contribute materially to the regulation of the manners. Pursuing a similar train of reasoning we maintain, that no small degree of intellectual improvement may be derived from contemplating the progress of errour. For if we discover the occasions on which great and enlightened minds have deviated from the paths of right reason into the mazes of falshood, our understandings will be gradually weaned from that implicit homage which we too fondly pay to a favourite name, and we shall become more scrupulous and circumspect in the admission of opinions which are not founded on the basis of truth. The survey of such deviations will extinguish, likewise, the petulance of dogmatism, and the pride of conceit. He who observes, that writers conspicuous for vivacity of fancy, extent of learning, and acuteness of penetration have some times been hurried into weak conclusions, or misled by trifling speculations; will advance with more deliberate and cautious steps in the progress of his inquiries; he will be more candid in his observations, and more inclined to compassionate than to censure the infirmity of the human intellect. When in the course of his studies he remarks that a great mind has in any instance deserted the dictates

SERMON I.

dictates of sober reason for the phantoms of paradox, he will feel a sensation of regret similar to that which is excited on seeing the virtuous fall a sacrifice to the allurements of casual temptation. Comprehensive knowledge and splendid talents afford no constant security against the delusions of fancy, and the wiles of imposture. Origen gave way to the most chimerical expositions of scripture, and Tertullian embraced the preposterous reveries of Montanus. Thus as the great art of life consists in extracting good out of evil; so even from the imperfections of these writers may be drawn those considerations which encourage Humility of mind, and are favourable to genuine Liberality of sentiment.

Considerable learning united with much critical skill has been employed, in endeavouring to expose the Credulity of the fathers. It has been urged that they have admitted many Facts and Opinions to a place in their writings, which were adopted upon insufficient grounds.

Upon an impartial examination of the passages, upon which this charge principally depends for support, it will appear, that many of the supposed errours arise from misrepresentation; that many relate to trifling circumstances, many are difperfed among the sentiments of individuals, and not among the tenets of the church; and have no relation whatever, to publick principles of belief, or publick terms of communion. How therefore thefe peculiarities confpire to make them generally unferviceable in the caufe of religion, it is difficult to comprehend. If any attempts to elevate the fathers to the high rank of the apoftles, were made by their advocates; if they were affirmed to have been affifted by infpiration; or to have been endowed, above the common lot of mankind, with infallibility; the objection would, doubtlefs, carry great force againft fuch ambitious pretenfions. But we contend only that they deferve our regard as witneffes of the opinions of their refpective ages; as hiftorians of the facts which were acceffible to their inquiries; and as teachers whofe piety and learning eminently diftinguifhed them from all their contemporaries. Sharing the imperfections of other writers, they fairly claim the fame indulgence. The faults imputed to them, ought frequently to be imputed to the times in which they lived; when accuracy of refearch was often precluded by numerous obftacles, and when ardent zeal induced them to prefs every circumftance into their fervice, which carried with it even the

appearance

SERMON I.

appearance of truth. If the plea of credulity deferves to be admitted as a ground of rejection, with equal or perhaps fuperiour force does it operate againſt ſome of the moſt celebrated authors of Greece and Rome. But while judgment can difcern the probability of facts; while it can appretiate the credit of witneſſes, and difcriminate the gradations of evidence; the faults of hiſtorians will be weighed againſt their excellencies, and ſuch of them will unqueſtionably be entitled to high eſteem whoſe veracity preponderates in the balance.

This charge, therefore, cannot in any degree induce us to conclude, that becauſe they admitted ſome diſputable facts with too much precipitation, they therefore embraced Chriſtianity itſelf upon infufficient grounds.

For ſuppoſing their credulity to have been as exceſſive as ſome writers are willing to repreſent, whence ariſes the probability that it was the baſis of their converſion? Had Chriſtianity been a *cunningly deviſed fable*, calculated to delude the imagination, and laying no reſtraints on the conduct, there would be ſome colour for the charge; but faith in a crucified Redeemer was not a merely ſpeculative point, which required no more than the paſ-

live

sive assent of the understanding. It by no means resembled an adherence to the Pagan mythology, which charmed the fancy by the beauty of its objects, and even authorized the most depraved corruptions of the heart. The Christian convert was obliged to turn aside from the prospect of worldly interest, to oppose the tide of ridicule and persecution, and to recommend himself to the church by a series of exertions the most opposite to his former pursuits, and the most painful to human nature. His sincerity was called to the severest trial by the austerities of mortification, and by the voluntary rejection of sensual pleasure. It was his daily endeavour to correct all his irregular desires, and it was his steadfast resolve to forfeit even life itself, rather than recant the vows of baptism, and bow before the altar of idolatry. His faith therefore must necessarily have been the result of sober and serious conviction, not of blind and headstrong credulity. In the exercise of his belief he discovered an enlightened understanding, which yielded a ready assent to the evidences of revelation, and followed the dictates of divine truth with alacrity and gladness.

The deficiency of the Fathers with respect to topicks of morality has likewise been much misre-

misrepresented. They have been charged with deviating from the standard of scripture, and with encouraging the subtleties and evasions of disingenuous casuistry. The accusation, however, carries not with it even the slightest plausibility, except when brought against one Father in particular, whose general sentiments are far from justifying so vague a charge. While their accusers censure the rules of conduct marked out by some of the fathers, they make the candid concession, that their characters and actions were eminent for piety and virtue. This tribute of just applause furnishes us with a strong presumption in favour of the soundness of their instructions; since it is highly improbable, that theory should degenerate into corruption, where practise is consistent with the rules of morality and religion. As a decisive argument in vindication of their ethicks, it ought particularly to be observed, that the most judicious modern writers upon the subject of Jurisprudence have derived information from them, and have gratefully acknowledged the favour. The general principles and particular sentiments of Chrysostom and of Basil have given solidity of argument and copiousness of illustration to the celebrated treatises of Grotius and of Pufendorf.

Even

Even the Author whose acute criticisms, and original remarks have given the greatest force to his censures, has candidly acknowledged that peculiar merit which constitutes the strongest recommendation of the ecclesiastical writers. " They abound in strong and
" solid proofs of the fundamental principles of
" Christianity, and they teach many excellent
" things which contribute to the clear under-
" standing of the scriptures, in which these
" mysteries are contained. In this respect,
" their authority is of great use, and may
" serve as a probable argument of the truth."

A declaration such as this, is of no small importance; since it manifestly points out the great advantage of their testimony, by deducing the fundamental principles of the faith through their works. Thus they become eminently useful by furnishing a new and curious illustration of the scriptures, and by supplying a safe repository for the doctrines of the gospel.

From the concessions, therefore, of censurers themselves, may be drawn no small degree of encouragement to prosecute ecclesiastical studies, and to investigate the labours of the wise and good, who zealously espousing

the

SERMON I.   13

the caufe of Chriftianity have written in its vindication, and facrificed every worldly object to its glory. In their works may be found fpecimens of elegant Compofition to gratify the tafte: interefting Facts to enlarge the circle of knowledge; and Examples of piety to amend the heart.

The reader of the fathers is convinced that although the prize of literature is borne away by the claflical authors of Greece and Rome; yet fimilar beauties diftinguifh the compofitions which are the objects of his purfuit. Neither the graces of fimplicity, nor the fplendour of ornament were confined to Xenophon and Plato, nor to Livy and Cicero; for every impartial critick will commend the pure ftile of Lactantius; the rich imagery, and appofite illuftrations of Theodoret; the claffical fluency of Minucius Felix; the uniform perfpicuity of Bafil; the glowing effufions of Gregory of Nazianzum; and the exuberant and attracting eloquence of Chryfoftom, and Cyprian.

To connect the different provinces of literature by new affociations, is a pleafing and a profitable tafk. If fcience has acted as the ufeful ally to theology, the learning of Greece and

and Rome has the beſt pretenſions to claim the ſame honourable employment in the ſervice of ſacred hiſtory. The works of Polybius, Livy and Diodorus Siculus, throw a ſtrong light upon the prophecies of Iſaiah and Daniel. The relations of Suetonius, Tacitus, and Pliny corroborate the evidence of the goſpels, and illuſtrate the early events of the church. The ſentiments of Plato are no leſs uſeful in developing the principles of the antient hereſies; and even from the ſarcaſtick ſallies of Lucian, and the illiberal repreſentations of Julian, may be derived conſiderable information reſpecting the conduct of their chriſtian contemporaries.

From the fathers we may learn with what unremitting care the Holy Scriptures were preſerved during ſucceſſive ages. The quotations which abound in their works furniſh ſtrong and convincing proofs of the authenticity of the preſent copies. By them we are informed that theſe ſcriptures were zealouſly appealed to and conſulted by writers who were unanimous upon no other ſubject. Their authenticity was held to be indiſputable. They were repeatedly made the arbiters of controverſy, and the guides of faith and practiſe. Hence alſo we eſtimate the veneration in which they were

SERMON I. 15

were held, and the vigilance with which they were guarded. Hence we derive the moſt perfect aſſurance and ſtrongeſt evidence that they have eſcaped unmutilated, and uncorrupted from the tumult of Controverſy, the artifice of Fraud, the hoſtility of Paganiſm, and the ravages of Time.

We may not only trace the progreſs of the ſcriptures until the ancient manuſcripts which now exiſt, give the ſtrongeſt aſſurance that no ſubſequent corruption took place; but we may remark likewiſe the various Revolutions of the church. The proſpect of primitive chriſtianity, in all its various ſtates of depreſſion and of triumph, is open to our view. We behold it riſing from the ſhade of obſcurity, oppoſed in its advances to general obſervation by formidable obſtacles, and at length eſtabliſhing an extenſive and ſupreme dominion.

The celebrated work of Euſebius ſtands firſt as a regular hiſtory, in the order both of time and of excellence, to throw light upon this intereſting ſubject. The variety and originality of its contents, as well as the diligence and judgment of the writer, ſuperſede in a great degree, the neceſſity of recurring to other ſources for early intelligence; and ſupply no ſmall conſolation for the loſs of many
monuments

monuments of christian antiquity which have long since perished.

In a survey so comprehensive, examples may be found of the purest and most exalted virtue. Here we may contemplate the strictest integrity of conduct, and the most unremitting attention to duty; zeal tempered by moderation in opposing the encroachments of heresy, and courage free from rashness in defying the malice of power. To the volumes of classical history we are directed by the wisdom of our early teachers, for incentives to the practise of whatever is fair and good. We admire the tranquil dignity of Socrates, the noble moderation of Cincinnatus, and the unconquerable spirit of Hannibal. But is not example more powerfully recommended, and ought it not to have greater efficacy when superiour virtues spring from superiour principles, and are productive of more valuable effects? When obedience to the Supreme Being is the leading inducement to action, and the attainment of everlasting happiness is its transcendant and invaluable end? For this reason, the commendation bestowed upon the illustrious characters of prophane history is languid and transitory, when compared with the sentiments with which we are inspired, on contemplating

SERMON I.

templating the conduct of those who have gone before us in the faith. The ingenuous mind is struck with the perfection of christian principles and with the most chearful obedience to the dictates of the gospel, when it remarks the frugality of the venerable Basil, who although he was the opulent Metropolitan of Cæsarea, bestowed all his revenues upon the poor; the noble moderation of Gregory of Nazianzum, who voluntarily resigned his bishoprick to preserve the harmony of the church; the benevolent condescension of the Empress Pulcheria, who frequently retired from the splendour of a court, to visit the abodes of indigence and sickness; and the mildness of the amiable and learned Pamphilus, when placidly resigning himself to the flaming pile.

Examples such as these, while they rouse the mind of a Christian to sacred emulation, have likewise an immediate tendency to confirm his Faith. The early Converts had the best opportunity to examine the grounds of their religion; since they lived so near to the period when its divine Author appeared upon earth. As they were prompted to act with such unshaken constancy, upon the most trying occasions of life, they must have had full assurance

assurance and perfect satisfaction for the truth and the importance of all they believed. Their conduct therefore naturally impresses upon our minds a stronger persuasion of the truth of their principles, than the most ingenious and acute reasonings of modern Theologists. The arguments in favour of a divine revelation may be opposed by the arguments for Deism, but the evidence of Facts can never be disproved. It is level to the capacities of all Mankind, and produces the speediest, the clearest, and the most durable conviction.

Such is the nature of these studies, such is the information which they hold out to the inquisitive, and such are the advantages which they confer on the impartial.

Far be it however from our design, to paint them in colours that are too splendid, or to bestow on them the commendation of equal and indiscriminate excellence. To render the study of the Fathers truly useful, a distinction must not only be made between the several works of one Author, but between the works of different Authors of different ages. Without subscribing to the censures which are frequently thrown upon the later Fathers of the Church, it may properly be remarked, that the

the manners and cuftoms, the inftitutions, and the literature of the two centuries which immediately fucceeded the Incarnation of our Lord, form objects of infinitely greater importance in the opinion of an ecclefiaftical Student, than any thing which relates to the following times. The feeds of chriftian degeneracy began to be fown in the fourth century. At that period, and perhaps not before, there are vifible traces of thofe rites and eftablifhments which encumbered Chriftianity with burthenfome appendages, and afterwards brought down upon the Church of Rome the juft and weighty charge of corruption. Many Writers have been led into uncandid and confufed mifreprefentation by lofing fight of this important diftinction, and by throwing the fame cenfure upon all the Fathers, have held out fallacious lights to miflead their unfufpecting Readers. The failings of a few have been unjuftly attributed to all; the fentiments of individuals have been reprefented as the language of communities; and the motives, which actuated degenerate ages, have been imputed to the pureft times. In vain therefore we may fometimes look for that accurate delineation of Hiftory which carefully affigns to each period of time its appropriate defects and virtues, and which never blends the difcordant cha-

B 2   racterifticks

racterifticks of various ages in one confufed mafs of unqualified generalization.

The utility of the writings of the Fathers is in many refpects difputable, if placed in competition with more modern Theologifts who have brought more extenfive learning and more found philofophy to the elucidation of fcripture, and have combated the attacks of Infidels with more profound and more fubtle arguments. The ftudy of the Oriental languages, in particular, which among the Antients was almoft intirely confined to Origen and Jerom, and the improvement of the general art of Criticifm, have given a manifeft fuperiority to the Moderns. If however the palm of victory be adjudged to them on account of more extenfive attainments, there is one advantage on the fide of the earlier Fathers which cannot be counterbalanced. Their antiquity places them in an exalted fituation, from which they addrefs us in a tone of fuch folemnity as excites our earneft attention. In the foremoft rank of Chriftians ftand the Apoftles, to whom we pay that reverential deference which is due to the infpired Ambaffadours of Heaven. The next in order are thofe, who enjoyed the unfpeakable fatisfaction and peculiar privilege of converfing familiarly

familiarly with them, and hearing from their facred lips the *words of eternal life*. Their evidence in the caufe of our religion is truly important and valuable, if we confider the high improbability of their deviation in any fundamental point from the principles of doctrine and practice laid down by their great Mafters. They will recommend themfelves more ftrongly to our notice, if we recollect any inftances in which the government of the primitive Churches was committed to their care. From the qualifications enumerated by St. Paul as requifite for a charge fo weighty, we may conclude that the Apoftles were particularly careful in confining the fuperintendance of the chriftian communities to thofe, who were not only eminent for moral graces, but for rectitude of fentiment in all the articles of the faith, as well as for peculiar abilities to communicate inftruction to their flocks. The immediate fucceffors of thefe apoftolical Fathers claim likewife great regard, if we confider their conformity in effential points with the precepts of the Gofpel, and the fentiments of their Predeceffors. Thus the connections with the Difciples of our Lord, although they are in fome degree remote, eftablifh the refpectability, and confirm the credit of the writers

writers to the first and second century; and thus the Apostles become not only conspicuous from their own lustre, but impart splendour to all around them.

Hence from the great store of literature which the Church has accumulated from age to age, there are certain productions which deserve to be selected with peculiar care. The works of those, whose names have been recited, are valuable for elegance of Stile, faithfulness of Narrative, fervour of Piety, or copiousness of Examples. But allowing the strength of these recommendations, we hesitate not to conclude that the first attention of an ecclesiastical student is most properly directed to Clemens Romanus, Ignatius, Polycarp, Justin Martyr, Irenæus, and Athenagoras.

If it be considered that their writings immediately succeeded the publication of the New Testament; that they are the repositaries of sacred History which in the order of time claim the nearest place to the Gospel; that they are the monuments of the sincerity of the early Converts, and the evidences of the authenticity of the New Testament, they become very interesting subjects of speculation.

SERMON I. 23

tion. We shall raise these works to a much greater height of esteem if we consider the situations and the attainments of their respective Authors. The ages in which they flourished were singularly propitious to the acquirement of evangelical knowledge, as they drew christianity from its source. Some of them were exalted to the highest rank in the Church, and others were distinguished by comprehensive learning. Clement, Ignatius, Polycarp and Irenæus, were Bishops of the most populous and celebrated cities of the Roman empire, and Justin and Athenagoras were instructed in the wisdom of the antient Philosophers. The lives of all were consecrated to the faith; and such was their unconquerable adherence to the christian cause, that Ignatius, Polycarp and Justin sealed its truth with their blood.

The field of information which their works open to our view is wide and interesting. Here are to be found the prevailing sentiments of the first Christians, the testimony borne to the inspired volume, and the interpretation first made of its contents. Here are described the first heresies, and what measures were adopted to confute them; the discipline esta-

blished

blished in the infant Church, the form of its government, and the various and cruel machinations of its enemies. Moreover, in them may be seen the earnestness of the primitive Believers for the glory of God, and their solicitude for the salvation of man; what was their support during the vicissitudes of life; and what the ground of their hopes, amid the sufferings of martyrdom.

Such topicks are at all times curious and edifying. In the present day an accurate inquiry into them is more particularly seasonable, when the actions and opinions of the first Christians have been placed in the most unfavourable light, and painted in the darkest colours. When one writer prompted by blind partiality to their implacable enemies, has stripped them of their most distinguished virtues, and defrauded them of their just praise: and when another has elevated the earliest Hereticks to the rank of Orthodox Believers, and drawn arguments from the supposed tenets of the primitive ages, in order to deprive Christianity of its essential doctrine, by reducing the Eternal Son of God to the common level of human nature,

Such

SERMON I.

Such manifeſt prejudice, and ſuch perverſion of hiſtory, need not diſturb the tranquillity of the timid, nor unſettle the principles of the pious; unleſs truth will relinquiſh her antient conqueſts, and leave her cauſe to be tried at the tribunal of the moſt unjuſt miſrepreſentation.

For the *elegant Hiſtorian of the decline and fall of the Roman Empire* is too precipitate in his deciſions, if he thinks that the Religion which has overcome the aſſaults of violence, and repelled the arguments of ſcepticiſm; which has triumphed over every obſtacle that has impeded its progreſs for the long period of ſeventeen centuries, is at length to be ſhaken by the cavils of ſarcaſm, and ſubverted by the artifices of ſophiſtry.

Before an implicit regard be paid to the indefatigable Author of *the Early Opinions concerning Chriſt*, juſtice and impartiality ſeem to require, that the deciſions of the eccleſiaſtical Writers ſhould be fully and accurately exhibited; and that their evidence ſhould not be tortured by prejudice to ſpeak the language of his favourite hypotheſis.

The

The air of novelty which is diffused over the productions of these Writers may operate as an attraction upon the inconsiderate and the unwary. But where novelty is sometimes supposed to exist, on a closer examination, it is not to be found. The dress may strike by its singularity, but on a more accurate inspection, the features of ancient errour will be recognized and detected. Many of their sentiments are the same, or nearly the same, to those which formerly prevailed. Like a subterraneous river they are concealed for a time, and again come forth to view. The fundamental errour of the Unitarians is a modification of the opinion of Socinus, which was derived from the Hereticks of the early ages. Their interpretations of scripture, and their sophistical arguments, are either drawn from the works of Zuicker and of Episcopius, or from the ample compilations of the Brethren of Poland. The degrading description which the *Historian of the decline and fall of the Roman Empire* has given of the Jewish nation may be traced through the popular narratives of Voltaire, and the obsolete works of Collins and Tindal.

To trace the progress of these sentiments and characters, and to ascertain their original Authors,

SERMON I. 27

Authors, is a pleasing pursuit to the ecclesiastical Student. His desire to make an accurate estimate of the conduct and sentiments of the primitive Christians gives additional vigour to his researches into the pious monuments of antiquity. He compares the antient portrait with the copies of modern artists, and carefully examines how far they have preserved a resemblance of those original features which he has been ever accustomed to contemplate with veneration and delight. In order to take as comprehensive a survey of the subject, as seems fully necessary for the occasion; he considers the CONDUCT of the Christians of the first and second century, by examining the six immediate causes which co-operated in the propagation of the Gospel; viz.

1. The MIRACLES wrought in the primitive Church.

2. The APOLOGIES addressed to Emperors in vindication of the Christian cause.

3. The Zeal of the FIRST PREACHERS in disseminating the Knowledge of Christianity.

4. The Fortitude of the early MARTYRS.

5. The

Church.

6. The Conformity of the MANNERS of the first Christians with the precepts of the Gospel.

He moreover considers their SENTIMENTS with respect to the evidence given to the New Testament; he examines certain Assertions made by the Writers before mentioned, and closes his Disquisition with practical inferences.

Such will be the subjects of the following Lectures. The advantages which the serious lover of Truth, and the sincere follower of Christ may derive from the investigation, are manifold and important. Justice will be rendered to injured merit and to aspersed innocence; the superintendance of the Almighty in the diffusion of the Gospel will be fairly stated; the estimation, in which the sacred volume was at first held, will be manifested; and the faith, which was once delivered to the Saints, will be vindicated and confirmed,

Moreover,

Moreover, this inquiry will enable us to afcertain the high refpect which the moft authentick and moft antient remains of chriftian antiquity merit; it will illuftrate the external evidences of Chriftianity, demonftrate that the doctrine of the primitive ages is the doctrine of the Church of England; and thus ultimately confirm the fteadinefs of our faith, and invigorate the motives of our obedience.

SERMON II.

Mark XVI. 20.

And they went forth and preached every where, the Lord working with them, and confirming the Word, with signs following.

OF all the Revolutions which have taken place upon the great theatre of the world, there is no one so calculated to attract the attention of the learned, to rouse the curiosity of the inquisitive, or to excite the gratitude of the pious, as that which has been effected by the Establishment of Christianity. The page of History displays to us various instances, in which conquered nations have been compelled to acknowledge the authority of one mighty Sovereign, and to yield a reluctant and temporary submission to the terrour of his arms. It also presents us with examples of Philosophers who have disseminated discoveries of science, and taught systems of ethicks within the narrow circle of their disciples. But to simplify the leading principles of social and religious obligation, to harmonize them in one comprehensive plan, to accommodate them to the capacity of every individual, and to propagate them by the gentle arts of persuasion, has never been the project of any Legislator, or of any Philosopher. Such a design was as far above human ingenuity to contrive, as surpassing human power to execute. The Plan, and the Execution, were reserved for the Prince of Peace; and the final cause for which he condescended to be so employed, and for which such essential changes have been made in the sentiments of the most enlightened part of the globe, equally includes the Glory of God, and the temporal and eternal Welfare of Mankind.

The obstacles however which opposed the first reception of Christianity were so numerous and formidable, and the human instruments employed for its diffusion so apparently weak and insufficient, that a comparison between them will not only shew that the passions and opposition of man far from impeding the divine designs, may ultimately become the means of their perfect accomplishment; but will

SERMON II.

will fully demonstrate the divine origin of Christianity, by displaying the powerful assistance which the Almighty supplied for its establishment.

The simple and illiterate Fishermen of Galilee and their Disciples, in converting a corrupted, were obliged also to propitiate an hostile world. They dispelled the bigotry of the Jew, and confuted the cavils of the Philosopher. Though aspersed by the slander of the malicious, and exposed to the sword of the powerful, in a short period of time they induced multitudes of various Nations, who were equally distinguished by the peculiarity of their manners, and the diversity of their language, to forsake the religion of their ancestors. The converts whom they made, deserted ceremonies and institutions which were defended by vigorous authority, sanctified by remote age, and associated with the most alluring gratification of the Passions. Their minds were purified as well as enlightened by the new Faith which they had embraced, and the incomparable excellency of its precepts was visible in the rapid growth of private virtues, and the gradual reformation of public enormities.

The Six grand Causes by which this Revolution was produced, were as extraordinary

C
in

in their nature, as salutary in their effects. On some occasions, the divine assistance was vouchsafed to the first christians, and they were endued with the power of working Miracles. The exertions of the Apologists were called forth to vindicate the Professors of the faith from slander, and to explain the nature and design of their Religion. Inspired by the most ardent zeal, the first Missionaries travelled into various countries to sow the seeds of the gospel. The fortitude of the most eminent Martyrs was brought to the severest trial by torture and by death. A peculiar form of Government was established in the infant church, and its institutions were accompanied by that regularity of Manners, which, as it was uniformly consistent with the evangelical precepts, gave to those precepts a powerful recommendation among the Gentiles, and left a bright example for the imitation of succeeding ages.

Of all these various causes combining to produce one great effect, we shall first consider the Miraculous Powers.

That Miraculous Powers were exercised after the death of the Apostles, upon certain occasions, is a truth supported by the unanimous

SERMON II.

mous and fucceffive teftimony of the Fathers down to the Reign of the Emperour Julian. The particular fpecies of miracle which the fathers defcribe as having been moft frequently wrought, was the expulfion of Evil Spirits from the bodies of Men. If however it fhould only be fuppofed that by demoniacal poffeffions are reprefented thofe difeafes which from their violent fymptoms refemble the influence of evil fpirits; fuch a fuppofition can make no difference with refpect to the fupernatural operation.

For as no ordinary means of relief were employed, the inftantaneous Recovery of the perfons afflicted, was altogether miraculous. Thefe wonderful interpofitions of Providence are recorded too, not as traditionary tales or vague reports, but as events publickly known, and credibly attefted. The fathers hold them forth as confpicuous marks of the Truth of chriftianity, and are fo far from confining their narrations to the chriftian communities who might poffibly be fufpected of too great a degree of credulity, that they confidently publifh them to the Pagans. In their addreffes to Magiftrates and to Emperours, they ftate them as incontrovertible facts, when the detection of falfhood and the difcovery of impofture,

SERMON II.

posture, would not only have sunk the cause which they wished to promote in irretrievable discredit; but have exposed them to the indignation and vengeance of insulted authority.

Modern writers have indulged so sceptical a disposition, as to question the probability of these miracles, or rather to deny that they ever were wrought. *The* ingenious *Author of the Life of Cicero* has employed the classical purity of his stile, and the comprehensive reach of his understanding, in the discussion of this subject. We pay with chearfulness the tribute of praise to his learning and abilities, but at the same time regret their misapplication and abuse. While endeavouring to demolish the outworks of the Church, he obliquely glanced at the fortress itself; and while he laboured to invalidate the credit of the fathers, seemed careless of the effect which his arguments might ultimately produce upon the general evidences of revelation. His observations, if admitted in their obvious sense, will lead to consequences the most alarming to Christianity; for they tend to invalidate the certainty of all such effects as exceed the common operations of nature, and differ from all such facts as are the daily objects of the senses. Although he admits with the greatest plausibility

of

SERMON II.

of conceffion, the truth of the Miracles of Chrift and his Apoftles, yet his arguments indirectly weaken their credit. He reprefents as a full and complete view of the poffible variety which may exift in the works of God, only thofe objects which our feeble intellect can comprehend, and our limited obfervation can fupply. But by confenting to fuch a reftriction as this we are led to adopt a principle as the refult of daily experience, which even daily experience itfelf, as it opens a more extenfive profpect of the phenomena of Nature, and elucidates the hidden properties of Matter, will rectify, and in fome cafes even vifibly contradict. Such reafoning would, moreover, confine the agency of the Deity within the narrow bounds of human prefcription, and would even arreft the power of his arm when extended to difplay itfelf in figns and wonders, and mighty deeds.

Having thus in a fophiftical manner affailed the credibility of the Facts, the author abovementioned next proceeds to attack the competency of the Witneffes. Diffatisfied with the teftimony of the honeft, the fincere, and the pious, he erects a fantaftick ftandard of judgment, and feems to lay it down as an indifputable pofition, that the acutenefs of a critick,

critick and the deliberation of a philosopher, are necessary to distinguish truth from falshood, and that a witness who sometimes betrays the marks of credulity, is always weak and generally deceitful. But if such principles be implicitely and indiscriminately adopted, we shall contradict our own mode of conduct in common life, in the course of which we expect not the greatest possible degrees of certainty, but determine and act upon high probability. We shall inevitably be seduced into the most complete scepticism, and shall find ourselves at a loss for the proper authentication of any facts. The existence of Julius Cæsar, and the event of the battle of Actium will be involved in equal doubt, and exposed to equal objections with the miracles of Christ, and the propagation of christianity.

It is moreover objected that the apostolical fathers are silent relative to the continuance of miraculous powers, and thence it is inferred that no such powers were possessed by their contemporaries.

But upon a careful examination we shall probably find, that although this subject forms no direct and material part of their disquisitions, yet some slight traces and occasional intimations

SERMON II.

timations may be difcovered fufficient to abate the confidence of the objector, and make it more probable that miraculous powers were poffeffed at that time, than that they had actually ceafed in the church. Clement, Bifhop of Rome, addreffed his epiftle to the church of Corinth, and defcribing the profperous and godly ftate of the converts, before an alarming diffention had arifen among them, exprefsly fays, " that they were all endued with a plen-" tiful effufion of the Holy Spirit." In what that plentiful effufion confifted, may be beft underftood from the particular defcription which St. Paul had not long before given of the various gifts of the Holy Ghoft, that were imparted to the Corinthian converts. They were endued with the fupernatural power of fpeaking various languages, of prophecying diftant events, and healing difeafes.

Ignatius, in his Epiftle to the Philadelphians, mentions a particular Revelation which had been made to himfelf; and in the fuperfcription of his Epiftle to the Smyrnæans, alludes to the fpiritual gifts which they poffeffed. Polycarp, the venerable Bifhop of Smyrna, congratulates the Church of the Philippians, by declaring, that " God had bleffed them with " every good gift, that they had been filled
" with

"with hope and charity, and were deſtitute of no ſpiritual grace."

If theſe expreſſions ſhould ſeem to afford little aſſiſtance to diſprove the aſſertion, we wiſh not to overrate their force, or draw from them unwarrantable concluſions. Rather than attempt to torture them into a ſenſe which may be thought harſh and overſtrained, we will admit the fact to be as it is ſtated; and conſider what advantage the opponent can derive from a conceſſion apparently ſo important.

Many Epiſtles may be found in the New Teſtament itſelf, in which miracles are not mentioned, even at the preciſe period when they are known to have been actually performed. The 2d Epiſtle to the Theſſalonians, the Epiſtles to the Philippians, Coloſſians, to Titus, to Philemon, and the Hebrews, are univerſally ſilent upon the ſubject, during the time that St. Paul and the other Apoſtles are acknowledged to have exerciſed, and communicated thoſe powers. The inference therefore which is drawn from this negative argument is inconſequential, and cannot be allowed to have any force whatever. It proves only that where the immediate view of the writer was

to

SERMON II.

to inculcate fome didactic, or to defend fome fpeculative propofition, he either faw no neceffity, or felt no defire to mingle a narrative of fact with the interpretation of doctrine.

In order to fhake the credit of the Fathers of the fecond century, they are accufed of maintaining vague and abfurd traditions. Juftin Martyr, Irenæus, and Athenagoras are affirmed to have been unanimous in embracing fuch frivolous doctrines as the approach of the Millenium; the Tranflation of Enoch into the Paradife of Adam; the Production of Demons from Angels and Women; and the Old Age of Chrift; and hence we are told it follows, that they are not to be credited when they affert the continuance of the miraculous Powers.

In the firft place, we may venture, without incurring the cenfure of precipitate petulance, to doubt the truth of the affertion. By what proof is the unanimity of thefe Fathers upon the points in queftion eftablifhed? The greateft diligence, in the perufal of their works will probably be ineffectual to make the difcovery.

Athenagoras, in his Embaffy for the Chriftians, and in his Treatife on the Refurrection, is filent upon the fubject of the Millenium. Juftin

Juftin Martyr, in his exhortation to the Greeks, in his Apologies, and in his Dialogues, as well as Athenagoras, neither mentions the Old Age of Chrift, nor the Tranflation of Enoch: nor does Irenæus in any paffage of his Confutation of Herefies, exprefsly affert that Demons were the offspring of Angels and Women.

How far it is fair to reafon from matters of opinion to matters of fact, is a fubject not fufficiently confidered by the objector. An inconclufive reafoner, may ftill be a competent witnefs. Now even if we fuppofe the judgment of thefe Fathers to have been ever fo unequal to the determination of abftrufe points, to the interpretation of the difficulties of fcripture, or to the developement of its myfteries, how can fuch a defect be an impeachment of their Veracity? They may, notwithftanding, be credible relators of thofe things which either immediately occurred to their own obfervation, or were conveyed to them by the workers of the miracles in queftion, by the fpectators, or by the perfons for whofe benefit they were performed. The Apoftles themfelves were fometimes remarkable for mifapprehenfion of the difcourfes of our Lord. They required the moft obvious parables to be explained to them, and they miftook

SERMON II. 43

mistook the allusion of their Master to the leaven of the Pharisees for an allusion to the means of ordinary subsistence. Yet such instances diminish not our veneration for them, as the Historians of the Son of God. Nor by parity of reasoning, ought such instances to lessen the credit of the Fathers who immediately succeeded them. The sentiments, therefore, which we may entertain respecting their opinions, and their evidence, ought to be kept distinct; by which means a decision will be made, more just to them, and more consistent with candour and impartiality. To exclude their evidence to miracles because they erred in the interpretation of dubious texts, is nearly as unwarrantable, as to declare a witness disqualified to appear in a judicial proceeding, because he does not satisfactorily explain the meaning of an intricate law of his country.

Hence it seems to follow as a necessary Corollary, that as these Fathers are competent witnesses, their attestations either must be opposed by contradictory evidence, or ought to be admitted as decisive.

From the misrepresentations of the ingenious Middleton, whose cavils we have endeavoured to expose, the *Historian of the decline*

cline and fall of the Roman Empire derived his objections againſt the miraculous powers ſubſequent to the time of the Apoſtles. He has, it muſt be confeſſed, given ſome embelliſhment, but has added little weight to the arguments of his great Maſter. He aſks what period of time is fixed for the ceſſation of miracles, and how are we to account for the inſenſibility of the chriſtians who then lived, to ſo remarkable a circumſtance?

The miracles may fairly be ſaid to ceaſe, with reſpect to our belief, when we can no longer obtain ſatisfactory evidence of their continuation. The cloſe of the reign of the Emperour Julian is the period at which that evidence begins to fail. Since about that time we diſcover, or imagine we diſcover cauſes for ſuſpicion, we may be allowed to ſuſpend our belief, and to make our deductions from the imperfect evidence which ſucceeds. For this ſtate of mind the learned Origen prepares us, by remarking, that in the Apoſtolical age miracles were frequent; that in the ſucceeding century their number conſiderably decreaſed; and that in the third century only a few traces remained of ſuch ſupernatural interpoſition.

Similar

SERMON II.

Similar to the remarks of Origen are the obfervations of Eufebius, at a later period. The fentiments of Jerom and Chryfoftom, although not perfectly confiftent with themfelves, will enable us to come to a determination. Sometimes they explicitely affert, that the extraordinary gifts of the fpirit were imparted in the early ages, and were gradually withdrawn as chriftianity was more extenfively propagated and the flourifhing ftate of the church lefs and lefs required fuch fupport. Sometimes they give particular relations of miracles performed, even in their own days; they confefs however that the genuinenefs of them was doubted, the fame of them was not fo extenfively fpread abroad, and they were not recommended with fuch authority as to be received without hefitation even by believers themfelves. As no fuch doubts are expreffed relative to thofe of the earlier ages, a clear diftinction is marked out, which amounts to an indirect acknowledgement of preceding miracles, or at leaft a ftrong prefumption in favour of their exiftence. The chriftians had for fome time been attentive to the gradual change which was taking place in the interpofitions of Providence; and fo far were they from being infenfible or carelefs, that they remark the decreafe and the

ceffation,

ceffation, with fufficient accuracy to fatisfy a reafonable and unprejudiced mind.

An Event happened in the middle of the fourth Century, which may perhaps not improperly be thought to have clofed the fcene of thefe extraordinary interpofitions. The conduct which produced it was marked by fingularity of enterprize, and confidence of fuccefs; and its confequences were in the greateft degree wonderful and tremendous, they difplayed a fignal proof of the temerity of Man, and of the manifeft and irrefiftable power of God.

Meditating the infliction of a fatal wound on chriftianity, the Emperour Julian determined to rebuild the temple at Jerufalem, and to reftore the ancient rites of Judaical Worfhip. His heart was elated with the vain imagination of fruftrating the Predictions of Chrift. But the Almighty who gave the Law in Thunder from Mount Sinai, and difperfed the rebellious Ifraelites, in conformity with the prophefies of his Son, fully manifefted his power to demonftrate the truth of revelation. A fudden Earthquake fwallowed up the foundations of the new Edifice, and flames afcended in vaft columns to the blazing firmament

SERMON II.

ment of Heaven. The moſt fierce and unconquerable of the elements was made the inſtrument of divine indignation. All the materials for the building were deſtroyed, and many of the workmen were deprived of life. Thoſe who eſcaped, bore on their bodies the deep marks of the ſcorching fire; and the ground on which the temple ſtood, for many years retained the diſmal veſtiges of ruin and conflagration.

If evidence for the truth of this awful interpoſition be required, our appeal may be made to the univerſal voice of the eccleſiaſtical writers. Some of them lived near the ſpot, others derived their information from thoſe who had viſited it. The teſtimony of the adverſaries to chriſtianity is equally ſtrong. Ammianus Marcellinus, the friend and companion of Julian, a writer equally remarkable for his learning, candour, and impartiality, gives a circumſtantial detail of the event. In dark and ambiguous terms, the Emperour himſelf alludes to it. A learned Rabbi of the fifteenth century, who appears to have collected his materials from Jewiſh traditions, records it; and even the *Hiſtorian of the decline and fall of the Roman Empire*, although he attempts with ſtubborn ſcepticiſm to invalidate

lidate some of its proofs, and insinuates a want of impartial authorities, is compelled not only to acknowledge the general fact, but many of the particular circumstances by which it was accompanied and distinguished.

It may be objected that this is a Miracle of a peculiar kind, as it was the immediate operation of the Supreme Being, without the intervention of human means; and consequently that it differs materially from other miracles whether of the disputed or acknowledged class.

To this objection we are prepared to answer, that although it may differ in the means of its operation, yet it harmonizes with them in respect to its design, which was the Establishment of the Christian Religion.

This was a publick demonstration of the veracity of the divine prediction. "Jerusalem "shall be trodden down by the Gentiles, until "the times of the Gentiles be fulfilled." The decree went forth, and the powers of Heaven and Earth were combined to establish it.— Whilst the *Heathen furiously raged and the People imagined a vain thing.* The period of desolation ordained by the Almighty was

not

not yet arrived, and therefore vain was the attempt of man to haften its approach. Upon the fame immoveable bafis was built that remarkable promife which our Lord made to his difciples, before his afcenfion to heaven: —*thefe figns fhall follow them who believe; in my name they fhall caft out devils; they fhall fpeak with new tongues; they fhall take up ferpents, and if they drink any deadly thing it fhall not hurt them; they fhall lay hands on the fick, and they fhall recover.*

That fuch powers were not intended to be imparted to the apoftles only, is evident from the context; as the promife refers to thofe who fhould believe in confequence of their preaching, without any precife limitation as to time, or exception as to perfons. This affiftance was firft given to the Corinthian Church, to which St. Paul fent directions for the proper regulation of miraculous endowments. St. James likewife, in his catholick epiftle, recommends the prayers of the Elders of the church, and the performance of a ceremonial rite as certain means to produce the recovery of the fick. Such examples, by furnifhing a probable argument for the communication of miraculous powers to different fo-
cieties

cieties of christians, confirm the veracity of the fathers.

From considering the nature of miracles as being not a contradiction of the great laws of nature, but only a deviation from the ordinary course of Providence for some salutary end, and from observing that the Deity can extend his power not merely to the performance of them himself, but to the performance of them likewise by the agency of mankind; there arises no absurdity from the supposition, that some of the primitive christians were employed for that purpose. In the earliest ages, when the church was in a low and persecuted state, when its adherents had no worldly comfort to support their drooping spirits, and animate their faith; there seems to have been a necessity sufficient to call for this divine assistance. So that although we are willing to concur with the adversaries of the fathers, in censuring their vague representations of events which ought to have been related in circumstantial details; yet we are justified in asserting, in direct opposition to their cavils, that the objections, brought from the silence of the apostolical writers, are inconclusive; and that the unanimous testimony of the second

and

and third century deserves to be received without hesitation, unless we violate the first principles of historical credit. We admit, moreover, that the interposition of heaven to prevent Julian from rebuilding the Temple at Jerusalem was the close of miraculous operations for the establishment of christianity; and that the promises of Christ himself, the example of the church of Corinth, and the directions of St. Paul and of St. James, confirm and illustrate the general argument.

The justness and the propriety of these conclusions may be inferred, in some degree, from the concessions of those who appear most unfavourable to the subject. For *the Author of the Inquiry into the miraculous powers*, at the conclusion of his controversy, found himself so closely pressed by the arguments of his learned and able opponents, that he changed the ground of contest. Instead of persisting in the unqualified denial of an occasional display of supernatural gifts, by any of the earliest christians, which was the leading principle of his first work, he maintained, and only maintained in his last dissertation, that there was no standing power in the church which enabled her members to perform miracles on whatever occasions they pleased. This manifest nifeft equivocation was an indirect acknowledgement of a defeat, and was a fignal proof that if fuch only was the object of his diligent inveftigations, his learning and his talents had been unprofitably exhaufted in combating a pofition, which even the moft bigotted friend to chriftian antiquity had never ftood forth to defend.

The Utility of miracles in the propagation of the gofpel, feems to be fo obvious, that it requires not to be enlarged upon. We might at firft conclude that they were calculated to fucceed where every argument failed. For if the precepts of the gofpel were too pure to engage the minds of the ignorant, and the uncultivated; if its rewards were too refined and fublime to warm their affections; a miracle was a proof of a divine revelation which was at once calculated to vanquifh prejudice, and to flafh conviction in the eyes of the fpectator. If the dead man was raifed, or the fick were inftantaneoufly healed, Bigotry we fhould fuppofe muft therefore have deferted her idols to embrace the crofs of Chrift, and Perfecution dropping her fword, muft have fallen proftrate to adore that Being who imparted fuch gifts to men.

But

SERMON II.

But proper reflections on the disposition of mankind, and the testimony of evangelical and ecclesiastical history, will rectify this amusing theory. The effects of miracles might be transient, and as it sometimes happens with respect to the more rare phenomena of nature, might leave no lasting impression on the mind. Our Saviour too often experienced in the Jews a stubbornness of prejudice, which reluctantly gave way to the force of his mighty works. His disciples were obliged to contend with equal difficulties among the inhabitants of other nations. The Pagans attributed miracles to the operation of magick, and refused their assent to them, when urged as an evidence of a divine revelation. As the idolatrous priests pretended that supernatural effects were produced by the interposition of their Gods, so the distinction between true and false miracles was liable to be confounded; and the enquirer after truth, from a latent suspicion of fraud even in the most specious, might have recourse to some other proof to fix his choice of a religious persuasion. Among the authentick instances of divine interposition, several were of a private nature, and were more immediately designed for the consolation of individuals, or the support of particular congregations. These and similar causes conspired, we may suppose, to prevent that wonderful and lasting effect of miracles which a display of them, more frequent and more conspicuous than that which is recorded by the fathers of the church, must necessarily have produced.

Let us now pass on to consider the method that was adopted, and the arguments that were adduced by the earliest vindicators of christianity, to make the true nature of their profession known to their enemies.

The apologies of the primitive christians were no less calculated to prove the zeal and sincerity of their respective authors, than to vindicate the honour of their religion. Christianity, for a long period of time after its first appearance in the world, was aspersed by the virulence of defamation, and oppressed by the insolence of power. The edicts of emperours gave a sanction to the most unjustifiable proceedings against its followers, and incited the bigotted multitude to kindle the flames of persecution. These eventful scenes were equally calculated to try the patience of the humble and uncomplaining, and to rouse the courage, and call forth the abilities of the intrepid and the learned. In the first rank of the champions of the faith we see St. Peter coming

coming forth to rectify the misconceptions of the Jews, and to declare the nature of the new dispensation. We likewise behold St. Paul inspired with more than mortal boldness, whilst he unfolded the awful scene of a future judgment to the trembling Felix. Upon occasions almost equally perilous, Justin Martyr and Athenagoras, two of the most eminent converts from the schools of the philosophers in the second century, followed these illustrious examples. From their apologies we find that they combated slander with the weapons of truth, that they exhibited the rules of their conduct as they are recorded in the gospel, and described with the warmth of charity, and the consciousness of rectitude, the virtues of their christian contemporaries. With the earnestness of men who were sinking under the weight of persecution, they solicit the indulgence of that religious toleration which was freely allowed by the Roman Emperours to all the rest of their subjects.

The works of many eminent men, who distinguished themselves in the same manner, are unhappily lost. There is one consolation, however, which may in some degree compensate for the misfortune, since the diligence of Eusebius has rescued their names, and some fragments

fragments of their works, from oblivion. Quadratus, Bishop of Athens, Aristides the Philosopher, Melito, Bishop of Sardis, Apollinaris, Bishop of Hierapolis, and Miltiades, presented their vindications of christianity respectively to Adrian, Aurelian, and Commodus. The frequency of such applications in successive reigns, is both a proof of the depressed and injured state of christianity, and of the opinion prevalent in the different periods of time when these writers pleaded its cause, that their labours would produce a proper effect, by dispelling the prejudices of its enemies, and that the Emperours were not implacable, or deaf to the voice of truth.

These earliest advocates of christianity have not escaped the severe animadversions of the Historian of the Decline and Fall of the Roman Empire. He laments with pretended concern the scantiness of their talents, and complains of the misapplication of their arguments to improper subjects. "He asserts that they ex-
"pose with superfluous wit and eloquence the
"extravagance of Polytheism."

Now, the whole system of Polytheism was the offspring of fiction, and derived its support from superstition and fraud. No obstacles could

could more powerfully retard the progress of truth. The luftre of evangelical light, and the corruption of idolatrous darknefs, could not maintain a divided empire over the minds of men. The altar of Jupiter, and the ftandard of the Crofs, could not be erected on the fame place. *For what concord hath Chrift with Belial? And what agreement hath the temple of God with Idols?* The prejudices of education, the general habits of life, and the fervour of the paffions, all united to plead in favour of rites and ceremonies which were clofely connected with the purfuit of the groffeft fenfuality. In what more important or more neceffary fervice, therefore, could the advocates for chriftianity be employed, than in demolifhing the fabrick of Paganifm, in order that chriftianity might be erected upon its ruins?

Whatever might be the incredulity which the more enlightened Gentiles fecretly entertained, their external refpect for their religion was a formidable impediment to the progrefs of the faith; as it rivetted more clofely the chains of vulgar fuperftition. The magiftrates, however deep their diffimulation might be, preferved at leaft the appearance of devotion, from motives of policy; and the philofophers, too prudent to make an oftentatious difplay

play of their sceptical tenets, professed the same specious veneration for the Gods of their country. The keenness of wit was therefore by the christian most judiciously directed against the motley mass of Polytheism which was so artfully countenanced by the united examples of the wise and the powerful. The force of eloquence was as properly employed in exposing the plausible tales of a popular mythology, and in recommending the doctrines and the precepts of a pure and spiritual religion.

The Historian next proceeds to censure the apologists, because " they insist much more " strongly on the predictions which announced, " than on the miracles which accompanied the " appearance of the Messiah."

It is somewhat doubtful how far the fact is correctly stated, and if it be correctly stated, how far the practise itself is unjustifiable. Justin Martyr, fully sensible of the powerful effect which the representation of miracles was calculated to produce, appealed to the Roman registers, which contained a full account of the most remarkable transactions of our Lord. An additional proof that the miracles of Christ were well known, arises from considering the labours of the preceding advocates for christianity.

tianity. A short time before Justin addressed his apology to Antoninus Pius, Quadratus, the learned Bishop of Athens, delivered an elegant oration to Adrian; in which he particularly insisted upon the miracles performed by our Lord. He represented that they were not of short duration, like the impostures which charm the eye of credulity with a momentary delusion, and produce no permanent effects. Their durarion was not merely limited to the period of our Lord's continuance on earth, but lasted for a sufficient time to give the fullest proof of their reality and efficaciousness. He confirms the truth of his assertions, by appealing to a fact which was open to common enquiry. He assures the Emperour, that some persons who had experienced the miraculous influence of the power of Christ, in healing the sick and raising the dead, had even survived until that age.

Since the evidence of miracles had been displayed on a recent occasion, it would have been superfluous for Justin Martyr to have rested the proofs of christianity upon that ground alone, when they might be strongly established upon another. The evidence of prophecy is so clear and conclusive, that it may reasonably be questioned how far the
proofs

proofs drawn from miracles, ought to supersede it. The Old Testament contains a long series of predictions which are gradually enlarged with more particular circumstances, and pointed with more striking and appropriate reference to a most extraordinary event recorded in the gospels. Like rays of light proceeding from different points, they all converge in the same focus. The history of Christ, related by the evangelists, is an exact copy of the prophecies, in which not only the proportion and the outlines are uniformly preserved, but the striking resemblance of every feature, and the peculiar effect of every expression are faithfully delineated. A prophecy is indeed a more refined and philosophical proof, because it appeals to the judgment which delights in the comparison of general descriptions and particular circumstances with the event which they anticipate. A miracle is more liable to the cavils of doubt; because the possibility of its existence may be disputed, it may be attributed to the artifice of fraud, or the agency of demons. A miracle rests for its confirmation upon the evidence of men, but a prophecy when fulfilled, may be said to be the immediate evidence of God himself. The Ethiopian Eunuch, struck with the pathetic predictions of Isaiah, expressed an eager
curiosity

SERMON II.

curiosity to know to what person they properly referred. Great was his astonishment, and instantaneous his conversion, when Philip held up to him the picture of the Redeemer, as their compleat and illustrious counterpart. Our Saviour himself appeals not less frequently to the prophets, for an attestation of his divine mission, than to his miracles; and seems to intimate that an inattention to the former, immediately led to the rejection of the latter; —*for if they believe not Moses and the Prophets, neither will they be persuaded though one rose from the dead.*

Exclusive of the propriety of having recourse to prophetical evidence considered in itself; there are other reasons which justify the introduction of such proof arising from the genius and disposition of the Romans. Their eagerness to explore the events of futurity may be collected from the invectives of their satyrists, the censures of their philosophers, and the narratives of their historians. They practised the arts of divination with ardour, and applied themselves with blind credulity to the occult studies of magick and astrology. The mysterious volume of the Sibyl, supposed to contain the destined revolutions of the empire, was preserved with the greatest

reverence in the capitol, and confulted in all emergencies of the ftate. This attachment to the predictions which it contained was improved to great advantage by the moft celebrated of their poets, in a beautiful anticipation of the happinefs ordained to fucceed the approaching birth of the Son of Jupiter. If the imagination of the Romans was delighted with the felicity which fhould fucceed the reftoration of the golden age, and with the return of Aftræa to the earth; with what aftonifhment might their minds be imprefled when they were guided to thofe ancient writers who foretold the tranquil ftate of the world at the advent of the Mefliah, the eftablifhment of his fpiritual and eternal kingdom, and the wide extent of his dominion. Even their own experience could convince them in fome degree with what exactnefs thefe fplendid defcriptions had correfponded with the event. The advance of chriftianity from an obfcure city of Syria to the metropolis of the empire, and its rapid diffufion through the provinces, formed an object too fingular and too confpicuous to efcape the publick notice. A perfuafion which was prevalent at that time contributed likewife to juftify the conduct of the apologifts, and to awaken an attention to the works of the prophets. For it was generally believed
" that

SERMON II.

"that the antient sacerdotal volumes had fore-
"told that the East should have the preemi-
"nence, and that those who came from Ju-
"dea should obtain the sovereignty of the
"world."

It appears therefore upon the whole, that the subjects of these Apologies are unreasonably censured, since they were well calculated to silence the clamour and abate the rage of the Pagans. They moreover excited curiosity to inquire into the nature of a religion whose professors had been so injuriously treated, and thus greatly contributed to the conversion of the enlightened and candid part of mankind.

Whilst the Apologists were exerting their talents to confute calumny and prevent persecution, the christian Missionaries were more actively engaged in publishing the new revelation to the world.

Of the fidelity with which the Apostles executed the final injunction of their divine Master, to proclaim to every land the glad tidings of the gospel, we may form the best judgment from the inspired records. Neither dangers, nor hardships, deterred them from any exertion which contributed to the glory of God by the diffusion

diffusion of the gospel of his Son. The steadiness of their conduct, and the ardour of their zeal, are best seen in the effects of that conduct and of that zeal on the various countries to which they travelled, and the multitudes of different nations whom they converted. The first advances towards extending the knowledge of the new dispensation beyond Judæa, were made by Philip the Deacon, who met with the greatest encouragement to prosecute his labours in the conversion of the Samaritans, and the inhabitants of the shores of Cæsarea. The disciples who were driven from Jerusalem when the persecution raged after the martyrdom of St. Stephen, converted their flight into an occasion of triumph, by planting the gospel in the opulent coasts of Phœnicia, and in the fertile island of Paphos; and in laying the foundation of the ancient and renowned church of Antioch. The labours of St. Paul and of St. Barnabas are recorded with sufficient particularity to display the unabating vigour of their perseverance, and the wide extent of their travels. The progress of the great apostle of the Gentiles may indeed be traced from the banks of the Euphrates, to the metropolis of the Roman world. The celebrated cities of Damascus, Ephesus, Corinth, and Athens by the number, and the respectability

SERMON II.

bility of their converts, bore teſtimony to his labours.

We are informed by the moſt authentick evidence of eccleſiaſtical hiſtory, that after St. Peter had with the aſſiſtance of St. Paul eſtabliſhed a church at Rome; he directed his attention to thoſe Jews who were diſperſed throughout various provinces of Aſia. St. Mark planted chriſtianity in Egypt, and the coaſts of the Egean ſea were diſtinguiſhed by the preaching of St. John, who fixed his reſidence at Epheſus, where he compoſed his goſpel. At this period, the moſt effectual means were taken to diſengage habit and prejudice from the popular ſuperſtitions of Paganiſm, to correct their impurities, and to give them a more becoming and more honourable employment in the ſervice of chriſtianity. St. John founded the catechetical ſchool of Epheſus, St. Mark that of Alexandria, and Polycarp that of Smyrna. Here the ſeeds of the goſpel were firſt ſown in the young and ductile mind, before the propenſities of more mature age had obſtructed their growth. The difficulties which might have accompanied inſtruction merely private were leſſened both to the teachers and their diſciples; and the experience of ſucceeding ages has only ſerved to confirm the confummate wifdom and utility of thefe apoftolical eftablifhments, by difplaying more fully the advantages of early piety and religious education.

From thefe general accounts it is highly probable that even within half a century from the death of our Lord, his religion was difleminated over all the Eaftern part of the Roman Empire. The period of the converfion of the Weftern provinces is enveloped in great obfcurity, as well as the particular hiftory of thofe miffionaries, who pioufly undertook and accomplifhed it. By the dim light however which is thrown upon this fubject by the Ecclefiaftical Writers, we diftinguifh the names of Pothinus and Irenæus, who travelled from Afia into Gaul, and there eftablifhed the churches of Vienne and Lyons, which were in the reign of Adrian moft eminently diftinguifhed by the faith and fortitude of their martyrs. In the reign of the Emperor Adrian many other fucceffors of the apoftles vifited remote countries, where they either confirmed the churches already converted, or made new profelytes to the faith. From the high antiquity of fome verfions, particularly the Italic, the Syriac and the Æthiopic, we may reafonably conclude that they left

left copies of the scriptures with their converts, and thus furnished the means not only of diffusing the knowledge of christianity, but of delivering it down in its original purity to succeeding ages.

In the primitive Missionary we may contemplate the greatest resolution, productive of the most assiduous and painful exertions. Impressed by the deepest sense of duty, and eager to diffuse that divine light of revelation which burned with undiminished heat in his own breast, he disengaged himself from the strong attachments to his native country, and went forth to convert an idolatrous world. As his life was devoted to the interests of his religion, all the causes by which its pains were aggravated, or its continuance shortened, were stript of their terrour. His imagination presented to him the scourge, the rack, and the cross, yet was his resolution unshaken by the apprehensions of persecution and death. At the loud and solemn calls of duty he was loosened even from the ties of consanguinity; and with a spirit not less dignified than that of the Roman Hero, he suffered principle to predominate over affection, turned aside from the tears of friendship, and was even deaf to the tender supplications of love. The bright object of
his

his ambition was not the barren praise of inflexible constancy, but the crown of immortal happiness. The dangers of travel, the precariousness of subsistence, the perfidy of pretended friends, and the violence of open enemies, were in his estimation no more than light afflictions which endure for a moment. Lost in the solitude of the wilderness, exposed to the tempests of the ocean, or assailed by the outrage of the multitude, he was not destitute and forsaken, for the Almighty was his guide, and his comforter. With patience he saw the frowns of the great, and heard the scoffs of the vulgar. He proclaimed with the unshaken confidence of truth, the wondrous tidings of the new dispensation, and exhorted a guilty race to repentance and amendment. Elate with the accomplishment of his pious task, in bringing many sheep to the fold of Christ, he gloried amid the flames of martyrdom, and breathed out his soul with joy.

Such was the situation of St. Paul, as well as of many others who shared his dangers and met his fate. By their unbroken perseverance, the knowledge of the Gospel was diffused through those regions, in which the Roman conquests had prepared the way. Yet the victorious progress which was made by the arms of the most

SERMON II. 69

most warlike people in the univerfe, in the courfe of a thoufand years, was equalled, or perhaps exceeded, by the chriftian religion in two centuries. From Judea it conveyed the bleffings of life and immortality to the most remote countries, and refembled the Nile, which rifing from a diftant and obfcure fource, gradually overflows vaft provinces, and fertilizes every foil which is watered by its ftream.

There is no fubject which feems to have infpired the early fathers with fuch exultation, or which they defcribe with more lively colours of eloquence, than the general diffufion of the gofpel. It was highly gratifying to their devout minds to obferve, that the fpiritual comfort which they enjoyed, was communicated to others; and that the extent of the faith was correfpondent with the declarations of prophecy. From the glowing reprefentations of Tertullian we collect that not more than a century and a half had elapfed from the afcenfion of Chrift, when the followers of his religion might be found among all ranks of fociety; in all cities and villages; in the fenate, in the camp, and the palace; in the vaft regions of Afia, on the coafts of Africa, in the provinces of Gaul, Germany and Spain; in the parts of Britain inacceffible to hoftile arms;

arms; and in countries much more remote from the metropolis of the Roman world.

The Historian of the decline and fall of the Roman Empire seems to labour with much solicitude to confine primitive christianity within the narrowest limits. Whilst he makes a partial allowance for the exaggeration of Pliny, relative to the number of christians in Bithynia; he condemns a similar exaggeration of Justin Martyr as too precipitate and partial. It is the part of candour to allow the same indulgence to both, and to recollect that the passions of both might be so highly inflamed by the different motives of prejudice and fear, as to produce a description not strictly consistent with truth. When the fathers expatiate upon the wide extent of christianity, they assume a licentiousness of description, which is not uncommon among the antient writers, of confounding the Roman Empire with the whole habitable earth. It is however somewhat remarkable, that even from those records which the Historian esteems the most indisputable and authentick, we may find expressions to countenance, if not to justify the representations of the Fathers. The warm declamation of Justin Martyr and of Tertullian, the energetick narrative of Eusebius, and the
exact

SERMON II.

exact parallel drawn by Chryfoftom between the Pagans and the Chriftians, derive very confiderable fupport from the exprefs declarations of Suetonius, Tacitus, Pliny, Lucian, and Porphyry.

In thus tracing the progrefs of the gofpel, and eftimating the zeal of its firft preachers, a melancholy reflection naturally arifes in the mind. The countries in which the faith was firft promulgated, retain at prefent very imperfect marks of its antient diffufion. The rich provinces of Afia Minor and Syria, which have been long expofed to the defpotifm of the Ottoman Princes, exhibit only in venerable ruins the antient edifices of magnificence and devotion. Moft of the feven cities immortalized by the writer of the Apocalypfe, difcover no remaining veftiges to gratify the eye of the pious traveller. In Damafcus, renowned in facred hiftory for the converfion of the great Apoftle of the Gentiles, a Turkifh Mofque is erected amid the ruins of a Chriftian Church. Jerufalem itfelf, the theatre of the ftupendous and mighty works of the Son of God, exifts only as a monument of the rapacity and extortion of its infidel tyrants. Even in that holy place where rending rocks and opening graves attefted the dignity of an expiring Redeemer, the proud crescent of Mahomet is displayed over the prostrate banner of the Cross.

Of this triumphant ascendancy the history of the middle ages can sufficiently explain to us the causes. The degenerate christians corrupted that faith which they were bound to have kept unsullied; they introduced those superstitious rites which they ought to have despised, and indulged in all those vices, which it was their duty to avoid. Hence the sceptre departed from them, and hence the wolves were permitted to ravage the fold of Christ.

But if christianity has been involved in the great revolutions of empire, the seat of her dominion is not destroyed, but removed. Her sound has gone forth into lands which were unknown to the primitive preachers. The vast regions of the north of Europe have been long added to the kingdoms of the Messiah. In a world unknown to the antients, the wide extended shores of America have received the religion, as well as the civilization, of the European colonists. The commerce of the East has afforded an opportunity, which the patrons of a most pious institution have embraced, and the coasts of Malabar can attest the successful labours of their Missionaries.

Thus

SERMON II.

Thus the acquisitions which christianity has made in some places, are abundantly more than a counterbalance for her depressed state in others; and thus the evidence of its divine origin is established, by the confirmation of the prophecies which declare that no power should be able to effect its subversion. Obscure to man are the events of futurity, and veiled in awful mystery are the councils of the Most High; yet from the goodness of the Almighty, and the wisdom of his dispensations, we may venture to conclude, that the gospel will, in some future age, be preached in all the world.

To that blissful period the benevolent and pious mind wishes to extend its eager view, and feels the most sublime gratification by anticipating the immense addition which will be made to human happiness, both temporal and eternal, when the follower of Mahomet, the disciple of Brama, and the votary of Confucius, with every worshipper of every Idol, shall bow with equal veneration at the name of Jesus; and when the Christian Religion, like the bright luminary of day, shall diffuse its auspicious influence over the whole race of Mankind.

SER-

SERMON III.

JEREMIAH I. 19.

They shall fight against thee, but they shall not prevail against thee; for I am with thee, saith the Lord, to deliver thee.

IN the perusal of ecclesiastical history we are often surprized by observing, that men have existed so ignorant of the human mind, as to imagine that its operations can be controuled by violence. The scourge of oppression and the sword of tyranny may indeed have very powerful effects over the outward actions, and may awe the wretch who is exposed to them, into sullen acquiescence, or reluctant silence. But the free born soul is subject to no such restraints; for amidst the severest oppression, it exerts the boldest energies of thought, and triumphs even in the agonies of torture.

Compulsion

Compulsion eventually defeats its own purpose, and either forces the object of its resentment to wear the temporary mask of hypocrisy, or excites that restless and determined resistance of the will which no force can subdue. To soothe the mind into compliance by the gentle arts of persuasion, and to allure it by the flattering prospect of advantage, is easy and practicable; but to restrain its inclinations by violence, or to implant opinions repugnant to its judgment, is not less impossible, than to arrest the flight of the winged lightning; or to imprint a durable mark upon the surface of the ocean.

Such are the reflections which naturally arise in our minds, on considering the folly of Persecution. That the meek professors of a pure and peaceful religion should have ever been exposed to its fury, may, abstractedly considered, be a just subject of wonder. The inoffensiveness of its institutions, and the benevolence of its principles, gave it the fairest title to security and protection. Yet the reception it first met with, was far different; for as a proof how much the best gift of heaven to mankind was undervalued, the christians of the three first centuries were engaged in almost a continual struggle, against oppression and cruelty.

That

SERMON III.

That we may be enabled to form the more compleat idea of this interesting subject, it will be proper to survey the causes of the persecutions, the conduct of the martyrs, and the effects of their fortitude.

Whilst the christian religion was effectually making its progress through various parts of the world, it became an object of sufficient magnitude and importance, to attract the attention of the Roman government. When first superficially noticed in the metropolis of the empire, it was confounded with Judaism, and excited only the derision of the vulgar, and the contempt of the learned, and the powerful. As soon however as the zeal of the christians, in making converts, and the simple ceremonies of their worship, had distinguished them from the adherents to the Mosaical law, they were exposed to the most cruel and most unmerited punishments. On considering the character of Nero, it can excite no surprize to observe, that the first prosecution raged in his sanguinary reign. Christianity recorded the event as an honour to her cause, that the first Emperour who destroyed her votaries, was the incessant foe of exalted merit. For the imputed conflagration of Rome, of which he was himself the insidious and unfeeling author,

they

they were condemned to the moſt horrid tortures, that ingenious malice could contrive. Their dreadful execution began that long and melancholy catalogue of martyrs which, like the myſtick ſcroll of the prophet, was inſcribed, within and without, with lamentation, and mourning, and woe.

The boaſted harmony of the antient world reſpecting religious worſhip, muſt be underſtood to have exiſted only under certain reſtrictions. The inhabitants of different nations enjoyed the liberty of ſerving their reſpective deities, without moleſtation, or reſtraint. Hence the chriſtians, in their apologies, complain of the injuſtice of their enemies, in not allowing them the common liberty of toleration, which was granted to all the reſt of the world. But when once this privilege paſſed its preſcribed limits, and thoſe who held ſuch tenets as differed from the received opinions of the public, began to propagate them; they became the objects of public animoſity and ſevere puniſhment. Many philoſophers, whoſe free opinions tended to undermine the common veneration for the gods of their country, were doomed either to exile or to death. This was the cauſe of the proſcription of Diagoras, and the chief pretext of the guilt of Socrates.

The Romans, adopting an antient law of Athens, guarded against the introduction of foreign rites with scrupulous precaution, and in various periods of their history, roused the vigilance of the magistrate, to prevent their diffusion. Tiberius prohibited the exercise of the religious ceremonies of other countries, particularly those of Egypt and Judæa. We must therefore have recourse to the general manners of antiquity, to account for their prejudices against christianity, and must impute the leading cause of persecution to the zeal of the christians in making converts from Paganism.

Urged by the purest motives of conscience the christians expressed the greatest abhorrence of idolatry. They not only abstained with unremitting care from the participation of its rites, but embraced every occasion to expose the prophaneness of them, and to gain proselytes to the truth. Their zealous conduct appeared highly criminal in the eyes of the bigotted magistrates, who saw the new religion increase with alarming rapidity, and were apprehensive that the number of the converts would endanger the publick peace. Moreover the religious establishment of the state was supposed to be too intimately connected with

its

its political conſtitution not to receive a violent convulſion, if this bold innovation was ſuffered to proceed with impunity.

The alarms of the Roman government were equally groundleſs, but more plauſible, when excited either by the frequency of the chriſtian aſſemblies, or the ſecret manner in which they were held. The Emperours ſurveyed the aſſociations of their ſubjects with ſo much jealouſy and ſuſpicion, that they were ſtrictly prohibited, even when holden for purpoſes the moſt inoffenſive and ſalutary. As the meetings of the chriſtians were confounded with factious and diſorderly ſocieties, they were expoſed to rigorous and unjuſt penalties.

To avoid interruption, they met together during the ſilence of the night, or at the dawn of the day. Their choice of ſuch unſeaſonable hours for their devotions gave great alarm to the Romans, ſince the laws from the foundation of the republick, had ſtrictly forbidden nocturnal meetings. In the celebration of the Bacchanalian rites, with which the chriſtian aſſemblies, on account of their external appearance, might poſſibly be confounded, the Senate was alarmed with apprehenſions of danger, on being informed that a multitude

was

SERMON III.

was often convened in the feafon of darknefs and repofe. The baptifmal vow likewife, gave no fmall caufe for fufpicion, as it was liable to be interpreted into an oath of criminal fecrecy, and a ratification of treafonable defigns.

That the meek and benevolent followers of Jefus fhould be miftaken for the abettors of fedition, is an evident proof with what a fuperficial glance the jealous Roman furveyed their affemblies. His fears of their defigns were vain, and his ignorance of their conduct was inexcufable. Had he carefully examined their fimple rites, and harmlefs tranfactions, he would doubtlefs have paffed a more equitable judgment, and rather have imputed their conduct to the delufions of pitiable fanaticifm, than to the machinations of a malignant and deftructive fuperftition.—*He knew not what spirit they were of.* They met not to drain the bowl of intemperance, or to indulge the exceffes of licentioufnefs; but to break the facred bread of the Euchariſt, and renew their refolutions of purity and holinefs. They were convened not to fan the flames of infurrection or meditate dark and fubtle ftratagems againft the State; but to invoke the Moft High for the profperity of the Emperour, and pay the

F tribute

tribute of adoration and prayer to the Prince of Peace.

Whilst they were thus irreproachable in their conduct and steady in their loyalty, their enemies meditated a decisive blow against their reputation, by devoting their moral character to the most heinous infamy. The calumnies which were industriously reported, probably took their rise from the superficial remarks and observations of those, who had been present at the celebration of the sacraments. The ceremony employed in the immersion of the infant, and the distribution of the consecrated elements, were aggravated by the inventive genius of scandal into the licentious indulgences of the orgies of Bacchus, and the horrid and inhuman banquet of Atreus. The diligence of the earliest apologists was therefore roused to confute, and in some degree to retort this infamous and glaring imputation; and the developement of its falshood failed not to acquire new honour to the church, by introducing and warranting the delineation of her virtues.

To the elegant Correspondent of Trajan we are indebted for an invaluable testimony relative to the primitive church. By the converts of

SERMON III.

of Bythinia, he was made acquainted with the principles of their faith, and the ceremonies of their worship. Although convinced by the cleareſt evidence, that the aſperſions which had been thrown upon them were wholly groundleſs, he ſcrupled not to aſſert in his celebrated Epiſtle to the Emperour, that whatever was the nature of their confeſſion, yet their inflexible obſtinacy and ſtubbornneſs deſerved to be puniſhed. Diſſatisfied with the aſſeverations of numbers who declared the inoffenſive purpoſes for which their aſſemblies were convened, he heſitated not to put two Deaconeſſes to the torture in order to draw forth a confeſſion of ſome imagined guilt.

From a magiſtrate ſo enlightened by learning, ſo converſant with mankind, and ſo compliant upon all other occaſions with the dictates of philanthropy, we naturally expect more candid deciſions, and more mild behaviour. This inconſiſtency with his general conduct and ſentiments is yet more peculiarly ſtriking, if it be conſidered, that the ſame virtues which were exerciſed in the adherence of the pious to their principles, were the ſubjects of admiration and applauſe, when exemplified in the illuſtrious characters of antient heroes and patriots. The partial and inconſiderate

derate Pliny denied to the followers of Christ, that praise, and that estimation, which, as a Roman, he must necessarily feel for the exulting patience of Mutius, the inflexible resolution of Regulus, and the unconquerable spirit of Cato.

Our candour wishes to throw a veil over the failings of an illustrious character. We look however in vain for even a partial justification of Pliny, unless we impute his conduct to the inveterate prejudices of the times in which he lived, or to the apprehensions of a conscientious magistrate, who by excessive solicitude to discharge his duty, is sometimes hurried into acts of flagrant injustice.

An additional reason for the persecution of the christians resulted from their conduct upon some occasions being interpreted into personal disrespect to the Emperour. To his name in all seasons of publick festivity, libations were made, and in his praise, congratulatory songs were composed. These honours were accompanied by rites, similar to those which were performed to the Deities themselves. Hence as the christians refused to join in this prophane flattery, the invocation of the Imperial name was adopted, as a snare for their loyalty, and

and a test of their abjuration. A refusal to comply was interpreted into an avowal of complicated guilt, and furnished a plausible pretext for punishing them not only as subvertors of the national religion, but as enemies of the supreme and established authority.

The severity of the Edicts enacted against them varied according to the temper and passions of the different Emperours. Under the cruel Nero and the pusillanimous Domitian, they were rigorous and sanguinary. The partial clemency of Trajan checked indeed the fury of persecution; but left the christians exposed to the malice of informers. Marcus Antoninus the philosopher listened with credulity to the calumnies thrown upon the christians by their enemies, and the effects of his severity were felt from the more southern provinces of France to the most distant cities of Asia Minor. Although the laws were often silent, yet they were not always repealed. Hence the interval of persecution, far from becoming a state of tranquility, was a season of awful expectation and anxious fear. A temporary calm was no security against the return of more violent storms. The church was kept in a continual state of alarm, and enjoyed no permanent repose until the reign of Commodus,

modus, when the flames of popular fury were at leaſt mitigated, if not extinguiſhed, and when peace reigned for ſome time, in all the churches of the world.

The conſequences of the Imperial edicts were calamitous and deplorable. As often as they were enacted, the rage of perſecution was let looſe, and her way was marked with blood. The furious multitude were inſtigated by the ſuperſtitious prieſts, and the ſelfiſh artiſts, to whom the worſhip of Idols was a ſource of ſubſiſtence and wealth. Often when aſſembled to view the publick games, they demanded, with loud and tumultuous acclamations, a ſa- crifice to their inſulted Gods; and crouded the ſpacious amphitheatre, to ſee the innocent Martyrs expoſed to the edge of the ſword, the jaws of the hungry lion, or the more excru- ciating tortures of the flaming pile. "In the "ſight of the unwiſe they ſeemed to die, and "their departure was taken for miſery. For "though they were puniſhed in the ſight of "men, yet was their hope full of immorta- "lity. As they have been chaſtiſed they ſhall "be greatly rewarded, for God proved them "and found them worthy for himſelf. As "gold in the furnace hath he tried them, and "received them as a burnt offering."

. Thus

SERMON III.

Thus are we led on to confider in the fecond place the behaviour of the primitive martyrs in the laft trying fcenes of their fufferings.

Whilft the moft eminent and refpectable adherents to the faith, were devoted to publick executions, the obfcure condition of common converts was generally the caufe of their fafety. The Romans adopted the policy of Tarquin, and concluded that by dooming the leaders of the rifing fect to death, the energy and fpirit of its inftitutions might effectually be broken. No plan, it muft be confeffed, could promife with greater hopes of fuccefs its complete ruin and extinction. The perfecutors feemed to think that by depriving piety of her brighteft ornaments, and moft firm fupports, they fhould ftrike terror into the whole body of chriftians; and either drive them to inftant defpair or difgraceful apoftacy.

Such were the vain and fanguine hopes which were formed from the condemnation of Ignatius Bifhop of Antioch, Polycarp Bifhop of Smyrna, and Juftin, who, with an emphatical allufion to his unmerited fate, was denominated the Martyr.

SERMON III.

A minute account of their pious lives and exemplary deaths has been ably and repeatedly given by various writers. To tranfcribe the particulars of their narrations, is altogether unneceffary, as they form the moft ftriking and moft obvious parts of the antient martyrologies. It may be more proper on the prefent occafion to exhibit the leading principles of their conduct, and to place their behaviour in that point of view, which is moft confiftent with the impartiality of truth, and moft productive of religious edification.

They were unanimoufly actuated by the fame motives of duty, and expired in the confeffion of the fame faith. A firm conviction that the bold avowal of chriftianity was abfolutely neceffary to difplay their fincerity, and fecure their eternal happinefs, made them rife fuperior to every worldly confideration. Their behaviour was equally remote from the enthufiafm of bigotted zeal, and the rafhnefs of obftinate folly. They difdained to facrifice the ardent love of their divine Mafter to the allurements of the world. No offers of impunity, no threats of malice, no profpect of temporal advantage diverted them from the ftraight though thorny path of duty. To temporize by fervile conceffion, or timid retractation, was equally

SERMON III. 89

equally repugnant to their integrity, inconfiftent with their refolutions, and injurious to the honour of their caufe. Supported by the animating fuccour of the divine grace, they rofe fuperiour to the fears and the tortures of untimely and agonizing diffolution. They confidered their light afflictions as duft in the balance; and with pious confidence, and ardent defire, looked up to the author and finifher of their faith, for the unfading crown of immortality.

On reviewing the conduct of Polycarp and of Juftin Martyr, we commiferate their fufferings, and admire their firmnefs. The language of their profeffions was temperate and chaftifed, and their conduct in the laft trying fcenes of life was in every refpect difpaffionate and heroick. In the epiftles of Ignatius are found more ardent effufions of zeal: he expreffes his eagernefs to fuffer death, and requefts the Roman converts not to defire his deliverance, nor to intercede with the magiftrates for his difcharge.

To the Hiftorian of the Decline and Fall of the Roman Empire fuch fervour for martyrdom appears unnatural and cenfurable. But let the zealous fpirit of the Apoftolical times

be

be confidered, as well as the fuffering ftate of chriftianity, and the ardent temper of Ignatius. The defire of immortality was the ruling paffion of his mind, and hurried him into expreffions of rapture and impatience. His enthufiaftic ardour, fo far from refulting from a cenfurable motive, arofe from an excefs of virtue. He was fteadfaftly and unalterably determined to perfevere unto the end, and to crown a long life of unfhaken fidelity with a magnanimous death. He fought not officioufly the occafion of fuffering; but when the accomplifhment of his fentence approached, he even difconcerted the malice of his enemies, and encreafed the confidence of his friends, by converting that event into a fubject of pious exultation. He panted for that clofe of his life from which Socrates, in circumftances not diffimilar, difdained to fhrink.

The Emperour Trajan intended to inflict the deepeft wound on chriftianity, by devoting to public execution one of its moft eminent Paftors. It may be concluded therefore, that the interceffion of the Roman converts for the deliverance of Ignatius would have been vain and fruitlefs. Had their application been fuccefsful, the favour obtained by it would have been totally repugnant to his principles, as well

well as his wishes; since he looked forward to his approaching sufferings as the necessary trial of his constancy, and the true and unequivocal test of his faith. The prospect of heavenly bliss, which was the end and the reward of his perseverance, made the means appear not only tolerable, but attracting; not only to be endured with patience, but to be anticipated with rapture. St. Peter, by whom Ignatius was initiated into the service of the church, had not long before sealed the truth of the gospel with his blood. St. Paul had made Rome, and probably the same amphitheatre in which Ignatius was to be exposed to lions, the scene of his last sufferings. The Apostle of the Gentiles, on a similar occasion, calmed the grief of his friends, and silenced their pathetic remonstrances, when they foreboded the fatal consequences of his journey to Jerusalem. Animated rather than depressed by the impending trial of his fortitude and sincerity, he zealously expressed his readiness not only to submit to the rigours of imprisonment, but to endure the pains of death, in order to promote the cause of christianity. Moreover, the disciples of our Lord, after their dismission from the Jewish assembly, had converted their ignominious treatment into a subject of joy and congratulation. These examples therefore

were

were too recent, and too applicable to his own situation, not to make the deepest impression on the mind of Ignatius. Hence he was inspired with sacred emulation, and was encouraged to extend his eager views to that martyrdom which he wished to participate with his great and holy predecessors, in full assurance of participating with them also, its transcendent and immortal rewards.

However the sentiments expressed by Ignatius may seem to exceed the bounds of calm and quiet resignation, they are by no means singular. Amidst the multitude of similar instances with which later monuments of ecclesiastical antiquity abound, our attention is first directed to the conduct of Cyprian and Basil. Their expressions, on approaching the spot which was destined for their execution, were the dictates of joy, rather than of grief. Their death, like that of Ignatius, far from being attended with indications of tame dejection, or sullen acquiescence, wore the dignified air of a triumph.

The elegant Author of the inquiry into the miraculous powers of the church has represented that the Martyrs were encouraged by peculiar incentives to bear their harsh sentences

SERMON III. 93

tences with patience and even with joy; becaufe they were animated by the expectation that earthly glory would crown their afflictions; that their memory would be celebrated by panegyrical orations, and annual feftivals; that the greateft veneration would be paid to their reliques; and that the merit of their fufferings would be a fufficient expiation of fin. Now, as no traces are to be found of fuch expectations, in the works of the earlieft Fathers, which our plan has led us to confult; it feems more juft and more neceffary to develope thofe principles of action which we may conclude with greater certainty to have influenced their conduct.

He whofe mind is deeply impreffed with the defcription of the fufferings of the early Martyrs, aggravated as thofe fufferings were, in many inftances, by all the tortures of ingenious cruelty; and endured at the fame time with the moft unruffled compofure; will eafily admit, that their extraordinary fortitude arofe from the immediate fupport of the divine grace. He may be led to exprefs his opinion in the following train of reprefentation.

There exifts in man an inherent love of life, which is fo deeply engraven by the hand

of

of nature, that it seems to form an essential part of the soul. Self preservation is the fundamental law of our being; it is the passion which precedes every other in the order of utility, and is implanted by the Creator, as the root, from which every social and religious obligation necessarily springs.

However strong this principle may be, and however uniformly it might be supposed to operate in every state of society, the page of history, and the authentic relation of credible witnesses, exhibit to us various instances in which it is sometimes counteracted and overcome. The antient inhabitants of northern Europe sought death with ardent eagerness in the field of battle, or welcomed its approach in the decline of age, with expressions of savage joy. The follower of Brama, to shun the wearisome decay of lingering sickness, anticipates the hour of death, and devotes himself to the flames. The Indian remains unmoved amid the dreadful preparations for his lingering execution, and defies, in the agonies of torture, the ingenious cruelty of his foes. The Gentoo, with steady pace and unaltered look, ascends the funeral pile, and becomes a willing sacrifice to her departed husband.

In

SERMON III.

In thefe cafes we behold the effect of national cuftom and inveterate habit. Such felf-devoted victims were trained up from their birth to the contemplation of fpectacles of torture and death; and their perpetual occurrence operating upon a general obduracy of manners and temper, prepared the way for the unfeeling facrifice of life.

On contemplating the fituation and circumftances of the early Martyr, his cafe will appear to be widely different: he was generally taken from the eminent ranks of chriftians; he was born in an enlightened country; his difpofition and education inclined him more neceffarily to the allurements of eafe and peace; unlike the favage, he was a ftranger to fcenes of turbulence and blood, and unaccuftomed to fituations that called for vigorous exertion, or unremitting and hardy activity; his mind was actuated by keen fenfibility, which is a quality that never exifts in a barbarous ftate of fociety; he was alive to all the exquifite endearments of focial life, and attached to the world by all thofe tender ties of friendfhip and affection which hold the heart in the moft permanent captivity. Hence arofe a conteft between the love of God and love of Life; between the fuggeftions of confcience, science, and the calls of affection; between the claims of rigid duty, and the expostulations of violated nature. Nothing less therefore than a divine interference seems capable of terminating the dubious contest, and of making religion triumphant over the reluctance of humanity, and the powerful attractions of the world.

Moreover, the tenderness of youth, and the delicacy of the female sex, were frequently exposed to the same punishments. They turned from the fascinating pleasures of the world, and met their fate with the same unruffled composure, which distinguished the victims of more mature experience. The conduct of Blandina, among the Martyrs of Lyons and Vienne, was as conspicuous and exemplary as that of the venerable Pothius. As the same temper of mind actuated all the sufferers, without distinction of sex or age; it becomes more necessary to advert to a principle, which from the energy of its effect, and the extent, and the uniformity of its operation, will obviously account for such heroick behaviour.

The powerful succour which gave ardour and confidence to the first christians, was by no means confined to them. It was graciously
displayed

SERMON III. 97

displayed whenever the confolations and affiftance vouchfafed to the faithful, were equally inftrumental to the glory of the chriftian caufe. The mercy of the Almighty was equally propitious to thofe whofe conduct was uniformly diftinguifhed by rational piety, and whofe unremitting zeal prompted them to contend earneftly for the faith. For evident inftances of fimilar affiftance the pious reader of the martyrologies will proceed to appeal to the hiftory of our own country. He will ftill continue to maintain, that when the Demon of Papiftical bigotry raged, and the fires of fuperftition blazed in every part of Britain, the affertors of the proteftant faith received powerful fupport from on high. To this aufpicious fource his gratitude will attribute the inflexible conftancy of Hooper, the unruffled ferenity of Rogers, and the reanimated zeal of Cranmer. Nor, when he looks back to the tranfactions of bigotry which occur in the annals of Oxford, will he think that any other adequate caufe can be affigned for the dignified refignation of Ridley, and Latimer.

In this divine interference, there appears moft affuredly to be nothing repugnant to the declarations of fcripture; nothing that offers an affront to the powers of reafon: fo far
G   from

from it, the suppofition is strictly confistent with the predictions and promises of our Lord, who gracioufly difplayed the glory of his divine perfon, to animate St. Stephen, when finking under the violence of his murderers. The particular attention of Providence, to virtue in diftrefs, was a tenet which reflected honour on the principles of antient philofophy. Without diftrufting the firmnefs of the ground on which the general hypothefis refts, the caviller may be challenged to prove that fuch an interpofition is in any degree derogatory from the honour of the Supreme Being. For he cannot have the hardinefs to affert, that it is at all inconfiftent with the goodnefs and mercy of God, to fuccour his faithful fervants in the moft momentous and trying conflicts of life; more efpecially, 'at a time when thofe momentous and trying conflicts were undergone in atteftation to that truth, which even his beloved Son died to eftablifh.

But however eager the reader of the martyrologies may be, to eftablifh his fentiments in the minds of others; he muft not precipitately urge his favourite hypothefis, as an indifputable truth. Confidered as a conjecture, it derives fome probability from the extraordinary nature of the chriftian difpenfation itfelf,

as

SERMON III.

as well as from the extraordinary difficulties which its advocates were forced to encounter. But the evidence for it is lefs complete and lefs ſtriking than might have been expected. The deficiency in this refpect may lead many into a different train of thinking, and a different mode of accounting for the courage of the martyrs.

Such may impute it to the full conviction with which the martyrs were impreſſed of the goodneſs of their cauſe; to their certain hope of immediate happineſs; to their reluctance to retract from the profeſſion they had ſolemnly made; to the approbation of their own conſcience, and to their defire of following the example of their predeceſſors, and of leaving an equal example to poſterity.

The ſuppoſitions which we have attempted to ſtate, have a certain degree of evidence and probability to fupport them. The adoption of either muſt ultimately depend upon particular modes of education, and particular trains of thinking. He who views the providence of the Almighty prefiding over every part of the world, and ſometimes more immediately interpofing his arm to fupport his diſtreſſed ſervants, will eagerly embrace the former. He who

who is an advocate for the dignity of unaffifted reafon, and afferts the unconquerable ftrength of human refolution, will not fail to efpoufe the latter.

Thefe arguments naturally lead us, in the third place, to confider the Effects produced by the fortitude of the martyrs.

Their conduct was eminently conducive to the diffufion of chriftianity. The people, after viewing repeated executions of the faithful, far from adopting the fentiments of informers and perfecutors, were impreffed with juft indignation and exceffive horror at their unrelenting malice. The tender emotions of pity to the fufferers were excited in their breafts, and a ftrong inclination was awakened to afk what principles had infpired them with fuch undaunted heroifm. The compaffion of the multitude rendered them curious, and their curiofity became the happy caufe of their converfion. Thus was the confummate wifdom of the divine decrees exemplified in the wayward and precipitate folly of man. The fanguinary meafures adopted to extirpate the new religion, operated as the means of its more rapid diffufion; and the church, far from finking under her repeated loffes, rapidly augmented the number

SERMON III.

of her profelytes. She refembled the fruitful vine, which, from the defalcation of fome branches, produces more rich and more abundant fruit.

Nor did the number of her fons only encreafe, but their refpectability alfo. From the patience of the fuffering chriftians, the more contemplative and rational Pagans inferred the innocence of their lives, and the purity of their characters. To them it feemed impoffible that men who undauntedly encountered the pains of premature diffolution, could be addicted to voluptuoufnefs or ftained with guilt. For they wifely concluded, that the indulgence of vitious gratifications inevitably tends to enervate the mind, and to render it incapable of fuch great and ftrenuous exertions. Thefe arguments made a deep impreffion on the minds of many who had been educated in the fchools of philofophy; and their converfion failed not to reflect additional luftre on the chriftian name.

From the particulars of the preceding difquifition it appears, that chriftianity was long expofed to dangers which were conftantly threatening its compleat and irreparable fubverfion. During its infant ftate, it was affaulted

faulted by the relentlefs rage of the moft cruel tyrants, whofe crimes contaminate the annals of hiftory. The poifon of flander, the fhaft of ridicule, the fcoff of contempt, and the fword of perfecution, were the active but ineffectual inftruments that were conftantly employed againft it. But its great Author permitted not his religion to be extirpated by the malevolence and the infatuation of man; fince he was gracioufly pleafed not only to invigorate the minds of his fuffering fervants by his all-fufficient aid; but converted the machinations of their mercilefs foes into the moft effectual and abundant fources of the diffufion of the faith.

If the perfeverance of the early martyrs was thus eminently conducive to the rapid progrefs of the gofpel, it is not difficult to afcertain, or at leaft to conjecture, what would have been the confequences of their recantation and apoftafy. The Pagans would have boafted, that chriftianity itfelf wanted a fufficient energy of principle, to arm its followers with intrepidity; and confequently, that it funk much below many inftitutions confeffedly of human origin; and was weaker in its attractions than many attachments which have influenced the couragious of all ages, to difregard the approach

SERMON III. 103

proach of danger, and contemn the frowns of death. This would have been their prefumptive argument againſt its pretenſions to a divine revelation; and if it was a ſyſtem founded on the ingenuity of man, by the violence of man alſo it could have been ſubverted. Satisfied with ſuch ſophiſtry, and elated with the ſuccefs of their firſt attempts, the enemies of the goſpel would obviouſly have proceeded to try the ſame methods, upon the more ignoble adherents to the faith, which had ſuccefsfully been purſued againſt its leaders. Their repeated ſuccefs would have given a ſevere check to the progrefs of chriſtianity. For it muſt have been driven for refuge to the receſſes of remote provinces; and its benefits would have been loſt to multitudes for many generations.

But the perſeverance of the martyrs proves the vigour, as well as the perfection of the chriſtian principles. They rightly underſtood that its great Author never intended to confine its operations within the narrow and degrading limits of worldly prudence and temporizing caution. Their behaviour was ſufficient to convince all ſucceeding ages, that whilſt it can inculcate the love of whatever is laudable, and the defire of whatever is good; it can likewife excite the endurance of all that is terrible,

rible, and produce the performance of all that is magnanimous.

From the blind partiality which the frequent contemplation of suffering virtue is too apt to diffuse over the credulous mind, and from too close and vehement a pursuit of those reflections which prove how greatly the progress of christianity was accelerated by the fortitude of the first proselytes; the christians of the middle ages were led to attribute a peculiar efficacy to their relicks. They advanced martyrs to the same honours which the gratitude of primeval ages had conferred on the founders of states and the inventors of useful arts. When, however, the christian of more enlightened times censures the misguided conduct of such weak and superstitious zealots, let him be careful not to imbibe the opposite sentiments of those, who contemptuously overlook or studiously depreciate such eminent instances of merit. Weighed in the balance of fair and dispassionate judgment, the conduct of the early martyrs appears to have shed distinguished lustre on their profession. When a desertion of the banners of christianity would have been detrimental to her best interest, they were the first who met the encounter of the enemy. By the ardour of their zeal, and

by

by the firmnefs of their refolution, they difconcerted his continued affaults; and though they fell victims to their determined fteadinefs, became more than conquerors by fecuring the ultimate triumph of their caufe. For all who were thus expofed to danger and to death in the gloomy feafon of perfecution, we cannot fail to cherifh a high degree of refpect and honour. They reached the true elevation of the chriftian character, and adorned the noble inftitutes of their religion with immoveable attachment, and unfhaken courage. They gave the moft convincing and moft valuable proof of their fincerity, by fealing the truth with their blood. In every inftance of their pious refignation, through a long fucceffion of illuftrious examples, they prefent us with that noble and awful fpectacle, which is the favourite theme of philofophical eulogy, and is the moft interefting and moft edifying object which can poffibly be exhibited to the contemplation of the world:—a virtuous man fuffering unmerited misfortunes with patience. —*They have fought a good fight, they have finifhed their courfe, they have kept the faith. Henceforth, there is laid up for them a crown of righteoufnefs, which the Lord, the righteous Judge, fhall give them at that day; and not to them only, but to all that love his appearing.*

SERMON IV.

Ephesians V. 27.

A glorious Church, not having spot or wrinkle, or any such thing, but holy and without blemish.

THE establishment of discipline is necessary not only to the existence of every community, but also to its continuance; as it connects the members by one common bond of association, and checks internal disorders by salutary and efficacious restraints. This principle extends to religious as well as to civil constitutions; for though the origin of religion be divine, yet the preservation of it is committed to human means; and therefore like every other trust in the moral dispensations of providence, it requires some directions for the understanding, and some restraints upon the passions. The christian church seems to have been

been formed upon the model of the Judaical synagogue, since they agree in many circumstances of their government. The principles of its polity were immediately founded upon the express declarations of scripture, and the constant practise of the apostles. As from no less an authority than that of our Lord himself, was derived the privilege of initiating converts by the water of baptism, and of confirming their faith by eating the bread of the eucharist; so from the conduct of Christ's immediate successors originated the power of pronouncing the sentence of excommunication.

This discipline, by the unabating vigour with which it was enforced in the infancy of the church, constituted a sure and infallible criterion of the sincerity of the proselytes. A conformity of manners with the institutes of the gospel was expected to be the immediate consequence of conversion. Hypocrisy could not for any long period of time elude the vigilance of strict observation, nor could any flagrant infringement of baptismal vows remain unmarked and unpunished. As the reputation of the church intirely depended on the irreproachable conduct of her members, she wisely preserved the greatest distinction

between

SERMON IV.

between the exemplary and the profligate. The refult was highly favourable to her beft interefts; for whilft her unfullied purity of morals fupplied her friends with the moft animating fubject of panegyrick, it gave the moft unequivocal confutation to the malicious calumny of her enemies.

To minifters felected from the body of the converts, the difcharge of the facred functions was entrufted. As the church was frequently groaning under the feverity of perfecution, or filled with the apprehenfions of its approach; and as the moft eminent chriftians were the certain victims of popular rage, the ambition of raifing themfelves to ecclefiaftical honours muft have been in a great meafure repreffed. Spiritual preeminence was accompanied neither with the comfort of fecurity, nor the gratification of emolument. So that a purer and more exalted principle neceffarily predominated in thefe early ages, when a fituation of more immediate danger made the moft confpicuous diftinction between the paftor and his flock. Hence a long life of vigilance and piety was often clofed by a fudden and cruel death.

If many paffages of fcripture feem not clearly to afcertain the difference between the

orders

orders of bishops and of presbyters; that difference may be best illustrated and defined, by the early establishments. In the beginning of the apocalypse, the bishops are peculiarly distinguished from all other members of the christian communities; and by a figurative allusion derived from the synagogue, are denominated the angels of the seven churches. The letters addressed by Ignatius, the venerable prelate of Antioch, to various congregations of Asia, plainly show that their order was generally established, and that they were invested with peculiar powers of superintendance soon after the decease of St. John.

The clear distinction which Ignatius marks out between the bishops, and the presbyters, is supported by the antient acts of the same martyr, and of Polycarp. It is confirmed in the succeeding part of the century by the epistle of the emperor Hadrian to Servianus; by the testimony of Dionysius of Corinth, the epistle of the churches of Lyons and Vienne; and by the fragments of Hegesippus, Polycrates, and Serapion.

Implicit obedience to these governours of the church was represented as a proper principle of action, and an indispensable branch of
duty.

duty. A high degree of deference and even veneration was recommended, as peculiarly due to their character and rank. And without doubt the moſt compleat ſubordination will appear to have been highly neceſſary, on conſidering the perilous ſtate of the early chriſtians. Recently formed into communities, they were at once aſſailed by open violence, and agitated by internal diſcord. No expedient ſeemed better calculated to invigorate their common efforts, and infuſe a ſpirit of unanimity, than a chearful obedience to their eccleſiaſtical guides. The riſing church reſembled a ſmall army ſtationed on hoſtile ground, whoſe only ſecurity againſt the perfidy of inſidious allies, and the aſſault of open enemies, confiſted in receiving the orders of their leader without murmurs, and following him without complaint.

Among the arduous employments which called forth the activity of the primitive biſhops, no one required more unremitting attention than to confute the errours of hereſy. The alarming diffuſion of falſe doctrines had required the repeated exertions of the apoſtles; and their ſucceſſors found by painful experience, that a great part of their employment muſt neceſſarily conſiſt in eradicating
the

the noxious tares which the enemies of the true faith still laboured to disseminate.

To accommodate the sacred volume to their own preconceived ideas, and not to sacrifice their preconceived ideas to the sacred volume; seems to have been the fundamental errour of the early hereticks. The causes of their desertion of the true faith, must therefore be traced from their original manners of life, from the bias of corrupt inclinations, from the stubborn influence of early habits, and their warm attachment to a spurious philosophy. In some, may be discerned the sallies of a licentious imagination, which delights to decorate truth, with the most incongruous appendages of fantastick mythology; in others, is equally evident a palpable perversion of scripture, interpreted upon the contracted principles of bigotted Judaism. They resembled the philosophers of Greece, who attributed such characters to their deities as were most conformable to the relaxed, or rigid maxims of their favourite schools. Thus the Gnostick represented the person of the Messiah airy and volatile as his general system of theology; whilst the Ebionite, whose mind could not soar above ritual and carnal ordinances, sunk him to a level with his own nature.

Although

Although the Gnosticks, and the Ebionites were remarkable for an early desertion of the true faith, they were not contemporaries. So that ineffectual is the attempt which has been made by the Author of the early opinions concerning Christ, to heighten their antiquity, by referring them to the time of the apostles. As a proof how detrimental to the interest of christianity their errours were thought, and how serious an alarm was given to the orthodox by their diffusion, the detail and the confutation of their opinions forms a considerable part of the more antient literature of the church.

The Oriental and Platonic philosophy, some fictitious writings of Zoroaster and Abraham, together with the pretended traditions of Christ and his Apostles, combined to form the visionary system of the Gnosticks. Their particular tenets are too extravagant, and too numerous, to admit of repetition, after the minute and curious catalogue which has been given of them, by the ecclesiastical writers. The Historian of the decline and fall of the Roman Empire has distinguished them by a circumstantial account of their opinions, and a favourable representation of their conduct. He has however made an omission which the

H   rigid

rigid impartiality of truth can by no means juſtify, by paſſing over in ſilence thoſe ſects of the Gnoſticks, who were cenſurable for the licentiouſneſs of their morals. If even great allowance be made for the unfavourable relations of Irenæus, and the more dark and diſguſting deſcriptions of Epiphanius; it cannot be imagined, that they were totally deſtitute of a foundation. For the latter of theſe Fathers had every opportunity of aſcertaining the facts which he records, and deſcribes circumſtances which were publickly known. We muſt conclude, therefore, that the ſenſuality of their conduct bore ſome analogy to the extravagance of their opinions. The cenſures, incurred by their profligacy of manners, may be applied, with too much juſtice, to the followers of Marcion, Saturninus, Baſilides, Marcus, and Carpocrates.

As the diſciples of Cerinthus, of Menander, and of Valentinus, held the paſſions to be the moſt dangerous enemies of the ſoul, they mortified them with the moſt rigid auſterity; whilſt thoſe Gnoſtics, who were more relaxed in their principles, indulged them with criminal licentiouſneſs. Such conduct, however oppoſite, may be reconciled to their grand and fundamental tenet; as they held the body to be

SERMON IV.

be the source of evil and corruption, and totally distinct and disunited from the soul when purified by religion. They maintained therefore, that the impulses of the passions, however irregular, might be obeyed or disregarded, without spiritual danger, or spiritual advantage.

They denied the humanity of Christ, from a supposition that it was highly unworthy of a divine being to be united to impure and gross matter. They affirmed that what appeared to be his body was a mere phantom, and that his crucifixion was illusive and visionary.

To confute these paradoxical and erroneous opinions, both Ignatius, Bishop of Antioch, and Polycarp, Bishop of Smyrna, impressed upon the minds of the christian converts the grand and awful facts of the incarnation, and of the crucifixion. They declare in express terms, and repeat the same sentiments in various passages of their epistles, that "who-
" soever does not confess, that our Lord suffered
" upon the cross, is from Satan. Jesus Christ
" was truly born, and did eat and drink; was
" truly persecuted under Pontius Pilate; was
" truly crucified and died; and was truly raised
" up by the Father."

SERMON IV.

The derivation of the name of the Ebionites is involved in some obscurity. It has been supposed to allude to their indigent condition, or to the degrading opinion which they formed of the Son of God. But probability seems upon the whole to incline to the conjecture that it was the appellation of the author of the sect. They sprang originally from the Nazarenes, who composed a more antient society of Judaizing christians. These two sects have been very improperly confounded with each other, by the Author of the early opinions concerning Christ; although the distinctions which subsisted between them is carefully marked out by the antient writers. As a characteristick distinction, they not only held different opinions of the fundamental articles of faith, but received different gospels. In the gospel of the Nazarenes the two first chapters of St. Matthew were admitted, which the gospel of the Ebionites wanted. The Nazarenes not only maintained the miraculous conception of Christ, but also that he partook in some limited degree of the divine nature. The Ebionites held St. Paul in great contempt, as a deserter of the law of his ancestors; the Nazarenes, on the contrary, placed him among the most eminent teachers of divine truth. The Ebionites maintained that the

laws

SERMON IV.

laws of Moses ought to be observed by all proselytes to christianity; the Nazarenes, that such an observance should be extended only to the descendants of Abraham. As a decisive argument that the Nazarenes held opinions more sound and more approaching to the true faith than their successors the Ebionites, they are not included in the heretical catalogue by the early writers, whereas the Ebionites are distinguished by a conspicuous place.

They drew their opinions from a spurious history of Christ, to which reference is probably made in St. Paul's epistle to the Galatians. It was their grand object to make an accommodation between the law and the gospel, by raising the former, and depressing the latter, and to combine them in one system of belief and practise, in order to render them equally obligatory. A part of this sect maintained that the conception of Christ was miraculous; whilst others more presumptuously asserted, that he was a mere man, the Son of Joseph and Mary; and that he was not distinguished from mortals by any miraculous circumstances of birth. Some at least of this latter description are known to have held, that at the time of his baptism, the Christ, who had been invested by the Supreme Being

H 3   with

with the sovereignty of the world, descended upon Jesus in the form of a dove, and continued the director of his actions to the time of his crucifixion; when he reascended to heaven, and left Jesus exposed to the pains of unassisted humanity.

As the Ebionites began to rise into notice at the commencement of the second century, Ignatius and Polycarp assiduously laboured to extirpate their opinions. That the division of Jesus Christ into two distinct persons was at once unscriptural and irrational, sufficiently appears from the expressions employed by these Fathers to confute the Gnosticks. There are, however, many other passages in their epistles, more particularly directed against the Ebionites, the substance of which is conveyed in the following declarations:—" That Jesus " Christ our inseparable life, is sent by the will " of the Father. That our God Jesus Christ " was according to the divine dispensation con- " ceived of the Virgin, of the family of David, " by the Holy Ghost. Again; Be not deceived " by heterodox doctrines, nor with antient " fables, which are unedifying; for if ye con- " tinue to live according to the Jewish law, ye " confess yourselves not to have received grace; " ye ought no longer to observe sabbaths, but " keep the Lord's day."

These

SERMON IV.

These words, in their general import, seem equally to affect all the heresies of that early age, and to be levelled against those who denied the miraculous conception, as well as the divinity of Christ. The latter part of the quotation, however, is more strictly appropriate. The converts are exhorted to quit their attachment to the law of Moses, because totally inconsistent with the principles of the true faith; and the prejudices attributed to them, are not so strictly applicable to any description of Christians, as to the Ebionites.

On a full consideration of the expressions of Ignatius, it may not be improper to apply to them the pertinent remark which Tertullian makes on the first epistle of St. John. "The " Evangelist particularly stigmatizes those In- " fidels by the name of Antichrists, who deny " that Christ is come in the flesh, and who do " not maintain that Jesus is the Son of God. " The former was the errour of Marcion, the " latter of Ebion."

The censures of Justin Martyr are directed against the same hereticks, in his curious dialogue with Trypho the Jew. He describes particularly the errours of the sect, and his omission of their name is similar to his practice with respect to the evangelists, of whom he speaks only in general terms. He marks out the wide distinction between the Ebionites and the orthodox believers; adverts to their desertion of the doctrines of scripture for the vain traditions of men. To him their opinions appeared so derogatory from the divinity of the Son of God, that he expressed his deliberate disapprobation of their opinions, and seems rather inclined to rank them among the believing Jews, than to include them in the number of genuine christians.

Irenæus in his elaborate work, in which he confutes the various sectaries of the second century, maintains that the Ebionites, by their perverse and degrading opinions, had wantonly deprived themselves of the benefits of the incarnation; and were deserving of the same severe and full reprehension which was due to all other deserters of the truth. He includes them in the general catalogue of those hereticks " who are so unlearned and ignorant of the " dispensations of God, particularly of his " gracious design respecting the redemption " of man, that they are blind to the truth, " and contradict their own salvation."

SERMON IV.

From this unanimous oppofition of the antient fathers of the church it appears how much the fentiments of the Ebionites were reprobated. To the different pleas which they confidently fet up, the moft cogent and unanfwerable arguments were oppofed. They boafted of various advantages which they enjoyed in common with the church, and their claims were difputed with that firmnefs, and vanquifhed with that irrefiftible power of confutation, which will ever be the recompenfe of prefumption and errour. Like the church they had traditions: but of what did they confift? Not of the pure and uncorrupted injunctions of the apoftles; but of the empty and obfolete ceremonies of the Levitical law. Like the church they had prophecies; but how did they interpret them? Not in the fpirit of the infpired writers; not by an enlarged and complete view of the predictions that difplay the exalted nature of the Meffiah, as well as of thofe which defcribe his humiliation; but by a fervile adherence to the falfe gloffes of the later and more contracted Rabbins, who maintained him to be a mere man. Like the church they had fcriptures; but were their fcriptures the complete and indifputable productions of truth? So far was this from being the cafe, that they contained

tained not the testimony of the beloved disciple, nor the epistles of the great apostle of the Gentiles, because they rejected such parts of the canonical code with disdain. On the contrary, they received a mutilated gospel of St. Matthew, and perused with eager credulity the romantick legends of false teachers.

Thus they were slow of heart to believe all that the prophets had spoken, and all that the apostles had testified. Whilst the true christian enlarged his mind with a full conception of his religion, the Ebionite with inflexible obstinacy submitted to bear the unnecessary burthens of the law, and with blind perverseness cut off the essential principle of the gospel.

Between the Ebionite and the Mahometan there is a close and striking resemblance. According to the creed of both, Jesus Christ is a mere man. They practice with scrupulous attention the rites of circumcision and of purification. They both appeal to the authority of spurious books; and as the Ebionites value the fabulous travels of Clement, so the Mahometans consult the false gospel of Barnabas. They have a high regard for particular places: The Mahometan indulges the most profound veneration for the holy city which contains the

SERMON IV.

the tomb of his prophet: the Ebionite glows with equal enthufiafm on contemplating the profpect of Jerufalem.

The pride of Mahomet would have fuffered the keeneft mortification, if when he adopted fome ceremonial parts of the Mofaical law, and degraded the fublime character of the chriftian legiflator, he had reflected, that he fervilely purfued the fteps of an obfcure herefiarch; and that the boldnefs of his enterprizes, and not the fertility of his invention, gave him the beft title to the admiration of his followers.

Such was the origin of the antient communities of chriftians. In conformity with the apoftolical appointment, the fpiritual governours undertook their fuperintendance. To their more efpecial cuftody, the facred volume was committed, and by them the moft authentick copies of it were preferved. They performed the facred offices of religion, oppofed the incroachments of hereticks, confirmed the converts in their fidelity, and invited the Pagans to embrace the fame aufpicious hopes, which they cherifhed in their own breafts.

The

The regulations of these establishments, and the salutary influence of their rules, were open to general inspection. The heathens saw effects produced in the church which were more beneficial to society, than the theory of the sublimest philosopher had promised; or the performance of renowned legislators had produced. Here was the republick of Plato, without its licentiousness; and the asylum of Romulus, without its reception of the outcasts of society. The grand object of the institutions of Lycurgus was the acquirement of barren conquest. The consequence of the sanguinary decrees of Draco was the depopulation of his country. But the church whilst she executed judgment, remembered mercy, and the final cause of her severity was the extinction of sin, not the destruction of the sinner. Even in her discipline, there was nothing to repel the advances of the timid, nor to confirm the aversion of the prejudiced. The sentence of excommunication was awful in its circumstances, and certain in its infliction; but it was not irreversible. During the solemn season of penance, indeed, the countenance and the dress of the spiritual exile discovered the strongest marks of dejection and sorrow. But after giving the most unequivocal proofs of his sincere contrition, he was again admitted into the

SERMON IV. 125

the church, and his return was welcomed by the moſt ardent congratulations of the pious.

The prudent adminiſtration and ſtrict regularity of eccleſiaſtical diſcipline made the moſt favourable impreſſion on the mind of the Pagans, more particularly, when they obſerved the cloſe conformity of the conduct of the primitive chriſtians with the precepts of the goſpel.

Now, the chriſtian precepts appear to greateſt advantage when contraſted with the laws of the Jews, and the maxims of the Philoſophers.

The moral laws of the Moſaical code breathe much of that ſpirit of philanthropy which conſtitutes the glory of the evangelical ſcheme. Yet the laſt injunction of the Decalogue was liable to be fettered by a partial interpretation, and made ſubſervient to the contracted views of local prejudice. *Thou ſhalt not covet the poſſeſſions of thy neighbour;* might literally be underſtood as a prohibition of ſuch deſires only, as were fixed upon the property of perſons in the ſame vicinity. That the Jews were diſpoſed to conſider this duty as confined to ſo narrow a circle, ſeems probable, not only from the general averſion

which

which they discovered against all other nations; but likewise from the question proposed by the inquisitive scribe. Our Lord with his accustomed readiness to instruct, and his peculiar felicity to illustrate, represented the sensibility and the benevolence of the good Samaritan. This interesting picture was admirably adapted to awaken the torpid feelings of a bigotted Jew, and to display to him that sublime scheme of universal affection, in which he was to extend his views of charity beyond his native country, and to consider himself as the general friend of mankind.

The superiority of the gospel over the Mosaical law, appears more fully by considering that the commandments of the latter, are, for the most part, negative; containing rather prohibitions of sin, than incitements to goodness. Whilst the disciple of Moses, adhering to his own principles, advances only the first step in the path of morality; the disciple of Christ leaves him far behind, adds to his innocence much positive excellence, and adorns his character with every virtue. So far from merely not invading the possessions of another man, he reaches out his liberal hand to minister to his necessities: so far from merely not retaliating injuries received, he stands ready

SERMON IV.

ready to embrace his enemy in the arms of affection, and breathes a fervent supplication to heaven, for his temporal and eternal happiness.

The philosophers of Greece and Rome present us with the most convincing proof, how far unenlightened reason carried her investigations towards the perfection of ethicks. The powers of intellect which they displayed, and the obstacles which they surmounted, before they discovered many valuable truths, are not fairly estimated, when viewed through the medium of the christian revelation. Their attainments ought to be compared with the ignorance of the multitudes that surrounded, and that preceded them. Then will they appear most wonderful efforts of the human mind. Then will they become the bright dawn of the intellectual morning which shone more and more unto the perfect day.

If moral wisdom descended from heaven to dwell with the most enlightened Sage of Athens, she quickly caught the contagion of earthly depravity, and forgot her dignity so far as to bend at the shrine of superstition. Her dictates were not built upon any certain foundation, or digested in a consistent plan.

They

They were difgraced with falfe notions, intermixed with frivolous refinements, and fcattered among difcordant fects. The indiffoluble union of confiftency, the powerful attraction of example, and the ftrong and awakening voice of authority were wanted to give to precept the energy of law. But the moft material obftacle to a ready compliance with their inftructions was the want of fuch fanctions as hold the mind in the moft permanent fubjection, by immediately addreffing its hopes and fears.

Thefe defects were diftinctly vifible to the antients themfelves. Ariftodemus declared to Socrates that he would willingly worfhip the Gods, whenever their embaffadours defcended to inform him what to perform and what to avoid. The enlightened philofopher himfelf obferved, on contemplating the infufficiency of natural reafon to reform the world, that the labours of moralifts muft be vain and ineffectual, unlefs the Supreme Being would commiffion fome teacher to inftruct mankind. The great Roman orator alfo, expreffed an ardent wifh for the difcovery of a new demonftration to prove that virtue alone was fufficient for happinefs. This general diffatisfaction clearly evinces the neceffity

SERMON IV.

necessity of a divine revelation, and may be considered as the voice of philosophy complaining of her own defects, and imploring the Supreme Being to point out the path of duty to her impatient and bewildered followers.

By the gospel, therefore, were supplied the deficiencies of all preceding institutions and systems. The Mosaical code was as far excelled by the religion of Christ, as the tabernacle of the wilderness was surpassed by the magnificence of the temple of Solomon.

The maxims of antient wisdom were not only refined and enlarged, but established upon a true principle, and made conducive to an exalted end. The scattered and feeble stars of philosophy which were visible during the night of ignorance, were obscured by the diffusive effulgence of the evangelical sun.

To complete the benevolent plan of revelation, the same volume which was filled with the most pure lessons of wisdom, contained likewise the most perfect exemplification of them. The adorable Son of God condescended to recommend his own instruction by his own practice, and to exhibit that lively image of

I   moral

moral perfection which had, indeed, sublimed the imagination of Plato and of Cicero; but which, antient experience in the widest circle of observation, had sought for in vain. The divine teacher not only spake, as man never spoke, but at once to combine the efficacy of example with the 'perfection of precept, became the unerring guide to all that was pious, all that was amiable, and all that was great.

If the Pagans were dazzled with the lustre of his conduct, and saw him soar to an elevation which mere humanity cannot reach; they were convinced that it was practicable in some degree to follow his steps when they directed their attention to the early converts, who were no less zealous in their professions of fidelity to his commands, than instrumental to his glory by their actions.

The basis of the primitive virtues was a steadfast and lively Faith, which consisted in a perfect conviction of the truth of christianity, preceded by a careful examination of its evidences, and accompanied with a full assurance of its rewards. This principle purified their taste, and exalted their desires above the gross pleasures of sense, and made all sublunary enjoyments seem as dust in the balance when weighed

SERMON IV. 131

weighed againſt the happineſs of eternal life. It difpelled the miſts which obſtructed their profpect of heaven; for during the vexations of adverſity, the diſtreſs of perſecution, and the agony of martyrdom, they behaved with the fame invincible perſuaſion of the truth of the divine promiſes, as if they had beheld their Lord and Maſter coming in the clouds with power and majeſty, and holding out the crowns of everlaſting life to his perſevering followers.

From this faith aroſe that ardent and rational zeal which is ſhewn in a chearful and prompt execution of the commands of God, whatever he enjoined, and an unremitting purſuit of duty wherever it pointed the way. Their conduct was equally remote from the languor of indifference, and the extravagance of fanaticiſm.

In the firſt rank of primitive virtues ſtood Humility, which was the chief characteriſtick of our Lord himſelf, and is the peculiar ornament of his religion. How far the cultivation of it was carried by his early followers, appears from the literary remains of the firſt and ſecond centuries. The writers of that period were not influenced by dogmatical arrogance, or dictatorial presumption; but uniformly discovered an amiable and unassuming diffidence. Clement Bishop of Rome, although honourably mentioned by St. Paul, as his coadjutor in the faith, aspires to no authority over the Corinthian church, when writing to compose its dissentions; and Ignatius, the venerable Bishop of Antioch, celebrated for his piety and constancy, scarcely presumes to take the name of a disciple of Christ.

The character of many congregations was marked by the same virtue which distinguished their teachers. Gentleness of manners and obedience to authority were the fruits of their instructions. No sufferings in the service of their divine Master induced them to arrogate the smallest degree of merit to themselves, or to think that their conduct entitled them to any distinction, until they had advanced to final perseverance, and finished their course with joy. Armed by humility they were invulnerable against the derision and contumely of their enemies. As they cherished not the conceit of excellence, the pride of rank, nor the insolence of power; vain were the attempts of malevolence and slander, to ruffle their tranquility, and provoke their resentment.

SERMON IV.

In the diffusion of this virtue we behold the wonderful triumph of christianity over national character, and deeply rooted prejudice. The Romans were elated with the prospect of their ample dominions, which exceeded the extent of all former conquests. Descended from ancestors whose achievements, and whose virtues swelled their breasts with conscious dignity, and rich with the spoils of the vanquished provinces, they wanted nothing to increase their sense of personal dignity. The Greeks, equally illustrious for the noble exploits of their predecessors, and distinguished by the cultivation of the most elegant arts, beheld with disdain the barbarous nations that surrounded them. The philosophers although divided into various sects, yet were all elevated by the same spirit of superciliousness, and as they soared above the multitude in the rejection of vulgar prejudices, and the cultivation of the intellectual powers, they esteemed themselves the wisest of mortals. These respective propensities, so dear to the human mind because so founded on self love, were softened and controuled by the precepts of christianity. The humility of the gospel checked the presumption of the proud; and that haughtiness of spirit which had never before submitted to controul was transformed into complacence and condescension.

The primitive christians were equally remarkable for the exercise of Charity in its most enlarged and proper sense. One considerable branch of this duty was their genuine liberality of sentiment. This was as observable in their general conduct to the Pagans, as in their publick and private supplications to the throne of mercy. In the midst of the most fierce persecutions they fervently prayed for the preservation of the Emperour, and the prosperity of the state. When defamed by the insinuations of the Jews, and mindful of their rebellion against their crucified Messiah; when exposed to contempt and calumny on account of the scandalous licentiousness of hereticks, they generously confess, that far from viewing them as objects of hatred and abomination, they entreat the compassionate Parent of the world for their amendment and happiness.

The fairest and most conspicuous fruit of this comprehensive virtue was Beneficence. Its effects were not confined to individuals, or to a particular congregation, but extended to the church at large. The accumulation of property

property for the relief of the poor in the infancy of the church, as well as the liberal contributions promoted by the apoftle of the Gentiles, atteft its early prevalence. Nor did the converts of fucceeding times degenerate from their predeceffors. The commendation which was beftowed on the munificence of the Corinthians by Clement, Bifhop of Rome, was with equal juftice and ardour returned by Dionyfius the Great. He defcribes the attention of the Romans to the generous cuftom which commenced at the firft diffufion of the gofpel, of alleviating the neceffities of diftant brethren. Nor did their liberality ftop here, but was reached out to thofe pious captives who, torn from their focial connexions, were condemned for their adherence to the faith, to labour in the imprifonment of the mines. This principle was in fome inftances elevated to the height of ardent affection, and led to that difinterefted facrifice of perfonal confiderations which realizes the attachments of romantic friendfhip. Many refcued their fellow chriftians from captivity by voluntarily occupying their places, and others fold themfelves into bondage, that by the price obtained by the forfeiture of freedom, they might fupply the neceffitous with food and raiment. To the Pagans fuch conduct was at firft a fubject of

I 4 furprize,

surprize, and afterwards excited the greatest admiration, when the humanity of the more opulent christians was not confined to the circle of their own community, but extended to the multitude at large. Acts of similar munificence were in some degree familiarized to the minds of the Romans, by the expences lavished by the opulent and the noble on the splendid exhibition of publick games, and the ostentatious prodigality of entertainments; but the christian liberality was directed to far more beneficial and disinterested ends. It was not dissipated among those who returned the obligation, by sacrificing their civil rights to the lust of power or of ambition, but it was conveyed to distant lands and foreign cities, to the naked and the hungry, who saw not the hand that reached out the kind supply, and could make no acknowledgment to their unknown benefactors, but the ardent benediction of gratitude, and the pious sacrifice of prayer.

The sarcastick Satyrist of the philosophers, in a strain of lively but malevolent irony, endeavours to fix the imputation of weakness and imprudence on the christians for their generous conduct. The Emperour Julian remarking its attractive influence on the minds of the people, determined to reform the religion

SERMON IV.

of polytheifm, by ingrafting upon its obfervances the pure precepts of the chriftian law. He confeffed that nothing had contributed more to the progrefs of chriftianity, than the kindnefs of the chriftians to ftrangers, the decent folemnity of their funeral rites, and the fanctity of their general conduct. It was then to virtues, not pretended but real, that the church was indebted for her enlargement; to virtues, which the moft acrimonious enemies of the faith combined unintentionally to commend, and by that means fupply an illuftrious confirmation of the veracity of thofe ecclefiaftical writers who record and extol them.

Whilft thefe were more particularly confpicuous, the chriftians recommended themfelves by their general conduct. Their firm attachment to the eftablifhed government, their facred adherence to truth and honour, their ftrict integrity, love of peace, and inoffenfivenefs, gradually difpelled the mifts of prejudice and calumny which firft obfcured the profpect of chriftianity, and brought them forward to the general obfervation of the world.

It was evident then that the chriftians rofe to that elevation of character which is the

moft

moſt difficult to attain, and at the ſame time the moſt valuable to poſſeſs. An elevation, not ſupported by the flattery of ſelf-love, but the firmneſs of confiſtency. Their practiſe reflected luſtre on their principles, and gave them the moſt perſuaſive recommendation. It was a ſevere and juſt reproach to the Phariſees that " they ſaid, but did not." They ſat in the ſeat of Moſes, and expounded the moral law; but they wore the maſk of hypocriſy, and liſtened not to the cry of the ſupplicating widow. The philoſophers adorned the dictates of wiſdom with the graces of eloquence; but they too often ſullied the purity of their ſchools with the ſtains of immorality. The Philoſopher and the Phariſee might confeſs with a bluſh, that they were far ſurpaſſed, and if ever a ſenſe of real merit touched their breaſts, they bowed with unfeigned deference to the unaſſuming followers of Chriſt.

In the chriſtian character, the oppoſite extremes of torpid apathy and boundleſs gratification were avoided. So that the Stoic might learn to relax his principles with decorum, and the Epicurean to find pleaſure in the purſuit of virtue. They ſaw that the chriſtian directed the natural propenſities of the mind, the

the love of pleasure, and the love of action, to their noblest ends; for he was temperate, just, benevolent and pious. These are the qualities which shed the most soft and pleasing lustre over the scenes of domestick as well as publick life, which refine the feelings of nature, and advance the happiness of society, which adorn the father in the circle of his family, and dignify the statesman in the consultations of the senate. So that such is the wonderful and intimate connexion between the true interests of this world and the next, that the same virtues which render man useful and agreeable among his fellow creatures, are the best preparatives and most unerring guides to the society of angels.

This imperfect display of the conduct of the first christians is not drawn from the solitary examples of individuals, or the vague assertions of rhetorical declaimers, but from circumstantial and authentick records, from the apologies of the converts, when on the assertion of truth depended all their earthly welfare, from the concurrent attestation of the ecclesiastical writers, and from the partial relations of their avowed enemies. A display of facts derived from such various sources, may therefore properly be regarded as the general voice

of

of antiquity proclaiming the virtues of true believers to the world, and calling upon posterity for wonder, applause and imitation.

Yet these virtues, great and illustrious as they are, *the Historian of the Decline and Fall of the Roman Empire* has confined to a bigotted zeal and a timid repentance. Such animating subjects would do honour to the talents and the exertions of any writer, because they display the best feelings and most exalted sentiments of human nature. Upon this occasion, the pencil of fiction is not necessary to give shade and colouring to the outlines of fact, to soften the frowns of tyranny, and beautify the features of licentiousness. The virtues of the primitive christians require not those flowers of fancy, nor that splendour of eloquence which are vainly lavished on the superstitious folly of Julian, and the consummate hypocrisy of Mahomet. They modestly ask to be enrolled in the records of impartial truth, *that men may see their good works, and glorify their Father which is in heaven.*

To the contemplative statesman the revolutions of government become subjects of curious speculation. He considers them in their immediate and remote effects upon laws and customs,

SERMON IV.

customs, and how far they contribute to the aggrandisement of the sovereign, or the extension of the privileges of the people. To the moralist, the revolutions of manners appear far more interesting, as the consideration of them leads to an intimate acquaintance with the mind; and shows to what a degree the fervour of its passions may be abated, and the stubbornness of its prejudices may be bent, by new and salutary principles of action. It points out likewise how those principles may become productive of the greatest comfort to individuals, and the greatest happiness to society.

The triumph of christianity was completed during three centuries after the ascension of its divine Founder, partly by the subversion of the most antient and most popular superstitions which had been ever known to the world, and partly by the gradual revolutions which it produced in publick customs and private manners. Its salutary influence was not only felt by the refined and luxurious citizens of the Roman Empire, but by the savage and warlike people of Europe and Asia, who successively came forth in mighty armies to subvert the vast fabrick of Imperial greatness.

As

SERMON IV.

As it was the firſt glory of the goſpel to call forth into action the moſt benevolent feelings of the mind, the treaſures of its more opulent converts were not laviſhed on votive offerings, and bloody ſacrifices; but were appropriated to the relief of the ſhip-wrecked mariner, the diſtant exile, and the fettered captive. The ſongs of gratitude and the ſupplications of diſtreſs were no longer waſted on ſculptured images, but were addreſſed to the high and lofty one who inhabiteth eternity, and who heareth when the righteous call. The dark and fraudulent oracles of the prieſts were deſerted for the predictions of inſpired prophets, and for the leſſons of the book of life. The parents who formerly expoſed their infant offspring to untimely death, or reared them to maturity, that they might barter their innocence for the wages of proſtitution, awoke to the exquiſite feelings of nature, and led them to the path of holineſs and virtue. The ſlave no longer dreaded the ſtripes of his deſpotick maſter, for as ſoon as he was purified by the water of baptiſm, he aroſe to a ſpiritual equality with him, and was entitled to all the benefits of a free-born citizen. The bloody combats of gladiators, which had long been the favourite ſpectacles of the polite as well as of the vulgar, gave way to amuſements

more

SERMON IV. 143

more refined, and more confiftent with humanity. The licentious feftival of the Saturnalia was fuperfeded by the commemoration of the birth of Chrift; and the feafts of Flora were abolifhed for the obfervance of his meritorious paffion. The prophane myfteries of Ceres and Bacchus, and the horrid barbarity of human facrifices, were fucceeded by the pure and fimple celebration of baptifm, and of the eucharift. The crofs of Calvary, which had been the contemptible inftrument of the execution of flaves, adorned the fummit of the churches, and was depictured on the ftandard of the legions. As foon as divine honours were paid to Chrift, the heathen acknowledged the weaknefs of his gods. He liftened no longer with eager credulity to the ambiguous predictions of the Delphick prieftefs, or to the oracular ftreams of Daphne. Whilft broken arches and proftrate columns fpread the floor of the deferted temples, and the mutilated ftatues of the gods were monuments of the fall of polytheifm; numerous edifices of chriftian devotion were erected, and opened their fpacious doors to receive the multitude of thronging profelytes.

The Pagan religion, although affifted by various expedients, gradually gave way to the
increafing

SERMON IV.

increasing influence of christianity. Alike inadequate to its popularity and its reformation, was the sanguinary malice of Nero against its assailants, and the ingenious devices of Julian to remedy its abuses. When no longer upheld by the arm of the civil magistrate, its internal weakness sunk it to the ground, and the refusal of idolaters to suffer in its defence formed a striking contrast to the illustrious fortitude of the christian martyrs.

The barriers of national enmity and inveterate prejudice, which had for ages obstructed the intercourse of mankind, were broken down; and the inhabitants of different countries with benignant looks of esteem and cordiality, met around the social hearth, or filled the solemn assembly. The jew, enlightened by the evangelical law, no longer viewed the Gentile with disdain, or refused him the common offices of benevolence: nor did the converted Gentile any longer survey the Jew, as the hater of mankind, and the advocate for an intolerant superstition. The nations who before the glorious advent of Christ had been only distinguished by their abject and coarse barbarity, rose from the condition of rude savages to a higher elevation in the scale of reason and of morals. The Egyptian idolater ceased to bend

SERMON IV.

bend at the fhrine of Serapis and Typhon, and to exalt the facred animals of his country to the rank of celeftial fpirits. The myfterious fymbols of the facerdotal hieroglyphicks were changed for the practical and intelligible precepts of the gofpel. The Parthian and Perfian tribes inftituted the decent rites of fepulture, abolifhed their inceftuous alliances, and reftrained the inordinate licence of polygamy. The warlike inhabitants of Scythia, of Germany, of Spain, of Pannonia and Britain forfook their gloomy fuperftition for the pure religion of Chrift, and whilft its precepts foftened their ferocious fpirit, they imbibed a tafte for literature and for arts. Their adoption of Chriftianity from their Roman foes was at once an atonement of its intrinfick excellence, and of their ardent and fincere veneration for truth. They relinquifhed the favage profpect of revelling after death in the gloomy palace of Odin, for the bright hope of a heavenly paradife. They no longer fhed the blood of human victims, at the altar of their fhapelefs idols, but bent a willing knee to the God of mercy. The Druids, who were wont to lead the rude inhabitants of Germany and Gaul from the deep receffes of the forefts to the field of carnage and death, and infpired them with the delufive hope that the foul

K would

would reanimate another body, were succeeded by peaceful orders of ecclesiasticks, who taught their converts the real value of life, and the true doctrine of immortality.

Thus as soon as the christian religion spread its sacred light around the world, the shades of superstition vanished, the manners of mankind were distinguished by gentleness and humanity, the rigours of war were softened, the insolence of conquest was curbed, and a solid and permanent foundation was laid, for a comprehensive and equitable system of jurisprudence and a general law of nations. The unbounded spirit of philanthropy, highly extolled indeed by the antient philosophers and poets, but never before cultivated, began to operate upon its noblest principle, by establishing the love of Man upon the love of God. The state of man in all his various circumstances, connexions, and situations was meliorated, the line of his duty was marked out with precision, his pains were alleviated by the supply of the noblest incitements to his fortitude, and his blessings were multiplied by new and inexhaustible sources of hope. The magnificent and vast scheme of providence was fully developed, by showing to man the immediate relation of a present to a future state

SERMON V. 147

state of existence. The clouds of darkness and doubt which had obscured the prospect of heaven were removed by the full assurances of a glorious immortality. The triumph of vice and the depression of virtue were no longer subjects of inexplicable difficulty to human reason; but formed consistent parts of that moral scheme, the prospect of which was closed by the awful scenes of a future retribution. The christian religion united the whole human race by closer ties of affection, as children of the same Almighty Parent, as partakers of the same redemption and heirs of the same felicity. It clearly proved its divine origin by purifying the corruption, and exalting the capacity of the mind; by subliming its moral energies, and by affording the most extensive scope, and holding out the most glorious reward for the exercise of every virtue.

From the whole of this disquisition it appears, what an important object the progress of christianity forms in the history of those people over whom its light was first diffused, and how highly it deserves to be brought forward as the cause of a revolution in publick and private manners which far surpassed the powers of man to accomplish by the exertions of the greatest diligence, or the most refined policy. We have therefore the justest reason to conclude that the providence of the Almighty was not only active in co-operating with its votaries for its establishment, but likewise in preparing the way for its reception.

The weakness of all those causes which we have reviewed as immediately conducive to the establishment of christianity, as well as a survey of the events which preceded the manifestation of the Son of God, concur to produce this conviction. When we recollect how much the discipline of the primitive church was broken by discord, and perplexed by heresy; when we calmly consider the rage of Paganism which so frequently exercised the fortitude of the martyrs; the calumny raised against the church, which as it was in some degree occasioned by the excesses of nominal believers, was inadequately opposed by the apologists; and the dissoluteness of manners which idolatry allowed so hostile to the primitive virtues; we must necessarily be at a loss for some other cause, which is fully and completely adequate to the rapid and extensive propagation of christianity in the two first centuries after Christ. The necessity of having recourse to this

this caufe appears more evident from confidering the violence of prejudice in favour of eftablifhments confirmed by habit, and endeared by education, the natural pride of the human heart, which difdains the puerile condefcenfion of imbibing moral inftruction at the age of maturity and reflection, and more than all, the influence of univerfal example, which unites man to man by the clofeft ties, and has an immediate and imperceptible influence on every action of life. This formidable tide of prepoffeffions and paffions augmented by all the preceding obftacles was too impetuous to be oppofed by human efforts alone.

We can difcern therefore no other method of finding an eafy and fatisfactory folution to the difficulty, than by concluding that a long and magnificent feries of events were all previoufly arranged for the introduction of chriftianity.

For a demonftrative proof that the greateft empires of the world had a connexion with the advancement of true religion, under the different difpenfations of Mofes, and of Chrift, we may appeal to the teftimony of the antient predictions. Abforbed by the bright vifions of futurity, the prophet Ifaiah calls by name on the conquerour of Affyria, and the reftorer of Ifrael, two centuries previous to his birth. To the eye of Daniel, the fucceffive monarchies of Perfia, of Macedon, and of Rome were reprefented by the moft exact difplay of emblematical imagery. The different periods of the Jewifh hiftory, when the Almighty raifed up the nations as the inftruments of his vengeance, or of his mercy, will fhow by what various modes they combined to execute the divine decrees. Sometimes the daughter of Babylon mocked the forrows of her captives, whofe neglect of Jehovah had been the caufe of their chains: fometimes when duly humbled by their calamity, their conquerour permitted them to regain the feat of their fathers, and to reftore the glories of the fallen temple.

From the ruins of preceding ftates arofe the ftupendous and auguft fabrick of the Roman Empire. Though long agitated by the ftorms of contending factions, it furvived every fhock of domeftick tumult, and gradually extended its dominion over the moft populous and warlike regions of the world.

The nations of Europe, of Afia, and of Africa, which at prefent compofe formidable kingdoms,

SERMON V. 151

kingdoms, were enrolled in the regifter of her tributary provinces. The privileges of the conquerours were generoufly extended to the vanquifhed, and Rome became the common country of her fubjects. Wherever the legions led the way, a free admiffion was opened to arts, to laws, and to commerce; and the unreftrained intercourfe of various nations promoted a general fpirit of obedience and fubordination. On the advancement of Auguftus to the imperial throne, the violence of inteftine diforders was extinguifhed, and the various parts of the empire enjoyed a degree of repofe unknown to former ages. The love of conqueft, which had for feven fucceffive centuries exercifed the courage of the Romans, fubfided into fudden and lafting peace; and the difpofition of the firft emperours to mark out the boundaries of dominion and to filence the clamour of arms, produced a ftrong and aftonifhing contraft to the fierce and ambitious temper of their anceftors.

In the tendency of all thefe circumftances to fome magnificent event, we may clearly difcern the directing hand of the Creator of the univerfe. To his difpofal alone, can properly be attributed that long and complex concatenation of affairs which led the Romans

K 4 by

by regular steps to the summit of dominion. The conflict of their passions, the various revolutions of their government, the ingenuity of the wise, and the ambition of the valiant, co-operated for one transcendent purpose. It was ultimately for this purpose that the legislators remedied the political evils which threatened the destruction of th Roman State, and laid the firm foundations of general order. For this, her heroes fought with unparalleled advantage, and victory was ever ready to lead her armies to triumph. For this, Scipio gloried in the fall of Carthage, Pompey returned with the spoils of Mithridates, and Cæsar bore his triumphant eagle from the plains of Egypt, to the shores of Britain. All their great achievements and all their splendid events, the boldness of their enterprizes and the frequency of their success, uniformly pointed to the fullness of time when the Son of God was made manifest, and were so wisely regulated as to prepare the way for the more easy progress and more ready reception of the christian faith.

The Almighty King of Kings, with the same power which brought the universe into existence, superintends from the highest heaven all the nations of the earth. He views instantaneously the most astonishing effects in their remotest

remotest causes, and the long series of sublunary events, which to the human eye are distant and indistinct, appear but one object to the rapid glance of his Omniscience. At his command, the rise and fall of the mighty empires, whose history comprehends the most important transactions of mankind, were successively displayed upon the great theatre of the world. To complete his stupendous and beneficent designs a new empire was formed, and the government was given to his beloved and adorable Son. Descending from the bosom of the Father, and veiling his majesty in a human form, he graciously condescended to lay the everlasting foundations of his kingdom, and directed his followers to erect the vast and sublime superstructure. Animated by his grace, and directed by his example, his ambassadours proclaimed the glad tidings of immortality, his first followers professed with boldness the sacred truths of revelation, and his martyrs bled with exultation in its defence. Holiness, Peace, Charity, and Hope are the fruits of his laws, and all the faithful in the wide circle of the globe are his servants and subjects. When worldly grandeur shall have passed away, like the visions of the night, this spiritual empire shall unite the regions of paradise to her dominion, and flourish with encreasing glory throughout the ages of eternity.

SERMON V.

Isaiah XLIII. 9.

Who among the people can declare this, and shew us former things? Let them bring forth their witnesses, that they may be justified: or let them hear and say, It is truth.

IF the productions of literature be estimated by their utility, the most elevated place among writers ought to be assigned to the historian. Although the severity of truth marks out for him a more regular line of conduct than the poet, or the orator is required to pursue; yet his obligation to follow her immediate dictates is made easy, and even delightful, by proper reflections on the dignity of his labours, and the animating anticipation of the reward which will succeed them. It is his peculiar and important province to investigate the latent principles of conduct, and pursue them to their remotest consequences; to delineate the diversified picture of actions and characters, and display the revolutions of government, and the fate of empires. If his subject be judiciously chosen, and his productions be stamped with the marks of genius and fidelity, successive generations will celebrate his name as the benefactor of mankind, for giving them an imaginary existence in past ages, for introducing them to the knowledge of departed excellence, and for enabling them to profit by the conduct of their predecessors. His praise will be the constant theme of their gratitude, whilst they shun the vices, and imitate the virtues, which his works have consigned to immortality.

This approbation, however, ought to be withheld, in proportion as an author is discovered to entertain sceptical notions, and to disseminate them with caution and subtlety. Any endeavour to loosen the ties of religious duty, is an affront to the pious principles of education implanted in every cultivated mind; and an act of hostility against the general interests of society. If it has always been essential to historical decorum, for a writer to support the character of the friend to virtue and morality, how flagrant a violation of it,

must

SERMON V.

must the attempt of any one be, who undermines the credibility of that Revelation, which is their best and firmest support?

Such a design may not unfairly be imputed to *the Historian of the Decline and Fall of the Roman Empire*. His disinclination to conform to the religious opinions generally received, is sufficiently evident; for who has discovered from the most careful perusal of his works that he is an advocate for any particular establishment, or even that he is convinced by the evidences of christianity in general? The want of such a discovery can only add to our regret, that the splendid powers of an enlightened mind, should be made subservient to sentiments, the confutation of which has so repeatedly added to the triumphs of learning and theology. Although his endeavour to communicate them to the world, by combining them with the history of a most renowned people, may add to their general notoriety, it can produce no commendation from those who look upon infidelity with surprize, and upon artifice with aversion.

In the mode by which an eminent Philosopher of the North divulged his sceptical opinions, there was a boldness which was respectable

spectable and manly, and which at least entitled him to the praise of plain dealing and candour. He attacked christianity in works evidently written for the purpose; but when he came forward as an historian, he suspended his endeavours to invalidate the proofs of revelation; and if a conjecture may be indulged from a consideration of his arguments at large, his mind appears to have been influenced by a bias favourable to religious establishments and ceremonies. The *Historian of the Roman Empire* pursues a design, which, as it is executed by the most ingenious stratagems, is infinitely more dangerous. His scepticism is sometimes insinuated in the language of diffident hesitation, and is frequently so distant and subtle, as to elude the force of immediate detection. The reader feels unfavourable impressions made upon his mind, which he scruples to impute to the writer, until repeated instances make it evident that it was his deliberate design to disparage our holy religion, and weaken the credit of its advocates. On no occasion therefore, was it ever more necessary, to rouse the vigilance, and alarm the apprehensions of all who are charmed by a matchless brilliancy of style, and attracted by the recital of the most important events which have occurred in the history of mankind. *Let them*

SERMON V.

them beware least any man spoil them by philosophy and vain deceit, by the rudiments of this world, and not after Christ.

The necessity of such caution, and the pernicious tendency of such principles, will be fully evident from considering how closely scepticism may be connected with a disregard and even a perversion of truth. Every historian professes to hold the scales of justice with an equal hand; but he will at once, if the weight of prejudice be suffered to preponderate, alarm the suspicions of his readers, and forfeits their confidence. For such a desertion of his duty, no other qualification is an adequate apology. The brilliancy of his imagination, and the acuteness of his judgment, the strength of his reason, and the extent of his learning, rather aggravate, than diminish the fault. His grand and primary object is to convey instruction through the medium of narrative, and this purpose can never be answered by partial representations of conduct, and mutilated sketches of character. Artifices of this kind transform the venerable portraits of history into the airy phantoms of romance, and are productive of an injury both to the dead and to the living. The former are degraded from their proper places in the temple

of fame, and may be ftigmatized with cenfure, when their conduct, if exhibited in its
true light, would entitle them to praife. The
latter, may be taught falfe opinions of mankind, and may be led to form principles of
conduct fubverfive of their happinefs and pre-
judicial to fociety. As fuch confequences are
likely to enfue from mifreprefentation, in what
efteem is that hiftorian to be held, who poi-
fons the fountains of antiquity, and recommends them as pure and uncorrupted to the
world?

That Gravity is effential to the character of
an hiftorian, is a principle that few will be
hardy enough to deny. The fimple and ma-
jeftic grandeur of narrative condefcends not to
form an affociation with unbecoming levity.
But if the general events of paft ages require
to be recorded in a manner totally free from
this unfuitable mixture, it muft furely be
much more decorous for a writer to preferve
the moft ftrict ferioufnefs of character, when
the fuccefs of a divine revelation, which has
the moft intimate connexion with the beft
interefts of mankind, and the mode in which
its moft upright and moft fincere advocates
have endeavoured to promote its glory, and
diffufe its benefits, form a part of his difquifitions.

SERMON V.

fitions. Let us imagine for a moment the divine origin of chriftianity, and its infinite importance with refpect to the deareft interefts of mankind to be out of the queftion, and let us place it only on a level with other fubjects. If in the difcuffion of the principles of fcience, in the developement of the intellectual powers, in commenting on the maxims of legiflation, or the rules of ethics, if in examining the characters of Newton, of Locke, of Montefquieu or of Bacon, a writer fhould indulge the fallies of humour, fo far as to fcoff at what he could not confute, cavil at what he muft know to be true, and ridicule thofe whom he ought to reverence; would he not provoke the indignation of the judicious, and incur the cenfure of the difpaffionate; and would not they determine that he miftook irony for argument, that his judgment was a flave to the petulance of his wit, and that his conduct was an infult to propriety, candour and truth?

How far the *Hiftorian of the Decline and Fall of the Roman Empire* is liable to this imputation, will appear to every one who perufes the fifteenth and fixteenth chapters of his work, and compares them with the original materials from which they are affirmed to have

have been compiled. He has deviated from his principal fubject to defcribe the progrefs and eftablifhment of chriftianity, and to reprefent the actions and characters of its earlieft profeffors. The chain of thofe events which took place in the reign of Conftantine is violently broken, to introduce a long and elaborate digreffion, at the fame time that the fcantinefs or fufpicious nature of the ecclefiaftical records, of which he complains, would have furnifhed him with a convenient apology for filence upon the fubject: but that filence, which he affirms to be inconfiftent with religious zeal, is much more inconfiftent with infidelity. In the chapters before mentioned we obferve with concern that chriftianity is vilified in the perfons of its primitive profeffors. Their real or imaginary failings are aggravated, and at the fame time that no palliation whatever is afforded to their errours, every art which ingenuity can invent is employed to fcreen the inhumanity of their enemies. So that on many occafions, if a juft and impartial eftimate be made of the firft chriftians, the fentiments of the hiftorian will be decidedly oppofed by the fentiments of his readers; the virtue which he has degraded will be raifed to diftinction, and the indirect or pofitive cenfure which he has expreffed,

will

SERMON V.   163

will be rejected with contempt, or exchanged for general and ardent panegyrick.

To shew how far the monuments of ecclesiastical history can justify such a difference of opinion, has been the attempt made in the preceding lectures. In order to render them more complete, it may be proper to review some passages of the fifteenth and sixteenth chapters of the *Decline and Fall of the Roman Empire*. Such a discussion will prove the weakness of certain opinions, represented as conducive to the propagation of christianity; alleviate the Fathers from a charge of excessive credulity and uncharitableness; and place the cruel proceedings of their persecutors in a proper light.

Among the various instances of misrepresentation with which this particular part of the History of the Decline and Fall abounds, there are Five which immediately force themselves on our notice; we will consider them in the order in which they occur, and conclude this Lecture with some general observations.

The First consists in assigning a visionary cause for the propagation of christianity.

L 2   The

The historian asserts, that the " assurance
" of a millenium was carefully inculcated by a
" succession of Fathers, from Justin Martyr and
" Irenæus, down to Lactantius, who was pre-
" ceptor to the son of Constantine. Though
" it might not be universally received, it ap-
" pears to have been the reigning sentiment of
" the orthodox believers, and it seems so well
" adapted to the desires and the apprehensions
" of mankind, that it must have contributed
" in a very considerable degree, to the progress
" of the christian faith."

That this persuasion should hasten the progress of the christian faith, is an hypothesis
which it is as difficult to support, by the suf-
frage of antiquity, as to reconcile to the conceptions of reason. For the belief of the millenium was an expectation grounded on the
preconceived ideas and faith of a christian.
A competent knowledge of the scriptures, a
peculiar interpretation of the predictions, both
of the prophets, and of our Saviour, and an
implicit reliance on the mistaken sense in
which they were understood by some believers,
were previous and necessary steps to the reception of this opinion. It was therefore an
object of hope derived through a series of pre-
paratory circumstances, from particular tenets,
and

and consequently could have no foundation whatever, until those tenets were embraced.

When the principle is laid down as a cause for the propagation of christianity, we naturally require something more substantial than mere conjecture, to prove the certainty of its existence. But can the historian appeal to facts to establish the truth of his position? Where has he obtained, among the remains of primitive antiquity, any positive information that the doctrine of the millenium was held out as an allurement for the Gentiles to become converts to the church? We may conclude, that the effects of such a doctrine would have been far different from those which he imputed to it, upon very strong and very respectable evidence.

For the learned Origen thought that the opinions entertained by some, respecting the millenium, were too gross and sensual to form a part of the christian system, and that even the Pagan conceptions of a state of felicity were more refined and spiritual. So far is he from affording any support to the conjecture of the historian, as to remark on the contrary, that if the heathens understood that such a tenet was countenanced in the church, the

report

report of it would fix the imputation of weakness on chriftianity, and ftain the purity of its fublime doctrines.

To fay that a fucceffion of Fathers inculcated this opinion, from Juftin Martyr to Lactantius, is an affertion which may be controverted without danger of incurring the cenfure of petulant cavil, or precipitate contradiction. That many of them maintained it, will readily be granted; that all inculcated it, will as readily be denied. Tatian wrote a learned treatife againft the Gentiles; Athenagoras, the philofopher, prefented an elaborate apology to the Emperour Marcus Antoninus, and wrote a differtation on the refurrection. Theophilus, Bifhop of Antioch, infcribed three argumentative difquifitions to his noble friend Autolycus. All thefe, with the copious works of Clemens Alexandrinus and of Cyprian, were written within the interval mentioned. Their authors difcufs the received doctrines of the church, and particularly the opinion relative to a future ftate; yet in what paffage is the flighteft intimation given of the belief of the millenium, or even of the exiftence of fuch a tenet, where is the flighteft mention made? Although the hiftorian, with a degree of prudence which does credit to his corrections, has

SERMON V. 167

has qualified his vague affertions in the laft edition of his work, and thus eluded the force of a pofitive denial of his ftatement; yet after all, his prefent text has but feeble pretenfions to the praife of perfect accuracy, or manly decifion of fentiment.

For if it can be proved that the fentiments of the chriftians were equally divided upon the fubject of the millenium, the fentiment in queftion was not the reigning fentiment. That this equality was highly probable, will appear from the particular relations of Juftin Martyr and Irenæus, and from the general accounts of other writers.

Juftin Martyr, in his dialogue with Trypho the Jew, draws his arguments to prove the divine miffion of our Lord, from the old teftament. In allufion to the former part of their converfation, Trypho afks him, whether he had been induced to bring his proofs from the prophets in favour of the millenium, in confequence of his ferious conviction of the approach of that extraordinary period, or merely to fhew his dexterity in accommodating the prophetical defcriptions to any fubject of difcuffion, which his fondnefs for argument induced him to advance. " You cannot,", replies

replies Juftin, " fuppofe me capable of ex-
" preffing opinions which I do not fincerely
" maintain ; I have on a former occafion in-
" genuoufly acknowledged to you, that my-
" felf and many others, think that the mille-
" nium will certainly take place. I have like-
" wife informed you, that there are many
" chriftians diftinguifhed by the purity of
" their fentiments, who embrace no fuch opi-
" nion." As Juftin Martyr was himfelf a zealous advocate for this opinion, it may fairly be
concluded that he ftated the number of thofe
who countenanced him in it, in as favourable
a manner as the accuracy of truth would allow. It appears, notwithftanding, from the
paffage above cited, that thofe who rejected
this opinion, were as numerous as thofe who
maintained it. This makes an important alteration refpecting the chriftians of that age,
half of whom at leaft, ftand thus far acquitted
of the charge.

In oppofition to Irenæus and the millena-
rians of his age, may be placed many of their
contemporaries, whom Irenæus himfelf repeatedly affirms to have confidered the paffages of fcripture, which feem to favour this
doctrine, as figurative and allegorical. His reprefentation of their fentiments coincides with
that

that of Juftin Martyr, and affords fufficient reafon to conclude, that the opponents of the opinion were as numerous as in the preceding times.

Without the regular citation of other paffages, it may fairly be collected from thofe writers who deduce the belief of the millenium from its origin, particularly Eufebius, Epiphanius, and Jerom, that they conceived it to have been limited to certain Fathers of different ages, becaufe they never reprefent it as the predominant tenet of the church at large.

Upon the whole, therefore, it appears, that the hiftorian had no fufficient grounds for attributing any efficacy to this opinion in the converfion of mankind, and that the fuppofition of its prevalence even in the church to the extent which he defcribes, is deftitute of fupport from ecclefiaftical hiftory.

The Second inftance of mifreprefentation confifts in an attempt to invalidate the truth of prophecy.

" In the primitive church it was univerfally
" believed, that the end of the world and the
" kingdom

" kingdom of heaven were at hand. The near
" approach of this wonderful event had been
" predicted by the apoftles; and the tradition
" of it was preferved by their earlieft difci-
" ples, and thofe who underftood in their li-
" teral fenfe the difcourfes of Chrift himfelf,
" were obliged to expect the fecond and glo-
" rious coming of the Son of Man in the
" clouds, before that generation was totally
" extinguifhed, which had beheld his humble
" condition upon earth."

Here the hiftorian evidently betrays an inclination to excite doubts relative to that moft awful prediction of our Saviour, circumftantially recorded by all the evangelifts, which in the opinion of the moft learned expofitors, has a double allufion to the deftruction of Jerufalem, and the confummation of all things. He infinuates, that it was not fulfilled in the latter fenfe, when the accomplifhment of it was the fubject of general expectation among the primitive chriftians. But what defcription of them interpreted the difcourfes of Chrift in the literal fenfe he intimates, it is as vain for us to conjecture, as difficult for him to declare.

" It was univerfally believed that the end
" of the world and the kingdom of heaven
" were

SERMON V. 171

"were at hand." This affertion is as deftitute of proof, as his affirmation "that the near approach of this wonderful event had been predicted by the apoftles." We are fully aware that fome indefinite expreffions of St. Peter may be wrefted into an allufion to it; but that it was not his defign to foretel the immediate end of the world is evident from his preparing the minds of the converts for a feries of approaching trials which were to prove their faith during the eftablifhment of chriftianity. When therefore St. Peter affirms, that *the end of all things is at hand,* he certainly fpeaks only of the fulfilment of thofe events which carried with them a full ratification of the truth of chriftianity, and accordingly, in every fucceeding age of the church, thefe words have been applied to the deftruction of Jerufalem, and the fubverfion of the Jewifh Empire. That the apoftles concluded the end of the world to be far diftant from their own times, is moreover clear from the exprefs declarations of St. Paul. For as a proof that fome peculiar expreffions in his firft epiftle to the Theffalonians were not to be ftrictly interpreted, as if himfelf and his contemporaries were to live until the fecond coming of their Lord and Mafter, he fpeaks on another occafion of his approaching death,

and

and the future corruptions of the church. *He laboured that he might attain unto the refurrection of the dead*, and affured the Corinthians that *God shall raife up us also by Jefus, and shall prefent us with you.* He explicitly befeeches the converts *not to be foon shaken in mind, or to be troubled, neither by spirit nor by word, nor by letter, as from us, as that the day of the Lord is at hand.*

To fay that the tradition of the approaching end of the world was preferved by the earliest difciples of the apostles, is a hasty and groundlefs affumption. Of their earliest difciples the moft eminent were Clemens Romanus, Ignatius, Polycarp, and Irenæus, who in no part of their works which remain, mention their expectation of this event, as if at that time about to happen. Irenæus indeed, held an opinion which feems to give fome colour to thefe mifreprefentations; for he maintained that the Meffiah would begin his reign upon earth when the world was fix thoufand years old. The hiftorian endeavours to make the fuppofed general expectation of the accomplifhment of the prophecy in queftion coincide with the clofe of this period. Unfortunately, however, for the object he had in view, his computation of time is as erroneous, as his arguments

SERMON V.

arguments are inconclusive. He maintains that the primitive church of Antioch reckoned almost six thousand years from the creation to the birth of Christ. This number, for which no authority is produced, is most probably that of Theophilus Bishop of Antioch, which, according to the most exact statement, is found to be very little more than five thousand five hundred. Thus the historian, not content with the calculation of the Septuagint, which so far exceeds the Era of the creation commonly adopted, has added to one of the longest accounts at that time received, very nearly five hundred years.

If the historian had consulted the works of some of those writers whose names decorate his note upon the passage in question, he would have found sufficient reason to correct his misstatement, and to have expressed more precisely the computations of chronology. Lactantius expresly asserts that six thousand years from the creation of the world were not completed in his time. He flourished in the reign of Constantine the Great, at the distance of two centuries from the successors of the apostles. The insinuation, therefore, of the historian respecting the prophecy, is untrue;

and his attack upon the credulity of the early chriftians is weak, and eafy to be repelled.

The prediction of our Lord and his apoftles reft upon the ftrongeft foundation, even the truths of the Almighty himfelf. They did not foretel that the world would end before the death of the generation to which Chrift appeared, becaufe, otherwife, that event would affuredly have been accomplifhed. They predicted, however, among other inftances of the depravity of future ages, the vain enquiries of mifguided fcepticks, and the event has fully confirmed their veracity. *Be mindful*, faith St. Peter, *that in the laft day fhall come fcoffers, walking after their own lufts, and faying, where is the promife of his coming? For fince the Fathers fell afleep all things continue as from the beginning,*

Let it abate the infolence of the fupercilious caviller to reflect on the wife and wonderful difpenfations of providence refpecting the eftablifhment of the gofpel. Even his own efforts to depretiate its truth are included in the fcheme of the evangelical predictions, and furnifh of themfelves clear arguments for its divine origin.

SERMON V. 175

The Third inſtance of miſrepreſentation conſiſts in an unwarrantable charge of uncharitableneſs againſt the primitive chriſtians.

The hiſtorian remarks that "the condem-
" nation of the wiſeſt and moſt virtuous of
" the Pagans, on account of their ignorance
" or diſbelief of the divine truth, ſeems to of-
" fend the reaſon and the humanity of the
" preſent age. But the primitive church,
" whoſe faith was of a much firmer conſiſ-
" tence, delivered over without heſitation, to
" eternal torture, the far greater part of the
" human ſpecies."

The primitive church will be found on a fair and cloſe examination, to be more conformable in point of humanity, with the preſent age, than the hiſtorian repreſents. Tertullian is the only father of the church on whoſe authority the above aſſertion is founded. It muſt undoubtedly be cenſured therefore as an impropriety in the hiſtorian to reſt an argument upon a ſingle authority, and to aggravate the deſcription of a warm and precipitate writer, at the ſame time that the fathers who expreſs more calm and more benevolent ſentiments are paſſed over in ſilence. Is it not in the higheſt degree contrary to the principles

of

of historical justice to represent the language of an individual as a tenet of the whole church? Is it candid in him to place the invectives of that individual in such a light as to make him appear to pronounce condemnation on the Pagan world at large, when his effusions were principally directed against false philosophers, against corrupters of morals, and persecutors of the faith? He professed indeed that he drew a veil over a part of the description which Tertullian gave of their future tortures; but at the same time he fully exhibits, and artfully heightens every circumstance of it, that can excite the aversion, and provoke the indignation of his readers.

In order to ascertain the more liberal sentiments of the Fathers, it is to be observed, that Justin Martyr not only entertained a hope, that Socrates, and those who resembled him in virtue, would escape the divine displeasure in another life; but with a peculiar allusion to the general benefits imparted by the divine Logos, dignified them with the appellation of christians. With respect to the destination of the Pagans in general, in another life, it was the opinion of Hermas, Clemens Alexandrinus, Origen, and many others, that Christ and his apostles preached to their departed souls

in

SERMON V.

in the regions of the dead, and that all thofe who were converted, were without diftinction made partakers of the benefits of the paffion. Whatever may be the propriety of their interpretation of a myfterious paffage in the firft epiftle of St. Peter, upon which this belief was founded, at leaft it fhewed their readinefs to frame fuch an hypothefis, as might impart to the heathen world, the falutary truths of the gofpel. The fair evidence of antiquity is therefore repugnant to the reprefentation of the hiftorian, and the benign fentiments of the early chriftians refpecting the Pagans who preceded them, are proved to be correfpondent with their wifhes and prayers for their unconverted contemporaries.

The excellence and the expediency of the evangelical virtues may be inferred even from the contemplation of thofe minds which act not under their influence; for this fevere charge, which is founded on no fufficient authority, and can be proved by no fair argument, would not have been made by the writer, had he been guided by that fpirit of charity, which he vainly endeavours to detract from the primitive church.

M   The

The Fourth instance of misrepresentation consists in drawing wrong conclusions from facts.

The historian asserts that "the Romans in "the conviction of any of their subjects, who "were accused of so very singular a crime as "that of christianity, proceeded with caution "and reluctance."

To establish this assertion, inferences are drawn from the celebrated letter of Pliny to the Emperour Trajan. From thence, the historian observes, "we may assure ourselves that "when Pliny accepted the government of "Bythinia there were no general laws or de- "crees against the christians."

Whoever reads this letter with attention will be more inclined to draw a different inference. Pliny informs the Emperour that he had never been present at any judicial examinations of christians. This manifestly implies that they had already been brought before magistrates, and if brought before magistrates, they must have been apprehended on suspicion of infringing some standing law of the empire. Pliny does not consult the Emperour whether

SERMON V.

the christians were deserving of legal severity, and therefore were the proper objects of a penal decree; for on this subject he was sufficiently decided by expressly declaring that their obstinacy deserved to be punished. His reason for consulting the Emperour seems to have been this: He was solicitous to know whether some gradations of punishment should not be adopted, and a line of distinction be drawn between the young and the old, the recent and the early converts. His ignorance proves nothing contradictory to the existence of laws against the christians. He only speaks from his own inexperience, and sufficiently intimates that he wanted not the establishment of a new law, but the modification of an old one, in order that it might more particularly apply to various cases.

That this was the object of his enquiry will appear in a stronger light from weighing the circumstances of the affair in connection with the testimony of other writers. Is it probable that a Roman Proconsul invested with the command of an extensive province, and occupied by the administration of its weighty and numerous affairs, would have wasted his time in listening to accusations against its inhabitants for holding certain singular opinions, which in no degree affected the tranquility of the state, if the infringement of some law had not called for his attention? Is it probable that he would have doomed any of its inhabitants to death on the deposition of officious informers, if a law had not justified his decisions? Had not such been the case, he would have followed the example of the impartial Gallio, and have driven both the accusers, and the accused, with impatience from his tribunal. Such conduct would have been far more consistent with the general character of Pliny, than to have been led upon insufficient grounds into the most wanton and unauthorized exercise of his power.

Notwithstanding the Senate had repealed the bloody edicts of Nero and Domitian against the christians, yet Trajan at the beginning of his reign, from a desire to secure the rites of Paganism from innovation, enacted that all the subjects of the empire, should either offer sacrifice, or suffer death.

The authority of the acts of Ignatius, which contain this remarkable fact, is confirmed by the proceedings carried on during the same reign against Symeon the aged Bishop of Jerusalem. He was seized by the multitude, and

SERMON V.

and brought before the Proconful of Judea, who deliberately condemned him to be crucified. If the multitude could not have obtained the object of their indignation under a legal fanction, they would not have brought the venerable martyr before the magiftrate; and if the magiftrate had not acted under the influence of the law, he would not have condemned him to an ignominious and cruel death.

With how much precipitation Pliny proceeded againft thofe unhappy chriftians who were brought before him, appears from his own circumftantial account. He informs us that he ordered thofe who perfevered in their confeffion of the chriftian name, to be led out to fuffer death, and that he put two women to the torture to extort a confeffion of fufpected guilt. The praife of reluctance and caution, fo profufely beftowed upon him by the hiftorian, would have been more confiftent with truth as well as humanity, if Pliny had folicited the determination of the Emperour, before he adopted fuch rigorous meafures. His conduct can only be accounted for by fuppofing he was actuated by a fenfe of duty to enforce the exifting laws. If however it fhould be granted to the hiftorian, that Pliny was left entirely to his own difcretion, and acted not in conformity with any exifting law, what treatment muft the chriftians have experienced from magiftrates of cruel and inflexible difpofitions, if fuch were the proceedings of one, who was on all other occafions eminently humane and benevolent?

This queftion may be beft refolved by making fome remarks on a fubfequent affertion of the hiftorian, viz. "That the Romans "were moderate in the ufe of punifhments "inflicted on the chriftians."

In the conftitution of laws, there ought always to be fome proportion obferved between the crime and the punifhment. But the Romans, when acting as legiflators againft the chriftians, betrayed the moft flagrant defertion of every principle of equity. A member of the church was condemned for holding fingular opinions, before it was difcovered whether they would lead him either to the commiffion of crimes, or to the violation of the publick peace. He was doomed to fuch inflictions as were barely juftifiable for the moft atrocious enormities. Forfeiture of property, imprifonment, exile to folitary iflands, condemnation to the mines, were the moft lenient fentences pronounced

SERMON V. 183

pronounced againſt the innocent ſufferers. On other occaſions, their fortitude was brought to a ſeverer trial by the mutilation of limbs, or a death aggravated by the barbarity of inſult, and ſharpened by the ingenuity of torture. To refer to no other proofs, the epiſtle of the churches of Lyons and Vienne, will furniſh as many inſtances of refined cruelty, as of invincible patience. If this be moderation, what is ſeverity? If this be mildneſs, what is rigour? If the inference of the hiſtorian be confirmed by ſuch indiſputable facts, our opinions of the moſt atrocious characters muſt undergo a complete revolution. Nero will be eſteemed a philanthropiſt, Domitian the father of his people, and Decius the protector of chriſtianity.

The Fifth inſtance of miſrepreſentation conſiſts in ſelecting paſſages manifeſtly inconcluſive, and ſuppreſſing others of the ſame writers more deciſive and equally connected with the ſubject.

The hiſtorian remarks that " the learned
" Origen, who from his experience as well as
" reading was intimately acquainted with the
" hiſtory of the chriſtians, declares in the
" moſt expreſs terms, that the number of
" martyrs

"martyrs was very inconsiderable. His authority would be alone sufficient to annihilate that formidable army of martyrs, whose relicks, drawn for the most part from the catacombs of Rome, have replenished so many churches, and whose marvellous achievements have been the subject of so many volumes of holy romance. But the general assertion of Origen may be explained and confirmed by the particular testimony of his friend Dionysius, who in the immense city of Alexandria, and under the rigorous persecution of Decius, reckons only ten men and seven women who suffered for the profession of the christian name."

How far the historian is justifiable in diminishing the number of martyrs upon the authority of the writers he has here mentioned, will appear from the following considerations. In the treatise of Origen against Celsus, Celsus objected that christianity had arisen to distinction in the world by supporting a spirit of sedition, against the established government of the empire. Origen disproves the assertion by assuring him, that the christians, in no attack made by their enemies, had ever resorted to arms, but on the contrary, had yielded with the greatest submission to the most rigorous execution

execution of the laws. It had, however, he observes, pleased the divine goodness, that few, and such as could easily be enumerated, had at different times been cut off, in order to prevent the extermination of christianity. It is obvious to remark on this passage, that the expressions denoting a small number of martyrs, are to be understood with reference to the whole community of christians at large. Although the disproportion subsisting between them might be very considerable, as christians at that time abounded in every province of the Roman Empire, yet the quantity of martyrs might nevertheless be in itself very great. That Origen himself embraced such an opinion is clear from other passages. He says that every city and every order of men was hostile to the christian name. Again, speaking of the conduct of the Pagans of his own age, he observes that many who are well convinced that the profession of christianity will be productive of the most fatal consequences, and that a renunciation of it will ensure their security, have shewn their contempt of the world, by enduring with patience the loss of life. In his commentary on the epistle to the Romans, he moreover says, that it was common to see persons who surrendered themselves with the greatest composure

sure to persecutors, and not only submitted to outrage, but even to death.

If we proceed to examine the support which is given to Origen by Dionysius of Alexandria, we shall find that among his invaluable remains, preserved in the ecclesiastical history of Eusebius, there is a circumstantial account of the Decian persecution in Egypt. A particular relation is given of the tortures and death of seventeen persons. But does he hint that these were the only sufferers, who were exposed to the fury of the Imperial decree? So far is this from being the case, that he mentions in general terms, many other christians, who were likewise condemned to die. He particularly relates, that the persecutors rushed into the houses of the christians, and plundered them of their most valuable effects. Such was the excessive tumult, that Alexandria exhibited the appearance of a city taken by storm. Many of the brethren fled, and recollecting the consolatory expressions of St. Paul, sustained the loss of their property with joy. In addition to these circumstances, it is to be remarked that Dionysius concludes his interesting narrative with this pathetic expostulation. " Why need I describe particu-
" larly

SERMON V.

"larly the multitude of thofe who were driven to wander in the deferts and on the mountains; who perifhed by the bittereft afflictions, by hunger, by thirft, and by cold; or who were cut off by robbers, by difeafe, and by wild beafts? Thefe difaftrous events are not recorded in vain, but that you may have an authentick relation of the calamities which befel us."

From the whole of this detail we may fee by what difingenuous methods the hiftorian has perverted the plaineft facts. From a multitude of writers he brings forward Origen to corroborate his hypothefis of the fmall number of martyrs, when it is evident that Origen muft, on fuch an occafion, be a very incompetent witnefs. For the moft cruel perfecutions did not rage whilft he flourifhed, or probably not till after his death; and the barbarity with which Decius, Valerian, and Dioclefian depopulated the church, can only be known from later Fathers. By violently disjoining one part of his obfervations from the context, the fenfe is wrefted into a contradiction of his general fentiments, as well as of the accounts of other writers. To make his teftimony, thus tortured, affume a more fpecious air of plaufibility, the hiftorian contrafts it with the moft moſt palpable fictions and dubious martyrologies; he then brings forward Dionyſius of Alexandria, and curtails many circumſtances of his narrative, which were of equal, or rather ſuperiour importance, with reſpect to the cruelties exerciſed by the perſecutors.

After deliberately weighing all this palpable mutilation, and ſophiſtical management, the judicious and the learned may eaſily determine how far it is conſiſtent with truth or juſtice to repoſe an implicit confidence in the ſtatement of antient authorities thus made by the hiſtorian.

Thus has an attempt been made to ſhew that *the Hiſtorian of the Decline and Fall of the Roman Empire* is a conſummate adept in the arts of miſrepreſentation, and that deſerting the open path of truth, he has attempted to lead his readers into the intricate labyrinths of errour. If the preceding developement be accurate, he has ſullied the purity of chriſtian antiquity by

I. Aſſigning a viſionary, and inefficient cauſe for the propagation of the goſpel.

II. Attempting to invalidate the evidence of prophecy.

III. Un-

III. Unwarrantably imputing uncharitableness to the primitive chriftians.

IV. Drawing wrong conclufions from facts.

V. Selecting paffages manifeftly inconclufive, and fuppreffing others of the fame writers equally connected with the fubject.

From mifreprefentation detected under fuch various difguifes, and fo infidioufly operating to the difparagement of virtue and of piety, it may fairly be concluded that the writer is as unfavourable to the firft advocates of the chriftian revelation, as he is deftitute of that fenfibility which is ever alive to the unmerited fufferings of others. He recounts the moft affecting calamities of the chriftians with cold indifference, and reprefents them rather as objects of contempt, than of compaffion and refpect. He forgets, or he wifhes to forget, that thofe who endure misfortunes with magnanimity are the moft edifying, if not the moft proper fubjects of hiftory; and that a particular account of Ignatius and of Pamphilus, would have done as much honour to his work, as the firmnefs and the piety of Strafford and of Laud have conferred on the productions of Hume. During the perufal of the fifteenth and fixteenth chapters of the

Roman

Roman Hiſtory, we imagine we are ſurveying the dark deſcriptions of the firſt chriſtians, given by Tacitus, whoſe ignorance of their real character is the beſt apology for his miſrepreſentation. We can with difficulty be perſuaded that we are liſtening to an hiſtorian, who profeſſes to form his judgment of facts and of men, upon the liberal principles of a Philoſopher, and who enjoys all the light, and all the learning of the eighteenth century.

SERMON VI.

GENERAL EPISTLE OF ST. JUDE.

Verse 3.

Earnestly contend for the Faith which was once delivered unto the Saints.

THE manner in which the Socinians of the present day conduct their controversy against the established church, is equally extraordinary and artful. For not content with perverting the obvious sense of scripture, with torturing every text to their own purpose, and with slighting the plainest declarations of the proper Divinity of Christ; they have endeavoured to press into their service the proofs arising from the belief of the earliest christians. This appeal evidently shews the veneration in which antiquity is, in reality, held by all parties, and the great advantage which may be derived from its declarations. In consequence

sequence of this perfuasion, the works of those who undertake to reprefent the fentiments of the primitive writers have been explored with indefatigable diligence by *the Author of the Early Opinions concerning Jefus Chrift*; and all the paffages which feem to confirm his argument, are exhibited in the ftrongeft and moft advantageous point of view, with copious comments, and plaufible illuftrations. His general plan of attack upon the divinity of Chrift is conducted with a fingularity of enterprize, of which it is fruitlefs to fearch for another inftance. His readers muft be prepared to reconcile the rage of innovation with the fubtlety of paradox, and to watch the moft bold and extraordinary procefs of hiftorical experiment. For to their great furprize they will find, that the Fathers of the church are made to contradict their own opinions; and that the books which were profeffedly written for the fupport of the faith, are changed into the inftruments of its fubverfion.

But if the belief of the primitive chriftians be fo important, that an endeavour is made to procure its alliance to the Unitarian caufe, even by difingenuous arts; it is certainly worthy of all the exertions to retain it, which can fairly be made by its rightful poffeffors.

It

SERMON VI.

It is the valuable property of the church of England, and the refolution of her fons to ftand forth as its guardians and defenders, neither has been, nor will be wanting. We have the animating encouragement of an apoftolical injunction *to contend for the Faith which was delivered unto the Saints*. We can eafily have recourfe to the evidences that prove what the nature of that faith was; fo that to be flow in its profeffion, and irrefolute in its defence, would prove us unworthy of bearing " that holy name by which we are called."

Still however it muft be candidly confeffed, that the ecclefiaftical ftudent ventures on this difquifition with hefitation, and with diffidence. He fees the powers of ingenuity and diligence combined againft him. He contemplates, in the author of the work before mentioned, an undaunted boldnefs, which no oppofition has intimidated; an inflexible perfeverance which has been tried in many a polemical field; and a refined fophiftry which can elude the grafp of confutation. But the danger decreafes as he approaches to the conteft; for a love of truth, and a fenfe of duty, encourage him to proceed, even againft an opponent fo formidable and fo experienced.

It will be the object therefore of the following discourse, to attempt a refutation of the three grand principles which form the basis of *the History of the Early Opinions concerning Christ*, viz.

I. That the apostolical Fathers held the simple humanity of Christ.

II. That Justin Martyr corrupted the primitive faith, by the adoption of the Logos of Plato.

"III. That the pastors of the church maintained a corrupted faith, whilst the illiterate christians continued to maintain the simple humanity of Christ.

As a necessary preliminary to this discussion, we must carefully mark the distinction which subsists between the doctrine of the divinity of Christ, as contained in scripture, and the opinions formed of it, which we collect from ecclesiastical history. The doctrine stands recorded in everlasting characters, which the folly of man may misinterpret, but his power can never efface. It is asserted in appropriate phraseology, marked by peculiar and plain characters, illustrated by undeniable facts, and confirmed by the fullest testimony. The member of the church of England is defirous of fettling the principles of his faith by an immediate appeal to fuch evidences. He determines the nature of the doctrine in difpute by the rules of legitimate criticifm, and the obvious meaning of fcriptural language. But his opponent, impatient of that reftraint to which thefe limitations may fubject him, adopts a new teft by which the doctrine muft be tried, far inferiour in point of weight and importance to that which is rejected; inafmuch as he quits contemporary for fubfequent evidence, and prefers the atteftations of fallible men to the records of infpired evangelifts.

Still, however, we are ready to admit that as far as the opinions of men can be of importance to its illuftration, thofe of the primitive chriftians are fo. They had the moft favourable opportunities of information, and drank chriftianity at the fountain head. The records, therefore, which they have left us, are the beft comments on the facred text, as they fhow the fenfe in which it was firft underftood. Senfible, therefore, of the value of thefe records, in confirming our interpretation of fcripture, we proceed to fhew the futility of the above ftated affertions.

In the first place, let us attempt to prove that the apostolical Fathers did not hold the mere humanity of Christ.

An opinion very unfavourable to their writings will be formed, if we do not so far attend to the particular object of their admonitions, as to place ourselves in that situation from which we can clearly ascertain their grand scope. To him who is not conversant with the history of the church, and the particular incidents which gave rise to the epistles written by the apostolical Fathers, many points may appear to have been slightly discussed, or partially represented, which in fact form only the subordinate or incidental parts of their design. When the infant church was assailed by open enemies, and internal dissentions, her teachers expatiated on the duties of charity, unanimity and subordination. We must not expect to find in their works any doctrinal points, introduced with systematic arrangements, or defined with logical precision. The primitive compositions were suited to the circumstances of the times, and whatever topick was introduced in them, had an immediate reference to the urgent exigencies of the church. In opposition to the heresies of the Gnostics and the Ebionites, the great articles

of

SERMON VI.

of faith are stated in general terms, not as matters of private opinion, but as subjects of received belief. No ingenuity is employed to recommend them, and no arguments are brought for their support, except the clear declarations of scripture, which were held to be decisive and irrefragable. The apostolical manner of writing, which is remarkable for plainness and energy, and free from philosophical subtlety, or nice refinement, is happily imitated in the literary remains of the apostolical Fathers. The unaffected simplicity and earnestness of Clement, of Ignatius, and of Polycarp, are very close imitations of St. John and of St. Paul.

The Author of the Early Opinions concerning Christ first appeals to the authority of these writings, then refuses to acquiesce in the plainest sense of passages which press him with insuperable difficulties, and afterwards affirms that they are greatly corrupted or entirely spurious. This inconsistency of sentiment discovers strong indications of distrust in his cause, and of doubts in what manner it can be tolerably supported. Such an attempt to shake the authenticity of these writings results from a conviction how much, when fairly and fully consulted, they can prove against him.

We are authorized by the moſt learned men of various ages to affirm their genuineneſs, and think the argument in favour of our creed, which may be drawn from the opinion of the firſt and ſecond centuries, too valuable and important to be ſacrificed to hypotheſis without ſolidity, and aſſertion without proof.

The earlieſt, and one of the moſt authentic monuments of eccleſiaſtical antiquity, is the epiſtle ſent by the church of Rome to the church of Corinth, many years before the end of the firſt century. It was written by Clement, Biſhop of Rome, who is numbered by St. Paul among his " fellow labourers," and this epiſtle fully ſhows how deſerving he was to be placed in ſo diſtinguiſhed a rank. The deſign of it was to compoſe a recent diſſenſion, and recommend the reeſtabliſhment of harmony and ſubordination. Now granting for a moment what has been aſſerted, that this epiſtle contains not the doctrine of the Preexiſtence of Chriſt, can it follow from thence that the writer did not maintain it? It was the profeſſed deſign of Clement to write for a particular emergency, and the epiſtle itſelf is not complete. How, therefore, can any concluſion be drawn with reſpect to his ſentiments at large? It is well known that Cyprian, the
eloquent

eloquent and pious Bishop of Carthage, wrote an epistle to Antonianus equal in length to the epistle of Clement, in which no express mention is made of the divinity of our Lord. If this epistle had alone escaped the ravages of time, the most flagrant injury would have been done to the memory of Cyprian, by a supposition that he did not maintain this doctrine, when he is well known to have been its most zealous advocate. Equally unwarrantable would such a conclusion prove against Clemens Romanus. If however the train of his argument, and his express declarations be considered, the objector will find that he has no grounds to presume upon his silence. For as a motive to induce the Corinthians to behave with humility, Clement affirms, that " the " sceptre of the Majesty of God came not in " the pomp of ostentation and splendour, " though he had it in his power; but in hu- " mility, as the Holy Spirit prophesied con- " cerning him." To infer from these expressions that it was the design of the writer to represent our Saviour as a mere man, seems an extraordinary perversion both of language and sense. For if our Saviour was no more than man, how could he with any propriety be entitled to the grand and dignified appellation of the " sceptre of the Majesty of God?" and thus

thus be diftinguifhed by a far more eminent title than is ever applied to the prophets who communicated the divine will on earth, or to the higheft order of angelic beings who execute it in heaven? That his coming " in the " pomp of oftentation and fplendour" cannot refer to his publick life alone, but muft neceffarily be applicable to his incarnation in general, is fufficiently evident from the following confideration. Clement limits his expreffions to no particular period of our Lord's exiftence, but fpeaks in general terms; and in the prophecy of Ifaiah which follows the before mentioned words, his birth is alluded to in the emphatic queftion, " who fhall declare " his generation?" If his coming referred only to his working miracles in the capacity of a publick teacher, how could he, who was reftrained by a commiffion given to him for that purpofe alone, be faid to have it in his power to affume fuch a character of magnificence and fplendour as was moft agreeable to his own inclinations? We are at a lofs for an example to reconcile the paffage to fuch a fuppofition. Mofes, the greateft of mortal prophets, had no fuch privileges; at the command of the Lord he lifted up his rod, and the fea divided to form a path for the children of Ifrael; but can it be afferted with the leaft

fhow

SERMON VI.

show of probability, that he was able to lead them into the land of promise? Accordingly, we find that those privileges which exceeded the powers of his commission were neither claimed by himself, nor attributed to him by others. The whole passage of Clement exactly represents the sense of St. Paul's declaration, that *Christ being in the form of God, thought it not robbery to be equal with God, but made himself of no reputation, and took upon him the form of a servant.* As if there was some essential difference of nature which placed the disciples infinitely beneath their Master, Christ is not mentioned so much as the direct example for them to follow, as an incitement to the emulation of their fellow-creatures. For Clement proceeds to mention those whose conduct came more within the reach of their exertions. " If the Lord so " humbled himself, what shall we do who " are come under the yoke of his grace? Let " us follow those who predicted his advent."

At the commencement of the second century, Ignatius the venerable Bishop of Antioch, who had been a companion and disciple of the apostles, was conveyed to Rome to suffer death for having professed the faith of Christ. During his journey, he wrote epistles to various churches. To give the precepts of christianity their full weight and importance, by shewing the transcendent dignity of their Author, he enlarges upon the divinity of our Lord, and to prevent any misconception respecting the person whom he designs to characterize, he uses the most remarkable precision of language. The title of *the Lord* is invariably given both by Ignatius and Polycarp to the Son of God. There is not a single passage throughout their epistles in which it seems with any propriety of application to denominate God the Father. This appropriation however, is by no means singular, for the same may be asserted of the two epistles of St. Paul to the Thessalonians. The writers of the new testament frequently apply this term to Christ, and in the version of the Septuagint it is invariably used as an equivalent translation of the Hebrew Jehovah. We are moreover authorized by the testimony of many of the antients to say, that it was frequently applied even by the Pagans to the supreme God.

The objection which is made to the epistles of Ignatius by *the Author of the early opinions*, because Eusebius does not mention his name amongst other authorities for the divinity of Christ, will be found on examination to have

no

SERMON VI. 203

no weight. Eufebius, when quoting the following words of an antient writer who proves the late origin of the herefy of Artemon, mentions a few out of many writers, who profeffed the doctrine of the church. "What "Artemon afferts of the mere humanity of "Chrift would be credible, if the divine "fcriptures did not contradict him; as well "as the antient works of the brethren, writ-"ten in defence of the truth againft the He-"reticks, and the Gentiles. We may appeal "to Juftin, Tatian, and Clement, by whom "Chrift is defcribed as God. Who is unac-"quainted with the volumes of Irenæus, "Melito, and other ecclefiaftical writers, by "whom Chrift is afferted to be both God "and Man? The pfalms likewife, and hymns "of the church written at the beginning by "the faithful, celebrate Chrift the word of "God, and apply to him the attributes of "divinity." If in this full and decifive paffage, which is fufficient of itfelf to annihilate the pretenfions of unitarianifm to high antiquity, any reftrictions had been made, and the writer had affirmed that the perfons mentioned, compofed the whole number of the orthodox writers, the objection would carry great weight; but on the contrary, the expreffions are fo general, as to comprize many

more

more than are individually named, and confequently Ignatius may be included among the reft. It was not the defign of Eufebius to enumerate every writer, any more than to fpecify the compofers of the ancient hymns. This indeed is evident from no notice being taken of Athenagoras, Theophilus, and Tertullian, who are well known to have been advocates for the doctrine in queftion. Confequently, if Ignatius be excluded becaufe he held not the doctrine, they are excluded for the fame reafon, which reduces the objection to a manifeft abfurdity.

In the fmaller epiftles of Ignatius, which are proved to be genuine by many eminent fcholars of the laft and prefent century, the divinity of Chrift is afferted and proved in fuch a manner as was beft calculated to confute the errours which then began to arife. The Ephefians are commended for their diligence, and the motives which had inftigated them to the performance of their duty. "They were fol-
" lowers of God, and excited themfelves by the
" blood of God." They are cautioned againft the impiety of thofe who made chriftianity a veil for licentioufnefs, whilft their prefumption prompted them to attempt the removal of the failings of others. As an antidote againft thefe pretended

SERMON VI.

pretended curers of mental diforders, he directs them to "one phyfician carnal and fpi-
"ritual, God incarnate, begotten and not
"made, true life in death, of Mary and of
"God, firft paffible, and then impaffible."

To filence the cavils of the proud, who were offended at the ignominious death of our Lord, he ftates the pre-eminence of his divine, above his human nature: "Jefus Chrift our God
"was born of Mary, according to the difpen-
"fation of God, of the family of David, of
"the Holy Ghoft." He fays alfo, that to remove the univerfal darknefs of the Pagan world, "God became manifeft in a human
"form, for the newnefs of eternal life." In order to encourage a diligent attendance on divine fervice, and to reprefent the importance of the minifterial offices, he reminds them of Jefus Chrift according "to the flefh of the
"race of David, the Son of Man, and the
"Son of God, who was with the Father be-
"fore all ages, and who finally was made
"manifeft." He declares the prophets to have been infpired, to convince the world of the omnifcience of that Being, "who manifefted
"himfelf by Jefus Chrift his Son, and his
"eternal Word; who in all things pleafed
"him that fent him." Convinced of the va-

nity

nity and wickedness of the world, he looks with the eye of faith to heaven, " where our " God, Jesus Christ, being in the Father ap- " peareth the more." Hence likewise arises his fervent desire to gain admittance to his Lord and Master, by a signal trial of his constancy, for which reason he intreats the Roman con- verts to make no intercession for his life, but to " permit him to imitate the passion of his God." Addressing the Smyrneans, he makes their spi- ritual improvement a subject of pious gratitude. " I glorify Jesus Christ, the God who hath " given you such wisdom, who really was born " of the race of David, according to the flesh, " the Son of God. He did eat and drink with " his apostles, although spiritually united with " the Father. He suffered truly, as he also " truly raised up himself." He holds out the future judgment to Polycarp, as a motive to perseverance in the faith, and concludes his admonitions " with wishing him to be well " continually in our God, Jesus Christ. Ex- " pect him who is above all time, eternal, in- " visible, though for our sakes made visible; " he was impalpable and impassible, yet for " our sakes he became subject to sufferings."

If Polycarp, the eminent disciple of St. John, and the venerable Bishop of Smyrna, had, in

his

SERMON VI.

his epiftle to the Philippians, confined his exhortations to the duties of morality alone, fufficient reafons might have been difcovered, to juftify his filence upon points of doctrine. He refers the chriftian converts to the epiftle not long before written to them by St. Paul, of whofe zeal in preaching the gofpel, he makes the moft honourable mention. He likewife afferts the fufficiency of that epiftle, to edify them in the true faith. As the Philippians, therefore, were fo well grounded in the doctrine of the proper divinity of Chrift, there was the lefs neceffity for Polycarp to expatiate upon it. We may however difcover the moft plain traces of this doctrine, concerning which St. Paul had expreffed himfelf with fo much precifion and copioufnefs. For example, Polycarp exhorts the Philippians " to believe in him
" who raifed our Lord Jefus Chrift from the
" dead, and gave him glory, and a throne at
" his right hand: to whom all things celeftial
" and terreftrial are fubject, whom every fpirit
" ferveth, who is coming as Judge of the living
" and dead; whofe blood God will require of
" every one who believes not in him." He declares that " Chrift has promifed to raife us
" from the dead." That the faithful ought
" to be fubject to the church, as unto God
" and Chrift." Again he fays, " if we entreat
" the

" the Lord to forgive us, we ought also to
" forgive: for we are before the eyes of the
" Lord and God, and must all stand before
" the tribunal of Christ: let us therefore serve
" him in fear and reverence, as he himself
" hath commanded, and the apostles who
" preached the gospel to us, and the prophets
" who foretold the advent of our Lord. If
" we suffer for his name, let us glorify him."
In short, he concludes his epistle with praying
" that the God and Father of our Lord Jesus
" Christ, and he himself our everlasting High
" Priest, the Son of God Jesus Christ, would
" build them up in faith and truth."

No doubt can arise as to the intention of Polycarp to attribute the subjection of the universe to Jesus Christ; the obvious sense and regular order of construction will be outrageously violated by any other interpretation of the first passage above adduced, for the different members of the sentence are respectively correlative to the same person, and that person is Christ. That such is the true sense, may moreover be collected from the application which the learned and accurate Author of the credibility of the Gospel History makes of this passage, as a parallel text to the celebrated declaration of St. Paul, that *at the name of Christ*

SERMON VI.

Chrift every knee fhould bow." Polycarp afferts that the Omnipotence of Chrift will be exercifed by the refurrection of the dead, and that the church is fubject in the fame manner to the Son as to the Father. Admitting the juftnefs of our remark, that the appellation of *the Lord* invariably refers to our Saviour in this epiftle, it is plain likewife that he is confidered not only as the object of prayer, but as the forgiver of injuries. His Omniprefence is afferted to be the fame as that of the Father, and from thence arifes an exhortation to reverence and fear him. When he is denominated the *eternal High Prieft*, his priefthood feems to characterize him as human, and his eternity as divine. The former typically expreffes his character as mediator and redeemer, and the latter alludes to the attributes, which are common to him with the Father. That fuch were the ideas of Polycarp will be more fully fhown from confidering the clofe of his animated prayer previous to his martyrdom. " I praife and glorify thee
" through the eternal High Prieft Jefus Chrift,
" thy beloved and bleffed Son, through whom
" to thee, with Him, in the Holy Spirit, be
" glory now and for ever."

O   We

SERMON VI.

We now proceed to show, in the Second place, that Justin Martyr did not corrupt the purity of the faith by adopting the Logos of Plato.

As far as the features of an author's mind are visible in his works, it is evident that sincerity and candour were distinguishing characteristics of Justin Martyr. He seems on every topick to express his unpremeditated thoughts, in a simple and inartificial manner, and to be influenced by a natural ingenuousness, which was superiour to duplicity and evasion. His ardour in the pursuit of truth, and his alacrity in its profession, will appear in the most striking point of view, when we recollect, that the sincerity of his conversion was brought to the severest trial, since his courageous avowal of the faith was the glorious cause of his martyrdom.

After attempting without effect to satisfy his curiosity, by exploring the tenets of the Grecian sages, he procceded to examine the evidences of revelation, and discovered that the christian religion was the only safe and excellent philosophy. He was far from retaining any invincible prejudices in favour of

SERMON VI.

his former studies, or of being blindly attached to the opinions of Plato. He deliberately weighed the merits of the great founder of the academy, and with a calm and unbiassed mind exposed his contradictions of other philosophers, and his inconsistency with himself. Justin Martyr expresly declared, that " as " Aristotle and Plato differed so much in ex- " plaining the nature of earthly things, they " are not worthy of credit, when they dis- " course concerning the invisible world." " If " any one should accurately inspect the opinions " of Plato, his opinions will be found to be " repugnant to each other; on which account " he cannot escape the censure of deliberate " falshood."

Justin Martyr moreover represents that the conduct of Plato, on his return to Athens from his travels into Egypt, exposed him to the imputation of duplicity and dissimulation. For apprehensive of falling a victim to the popular clamour, which had caused the death of Socrates, he professed a " belief in a plu- " rality of Gods, though contrary to the evi- " dence of his first principles. Therefore " since nothing true can be derived from such " teachers concerning the real nature of God, " it remains that we listen to the inspired prophets

" prophets who lived long before the philoso-
" phers of Greece, and taught nothing from
" their own imagination, but received con-
" sistent and harmonious instructions from on
" high. For it is impossible that their pre-
" dictions should be the result of human in-
" genuity, or be imparted merely by the light
" of nature. In sublime subjects the philoso-
" phers have no accurate knowledge. What-
" ever is well expressed in all respects, belongs
" to the disciples of Christ.—We do not think
" the same as others; but all others, being de-
" sirous to resemble us, assert our doctrines."

From this, and a variety of similar passages, it is plain that Justin's acknowledgment of the excellence of christianity, amounts to a deliberate renunciation of his former philosophical opinions, relative to the nature of God; and that the force of divine truth had so influenced his mind, and corrected his judgment, that he saw the defects of Plato in the strongest light, and exposed them to censure without reserve.

Still however we are ready to confess that the Platonic philosophy had many great though subordinate claims to his attention. It conveyed such sublime notions of the Deity, in comparison

comparison of all other systems, that he thought it could not be the production of human sagacity and invention. He therefore attributed its excellence to the light afforded by the Old Testament. The travels of Plato, which extended to Babylon as well as into Egypt, favoured the supposition that he had consulted the sacred volume. From this source Justin Martyr imagined that the philosopher had borrowed his most sublime speculations, and more particularly the doctrine of the christian Trinity. He continually reasons upon this supposition, and from thence deduces all those constructions of the Platonic writings, and accommodations of them to scripture, which, to a mind uninfluenced by the same bias, must necessarily appear forced and unnatural. In his exhortation addressed to the Greeks, and his apologies dedicated to the Emperours, which form the most considerable part of his remaining works, he recommends the prophecies as an introduction to christianity. He endeavours to prove that the philosophy, of which the Greeks and Romans were such ardent admirers, was indebted for all its excellence to the sacred books of the Jews. " Plato derived from Moses that pe-
" culiar name of the deity, which so strongly
" indicates his self-existence and eternity. His
" doctrine

"doctrine respecting the divine ideas was bor-
"rowed from the commands of the Almighty
"to Moses, who was commissioned to con-
"struct the ark of the covenant correspondent
"with the archetype, which was shown to
"him on the mountain. By the prophets he
"was instructed to give the sublime descrip-
"tion of Jupiter, when he drove his winged
"chariot through heaven, for he had read
"that the glory of the Lord went forth upon
"the cherubim, and the cherubim lifted up
"their wings, and the glory of the Lord was
"upon them."

From a proper attention to these passages, it is evident that the writings of Justin Martyr have been grosly misconceived, or unfairly misrepresented; and the reverse of what has been confidently asserted will be found to be the true state of the case. It was not his object to accommodate the scriptures to Plato, but to accommodate the writings of Plato to the scriptures. With respect to the articles of his christian belief, he states fundamental doctrines in clear and direct terms, as he received them by the tradition of the church, and as he collected them from the sacred books.

We

SERMON VI.

We are now advanced to the moſt critical point of the argument. That Juſtin Martyr endeavoured to bend the tenets of the academy to the principles of chriſtianity, we are ready to affirm. That he corrupted the chriſtian faith by the introduction of Platonic ideas, we are inclined moſt confidently and moſt unequivocally to deny. We cannot fail in this ſtage of the diſquiſition to remark the evaſion to which *the Author of the early opinions* has recourſe. He is aware that the cloſe examination of the genuine principles of the academy will produce the ſubverſion of his hypotheſis; for in what part of the works of Plato is the ſlighteſt mention made of the perſonification of a Logos? And therefore he ſuddenly changes the ground of conteſt. After fatiguing our attention with a deſign to delude our judgment by an oſtentatious parade of the ſentiments of Plato, and his followers; after raiſing our expectations, to ſuppoſe that Juſtin Martyr will be detected in ingrafting Platoniſm upon Chriſtianity, he inſinuates that he adopted the Logos from Philo, who improved upon the principles of Plato. So that from the conceſſions of the author himſelf, Juſtin Martyr is proved to have been a Platoniſt in name only, and with equal reaſon might be denominated a Pagan, becauſe previous to his

his converfion, he had conformed to the popular fuperftitions of his country.

Let us not be deterred by the evafion of the enemy, from purfuing him in his retreat, and examining whether the poft, to which he flies, be more tenable than that which he has fagacioufly quitted.

Philo, an eminent Jew of Alexandria, who flourifhed in the time of the apoftles, in different parts of his works makes ufe of the word Logos, to which he affixes various fenfes. Sometimes it denotes the mind of God, fometimes the invifible world, according to the pattern of which, the vifible world was made, and in other places only wifdom, an attribute of the deity. When it is ufed to fignify an emanation of the divine mind, it is defcribed as an effect not permanent but occafional. In its higheft fenfe, the Logos is the moft antient Angel, the perfect Image of God, who revealed to Abraham the divine will.

However probable it may be that Philo derived fome of thofe ideas annexed to the Logos from Plato, he could not borrow from him the application of it to a Perfon. His defcriptions therefore of the divine Being, whom he invefts

SERMON VI. 217

invests with such lofty attributes, must be derived from some other sources, which will be found not to be remote from our observation. In the pentateuch and the prophets, whose sense Philo laboured to refine by allegory, several passages occur, which obscurely intimate the agency of the divine Word in the creation of the world, and in many subsequent dispensations. In the psalms, the Son of God is more clearly revealed, in terms expressive of the highest dignity and exaltation. According to the glosses of the antient Rabbinical writers, this was the Son of God, who was of the same substance with the Father, and who existed from all eternity. So that as from them the elevated descriptions of Philo are undoubtedly derived; vain and ineffectual is the search for that doctrine among the schools of Greece, which the schools of Greece never taught.

A tradition has prevailed in the church from a remote period, that St. Peter was preaching the gospel at Rome, during the time that Philo resided there in the quality of ambassadour to the Emperour Caligula. He contracted an intimate acquaintance with the great apostle, and from the high esteem which he entertained for the sanctity of his manners, was induced to make honourable mention of the

the disciples of St. Mark, who were at that time educated in the celebrated school of Alexandria. It is not improbable that his intercourse with the christians might enlarge his ideas upon the subject in question, and raise his mind to a more adequate conception of the nature and attributes of the christian Logos.

But of any adoption of the sentiments or approbation of the principles of Philo by Justin Martyr, where is the positive proof? In his authentic works, where is he even once mentioned? If however we grant for the sake of argument, that all the writings of Philo were as well known to Justin Martyr, as the *Author of the early opinions* may be willing to suppose, is it probable that his sentiments, merely as such, would have been implicitly embraced? Philo was a Jew, who had frequent opportunities of being converted to christianity, yet he resisted or slighted its evidences. His attachment to the law of Moses was so firm, that he laboured to establish its authority and give it the most refined interpretation. Thus tenacious of his religion, he held out no inducements to the christians to adopt his opinions. Whatever elevation of character he attributed to the divine Logos, he

SERMON VI.

he never spoke of him as the promised and expected Messiah. However conversant he might be with the predictions of the inspired prophets, and animated by their descriptions, he is altogether silent as to the Redeemer of Israel. The Fathers must clearly have perceived, that all his forced refinements and airy speculations were built upon the Old Testament. What therefore could induce them to borrow from the commentary, when they were in possession of the text? Why should they imitate an unskilful copy, when they possessed the bright and masterly original? They had Moses and the prophets to announce the future kingdom of the Son of God, and gradually to unfold his power and glory; they had the evangelists and the apostles, who jointly recorded his advent, fully developed his character, and clearly displayed his attributes.

If Justin Martyr had corrupted the doctrines of christianity, how comes it to pass that all the contemporary christians, all the Fathers who were not educated in the schools of Plato, have passed over so striking an event in silence? We must conclude that the members of every church were grossly ignorant, or culpably indifferent; that they knew not the meaning of the sacred names of Father, Son,

and

and Holy Spirit, which they conftantly repeated, and continually employed in all the publick and private acts of devotion. We muft fuppofe that all the bifhops and paftors, who have given fuch numerous proofs of their defence of the truth againft the incroachment of every innovation, were plunged in the moft profound lethargy, or abandoned to the moft culpable indifference. We muft fuppofe, moreover, that the authority of Juftin extended over the whole chriftian church, and that it unanimoufly obeyed his call to embrace a new faith. We muft fuppofe that the peaceful philofopher of Paleftine, produced the confequences without purfuing the meafures of the bloody prophet of Arabia, and effected that revolution of opinion without the aid of the fword, which the fword itfelf, deftructive as it was in the hand of Mahomet, could never fully accomplifh.

If Juftin Martyr had been guilty of the charge of corrupting the primitive faith, the fame rigorous fentence would have been pronounced againft him, which was directed againft Cerinthus, Marcion, Bafilides, Paulus of Samofata, and other herefiarchs of the early ages. As foon as they began to diffeminate their tenets, they were cut off from the communion

of

SERMON VI.

of the faithful, and their errours were combated by the united powers of fcripture and reafon. If the difciple Tatian, notwithftanding his learning and acutenefs, was enrolled in the heretical regifter, for what reafon was his mafter forgiven for a fault, which in the opinion of the church, the moft fplendid powers of genius, the greateft acquifitions of knowledge, the warmeft profeffions of zeal, and even martyrdom itfelf could not expiate.

To this argument Irenæus adds the moft fatisfactory confirmation, when he refutes the Valentinians. When they affirm that all objects of fenfe are only the " images of thofe " things which really exift, they only repeat " the fentiments of Plato. They transform " his ideas into Eons, and make them the " creators of the archetypal world, which " that philofopher invented. This opinion, " together with the corruption and depravity " of Marcion and Saturninus, was embraced " by Tatian, who after the death of his maf- " ter was fo elated with a vain confcioufnefs " of his fuperiour attainments, that he laid " the foundation of a new fect."

From a complete furvey of the fuppofed Platonifm of Juftin Martyr in all the various

points

points of view from which it can fairly be seen, it appears evidently not to affect in the smallest degree the value of the testimony, which he bears to the faith. His avowed sentiments, as well as his general character, equally militate against the accusation. The tenets of Plato, as far as they can clearly be ascertained, bear only a distant and faint resemblance to the christian doctrines. It does not appear that Justin was acquainted with the works of Philo, and if he was, they were not of sufficient importance in comparison with the scriptures for him to borrow from them. To assert therefore, that he had recourse to these authors to assist him in the alteration of his creed, is a groundless assumption, alike destitute of all probability and of satisfactory evidence.

In the Third place, we proceed to prove, that the Pastors of the church did not maintain a corrupt faith, whilst the other christians continued to be Unitarians.

That the great body of christians in the primitive times maintained a belief, relative to the nature of Christ, which was contrary to that of their teachers, seems as highly improbable in itself, as it is incapable of proof from
fair

SERMON VI.

fair and full authorities. It is highly improbable in itself, because every one of those teachers who wrote as well as discoursed on the articles of the faith is thus made an artful innovator, and muſt have endeavoured to work upon the credulity of the world by representing what were merely the corrupt perversions of his own mind, inſtead of the genuine doctrines of the church. Such conduct ſtands expoſed to the complicated imputation of matchleſs effrontery, profound hypocriſy, and deliberate falſhood; and is replete with all that can ſully the reputation, and undermine the credit of a man and a chriſtian. But ſo totally repugnant are ſuch injurious ſuſpicions to the general character and conduct of the eccleſiaſtical writers, to their proteſtations and ſincerity, to their integrity and piety, to their fear of God, and their charity to man, that the candid and the judicious will be diſpoſed to diſmiſs without examination, any hypotheſis which is ſupported upon ſuch diſingenuous inſinuations.

The vindication of Juſtin Martyr from the charges juſt confuted more particularly tends to ſubvert this aſſertion; for if he was not inſtrumental to the corruption of the faith, the pretended diverſity is attributed to no oſtenſible

ostensible author, and derived from no acknowledged source. As however direct proof will corroborate the preceding observations, we will endeavour to state a few passages selected from a considerable number, which strongly, directly, and unequivocally support them. Justin Martyr in his first apology endeavours to reconcile the faith inculcated in the scriptures to those who were attached to the popular philosophy, by showing that Plato derived some of his principles from the books of Moses. "We do not," says he, "therefore, "derive the opinions which we maintain from "others, but all others derive them from us. "Among christians, you may hear and learn "these things, even from those who are un- "acquainted with the first principles of learn- "ing, who are vulgar and untutored in speech, "but wise and faithful in mind; from the in- "firm, and those who are deprived of sight; "so that you may be sensible, that these "things were not the production of human "ingenuity, but were declared in the power "of God."

This remarkable proof of the reception of the christian creed among all ranks has been misrepresented by *the Author of the early opinions,* but it is too clear to be misunderstood.

The

SERMON VI.

The previous obfervations on the Mofaical hiftory of the creation, do not conftitute the main argument, but is merely an incidental circumftance of it. It is not the point in debate, but a fubject of illuftration introduced to reconcile the heathens to that faith which the vifionary fyftem of Marcion was defigned to fubvert. Juftin Martyr therefore clearly defigned to reprefent how much the moft illiterate of the chriftians furpaffed the moft learned of the philofophers. To fay that they furpaffed the philofophers, by poffeffing the Mofaical account of the creation, is no proof of their fuperiority, for it was a general opinion of the primitive church that Plato himfelf derived his principles from the pentateuch, and the prophetical writings. But to affirm that they had full evidence of the fublime doctrines of chriftianity, which had eluded the difcovery of unenlightened wifdom, is a declaration of fuperiority which is alike confiftent with the context, and with the reality of the fact itfelf.

Not long before the clofe of the fecond century, Irenæus defcribes the actual ftate of the faith at that time, and in a full and fatisfactory paffage expatiates on the unity of its principles, and the univerfality of its extent.

" The

" The Church, although dispersed throughout
" the world, having heard the preaching of
" the apostles, and embraced their belief, pre-
" serves it with the same diligence as if her
" members composed only one family. This
" it unanimously preaches and delivers as with
" one mouth. The languages of man are di-
" verse, but the power of the tradition is one
" and the same. As there is only a single sun
" to illuminate the world, so the gospel ap-
" pears in all places, and enlightens those who
" are willing to come to the knowledge of the
" truth. For neither do the churches planted
" in Germany believe or deliver any other,
" nor those that are in Spain, in Gaul, in the
" East, in Egypt, in Libya, or in Judæa.
" Nor do any of those who preside in the
" congregations, whatever be his eloquence.
" profess a different creed; nor will any one
" who is unlearned detract from this tra-
" dition."

The whole controversy might fairly be set-
tled by an appeal to the close of this memo-
rable passage. Irenæus, as if aware that some
insinuations might be thrown out of a diversity of opinion in the church, discriminates
between the members who composed it with
respect to their situation and talents, and declares

clares that however they differed in such respects, their principles of faith were still the same. This is a testimony in favour of the early belief which cannot be evaded, and among all the proofs which antiquity can furnish, is one of the most convincing and irrefragable.

About twenty years after the time of Irenæus, Tertullian makes a similar reference to the general belief, in order to point out a clear distinction between the novelty of heresy, and the antiquity of the genuine faith. " The " doctrines which are generally preached, that " is what Christ has revealed, can by no other " means be proved than by the churches " founded by the apostles, and either edified " by their personal or written instructions. It " is evident therefore that all doctrine which " agrees with those apostolical churches is " consistent with truth. So that without " doubt, that must be embraced which the " christians have received from the apostles, " the apostles from Christ, and Christ from " God."

In order to render Tertullian consistent with himself, it is necessary to advert to his observations in another part of his works. The Author of the early Opinions has given such

such a colour to a passage extracted from the treatise against Praxeas, as to make the mere humanity of Christ appear to have been the belief of the great body of the christians who lived in the second century. A careful examination of the subject at large, will free Tertullian from a palpable misrepresentation, and show that the passage in question is so far from being capable of the sense alledged, that it proves a point which is directly the reverse; since the persons who are asserted to have held the mere humanity, were advocates in the highest sense for the divinity of Christ. Praxeas maintained that Jesus Christ was no other than the supreme God, that he was born of the Virgin, and that he actually suffered death upon the cross. This errour, which its author had carefully disseminated during his journey from Asia to Rome, is combated by Tertullian with metaphysical subtlety of argument, and manly vehemence of declamation. Desirous of giving a just idea of the capacity and talents of the advocates of Praxeas, he observes, that they were persons of that plain understanding, which usually characterized the majority of believers, who might, without any great impropriety of language, be called dull and senseless. Such men, he observes, when first weaned from the errours

SERMON VI. 229

of Polytheifm, and converted to the belief of God, expreffed fome reluctance againft the myftery of the Trinity. Praxeas took advantage of this difpofition of the common people, to inculcate his erroneous tenets. His difciples boafting that they only were the worfhippers of one God, accufed the orthodox believers of Tritheifm. Such was their weaknefs as not to difcern that by confounding the perfons of the Deity, and making Jefus Chrift the fole God, they ran into a palpable errour, and that the creed of the church properly explained, was the true faith. The Latin converts of Praxeas, whom he had made in Italy, and the Greek whom he had made in Afia, repeated the terms of theology which he perverted, with as much clamour and vehemence, as if they clearly underftood, and properly maintained them.

By thus taking an enlarged view of the meaning of Tertullian, the paffage is reftored to its original fignification. As tranflated by *the Author of the early Opinions* it is an inftance of invalid proof. In his verfion he omits a complete fentence of the text of Tertullian, which is of great importance to the general fenfe of the paffage, becaufe it explains in what an erroneous fenfe the divine unity was held by thofe, who in the time of

P 3 Tertullian

Tertullian miſtated the catholick faith. This omiſſion rendered it an eaſy taſk to turn the general purport of the argument out of its natural courſe, and to throw an air of plauſibility over a weak opinion. By cutting off this paſſage from his liſt of proofs, the author is deprived of his fundamental ſupport; for of all the antient evidences which he preſſes into his ſervice, there is no one which he exhibits with more oſtentation, which he decorates with greater parade of argument, or which he introduces with greater confidence of ſucceſs. The chriſtians mentioned by Tertullian as the followers of Praxeas were as remarkable for their deviation from the opinion of the modern unitarian, as from the true faith of the church; unleſs the modern unitarian will reverſe his creed, and maintain him to be God whom he labours to prove to have been mere man. If he thus becomes the diſciple of Praxeas, he muſt be combated with the weapons with which Praxeas was defeated, and the treatiſe of Tertullian inſtead of furniſhing him with armour againſt the church, will become the inſtrument of his deſtruction.

All the authorities which have been conſidered, form a chain of evidence, including a period of more than ſixty years, which is

ſtrong

SERMON VI.

strong and closely connected. The declarations stated are strictly and undeniably to the purpose. For it is very particularly to be observed, that the Fathers are not speaking of any points of christianity independent of the faith. They are not discoursing on the prevalence of the christian morality, or the establishment of its positive institutions, but on the unanimous consent of the catholick church in their belief in the proper divinity of the Son of God, as constituting one of the fundamental principles of their religion.

Fortunately for the determination of the present question, we are not obliged to confine our inquiries to the church alone for evidence of its primitive belief. Although the prophane writers surveyed christianity with a superficial eye, some scattered notices of its principles may be collected from their works, which however general, are very important. Contemporary with Ignatius was the learned and accomplished Pliny. He found as soon as he entered upon the proconsulship of Bythinia, that christianity had prevailed among all ranks of its inhabitants. He was officially informed of the grand object of their religious solemnities, as well as of their institutions and manners. " They met on stated days before the
" dawn,

" dawn, and fang choral hymns to Chrift as
" a God."

Contemporary with Juftin Martyr was Lucian the Syrian. In his hiftory of the death of Peregrinus he obferves, " that the chriftians " defpife all things, and even death itfelf, in " hopes of immortality. For their firft Legif- " lator made them believe they were all bre- " thren. They adore their crucified Saviour, " and live according to the laws of their own " religion."

In the dialogue entitled Philopatris, which is afcribed to Lucian, there is a paffage which more fully expreffes the faith of the chriftians of that age. It was the evident defign of the writer to ridicule the catholick doctrines. The characters introduced as converfing are a chriftian and a heathen. The former propofes to the latter, that inftead of invoking Jupiter, he fhould fupplicate " the moft High God, the " Son of the Father, and the Spirit proceeding " from the Father." The heathen replied, that this was a belief which he could not comprehend. The value of this teftimony may rife in the opinion of fome, when it is recollected that fuch was the deference paid to it by Socinus, that he efteemed it the moft
undeniable

SERMON VI. 233

undeniable evidence which antiquity gave to the prevalence of the doctrine of the Trinity.

And here we could multiply the number of our proofs. We might appeal to the attestation given by the chriftians to the worſhip of Chriſt, when accufed by the Pagans of a defign to pay divine honour to the relicks of the martyred Polycarp. We could advert to the practife of the Jewiſh converts, who in the reign of Adrian refided at Jeruſalem, and maintained Chriſt to be God : and we could dwell with more copious obfervations upon the teſtimony of the Emperour Julian, who expreſsly maintained that St. John was induced to aſſert the divinity of Chriſt in his gofpel, from obferving that a confiderable number of the Greeks and Romans had already embraced that opinion. But a minute inquiry into theſe important atteſtations would demand more time than is allowed to difcourfes like the prefent. We recommend them to the earneſt attention of thofe who deny the early prevalence of the doctrine in queſtion among all ranks of chriſtians, and we hefitate not to aſk in the fame terms indeed, but not with the culpable precipitation of the Jews, *what need have we of any further witneſs?* An appeal is made by our opponents to the general opinion

opinion of the firſt chriſtians. We have carefully inveſtigated the proofs for that opinion, and find them to be as ſtrong and as conſiſtent as can be adduced for the ſupport of any fact in antient hiſtory. The witneſſes did not collect their information from vague reports, conveyed through ſuſpicious channels, neither did they live in places remote from moſt of the countries of which they ſpeak, or truſt to the tradition of former ages. Their teſtimony is for the moſt part, the reſult of actual obſervation. The friends of the church are ſupported by their avowed enemies, and thoſe who diſagreed upon all other ſubjects, combine to eſtabliſh the argument in queſtion. At the ſame time that Ignatius vouches for the churches on the coaſts of Aſia, Pliny cooperates with him by his account of chriſtianity in the ſpacious province of Bythinia. Juſtin Martyr extended his obſervations from Paleſtine to Rome; Irenæus travelled from Aſia to Gaul; and Tertullian was well acquainted with the congregations of Africa. Within the period of time that theſe writers give a ſtatement of the faith in all theſe countries, Lucian does the ſame for the extenſive kingdom of Pontus, and not only brings an additional proof of its wide diffuſion, but corroborates the credit of the writers who aſſert its uniformity. Their general

SERMON VI.

general evidences give us for that period of time, in which the corruption has been afferted to have taken place, a diftinct view of unanimity in the moft remarkable parts of the antient world.

To conclude—The proper confideration of the prefent fubject would lead us into a much wider field of difcuffion, than is confiftent with the limits marked out for difquifitions like the prefent. Let what has been advanced, be thought fufficient to fhow the weaknefs of their efforts, who attempt to wreft from the church of England the fupport of the primitive chriftians in the faith which fhe profeffes. We have reviewed the cleareft proofs that the apoftolical Fathers maintained the nature of Chrift to be human and divine; that he was God incarnate; that the incommunicable attributes of omnifcience and omnipotence, and the divine prerogatives of glory, praife, and power, are frequently and fully afcribed to him.

We have feen the weaknefs of the afperfions thrown upon Juftin Martyr; we have remarked that he built his faith neither upon the profound difquifitions of Plato, nor the airy fpeculations of Philo; but upon the folid and clear teftimony of the apoftles and evangelifts:

gelifts; and that every page of his works is expreffive of the fame exalted ideas of the Son of God. We have obferved that the authority of Irenæus, in a particular paffage, is fufficient to decide the point in queftion; and that the Pagan writers, among whom the Emperour Julian ought particularly to be diftinguifhed, are important and confiftent witneffes of the truth of our affertions.

Thus the friends and the enemies of chriftianity have concurred to record in general the prevalence of that faith, which has been illuftrated in detail. The fentiments, therefore, of the primitive church appear to have been unanimous; and vain is it for the gainfayer to attempt to eftablifh a difference among thofe, who, influenced by the power of the fame truth, united in the moft perfect harmony.

SERMON VII.

2 TIMOTHY III. 15.

All Scripture is given by inspiration of God.

THE glad tidings of the gospel were neither confined to the Jewish people, nor to the generation which was eminently honoured by the appearance of the Messiah. It was the great object of his mission to establish a church collected from the various parts of the world, and to extend its duration from age to age. Christianity was manifestly designed by its great Author for an eternal monument of the divine will, intended to survive the decay of human institutions, and to escape even from the wreck of empires, uninjured and triumphant. This was the light appointed to shine upon every one that cometh into the world, that *all flesh might see the salvation of God.*

In order therefore that an intention so gracious and beneficial, might be most effectually fulfilled, the history of our Saviour, the transactions of the apostles after his ascension, and their instructions upon particular emergencies, were committed to writing; by which expedient, the purity and the duration of the christian principles have undoubtedly been secured, more particularly if it be considered that the frequent and sanguinary persecutions, which raged in the primitive times, endangered the continuance of the faith, and that numerous heresies threatened its corruption. Even its escape from these early alarms was no security for its final preservation. In passing down to successive ages, it was liable to contract that mixture with falshood, which is inseparable from oral tradition, and to lose by continued corruptions its original spirit and purity.

The motives which induced the Sacred Writers to undertake their literary labours, may in some degree be ascertained from their respective situations. The urgent necessity of impressing the faith with exactness on the minds of early converts, among whom errours of an alarming tendency had actually taken root, called loudly upon some of them for written instructions.

SERMON VII.

inftructions. Publick as well as private folicitations induced others to ftamp on their writings the indelible characters of Chriftianity, and place it out of the reach of innovation.

The gofpels and epiftles are intended to perpetuate the important truths they contain, and to fupply the place of thofe holy witneffes whofe names they bear. They breathe the fame fpirit of fimplicity, zeal and godlinefs, which diftinguifhed their authors, *who being dead, yet fpeak; who endeavoured that after their deceafe, we might have thefe things always in remembrance.* They fulfil in a fecondary, though important fenfe, the gracious promife of our Saviour, that his animating prefence fhould continue in his church, for *they are with us always, even unto the end of the world.*

There is the ftrongeft reafon to conclude, that the books of undoubted authority were expeditioufly circulated. They were not addreffed to individuals in whofe poffeffion they continued in concealment, but to the rulers of large congregations; or more ufually to large congregations themfelves, before whom they were frequently recited. They were communicated

municated with pious diligence from church to church, and their reciprocal notoriety was sometimes haftened by apoftolical injunctions. Thofe who received them, had full affurance of their authenticity from thofe who delivered them, and the multiplication of copies not only contributed to make them more generally known, but effectually fecured them from the lafting injuries of interpolation.

That the gofpels and epiftles were generally known foon after they were communicated to different churches, may be concluded from the interefting nature of their contents. Novelty in general is calculated to excite attention. In the prefent cafe, in which novelty confifted in the developement of a recent revelation of the divine will, the moft eager curiofity was roufed into action. The new converts likewife fought after thefe authentick documents of their faith with ardour, and divulged them with zeal. They drank the waters of life themfelves, and conveyed it to the thirfty who were at a diftance. The teftimony of hiftory confirms the truth of thefe obfervations. The works of Matthew, Mark, and Luke, which had been for fome time well known to Chriftians in general,

were

SERMON VII. 241

were fanctioned by the exprefs concurrence of St. John, previous to the compofition of his own gofpel, and the moft authentick evidence remains, that at a period not later than thirty years after his death, all the gofpels were recited on ftated days in the general affemblies of the faithful.

As foon as they were thus divulged, they were held in the higheft eftimation, as the rule of faith, and practice. They were particularly confulted by teachers to confirm their admonitions, by difputants to eftablifh their arguments, and by apologifts to vindicate their caufe. For fuch fupport, Clement, Ignatius, Polycarp, Juftin Martyr and Irenæus were eminently indebted to them. The atteftations which they afforded to thofe books of fcripture, which they had occafion to cite, are curious and important, as they furnifh a ftrong argument for their integrity and authenticity. Many paffages are very fimilar, others exactly reprefent thofe which occur in our prefent copies. From what is known, conclufions may fairly be drawn refpecting that which is not. Hence it may be prefumed, that the revolutions of feventeen centuries have left the New Teftament in the fame ftate as in the primitive times. The difficulty of intermediate corruption has not only been increased in proportion to the multiplication of copies, but in proportion likewise to the number of those who inserted any part of the sacred text into their writings. Hence an argument is furnished, that the stream which was not polluted at the fountain head, still runs pure and uncontaminated. If we are able to prove that it was not polluted at the fountain head, by shewing that the early Fathers used and quoted our scriptures, a complete and unbroken chain of evidence might be formed, and no generation be left without witnesses to the genuineness of the Christian records.

I. Since this investigation is so curious and important, an attempt will be made to remove the objections raised against the high probability of the apostolical Fathers having used our gospels.

II. It is intended to shew that the apostolical Fathers, as well as Justin Martyr and Irenæus, made quotations from most of the epistles.

III. The persuasion of the primitive church that the sacred writers were divinely inspired, will be shown; and the reasonableness of the persuasion

SERMON VII. 243

perfuafion will be confirmed by additional arguments.

The noble author of the Letters on Hiftory, whofe fpecious eloquence is frequently the difguife of unfounded affertions, maintains, " that the Fathers of the firft century either " made ufe of different gofpels from ours, or " the paffages which refemble thofe that oc- " cur in our gofpels, were preferved by un- " written tradition. To fay that they had the " works of our evangelifts before them, is a " manifeft abufe of hiftory, as they never ex- " prefsly mention their names."

It is an object of importance to examine thefe affertions with particular attention, becaufe they include the ftrongeft objections that can be brought againft the opinion moft reafonable to be maintained; refpecting the early reception of the New Teftament.

The Firft charge to be confidered is, that " the Fathers of the firft century might make " ufe of different gofpels from ours."

This fuppofition at firft fight appears highly improbable to thofe who recollect that Polycarp was the difciple of St. John, that Ignatius was inſtructed by ſeveral of the apoſtles, and that Clement was a fellow labourer of St. Paul, who was accompanied during his travels by the evangeliſt St. Luke. Connexions ſo intimate with theſe eminent inſtructors would naturally produce a high veneration for their ſentiments, and a decided and excluſive predilection of their works. Hence ariſes the extreme improbability of their having recourſe to any other goſpels than ſuch as were written or authenticated by thoſe from whom they received the firſt principles of the faith.

The improbability becomes much greater if it be conſidered, that the authors of apocryphal goſpels were either contemporary with the apoſtolical Fathers, or lived at a later period. If they lived at a later period, the ſuppoſition of the writer falls weak and inconcluſive to the ground: if they were contemporaries, the works of theſe heretical writers could be immediately referred to their reſpective ſources, and their omiſſions or interpolations of the true goſpels be inſtantly detected by being brought to the teſt of the uncorrupted originals. That this taſk was zealouſly performed, may fairly be preſumed from the frequent alluſions which are made to the hereſies of Ebion and Cerinthus, and the frequent cautions

SERMON VII.

cautions which are given to guard againſt their errours. To maintain that the apoſtolical Fathers were betrayed into the prepoſterous and weak inconſiſtency of borrowing from thoſe whom they inceſſantly attacked, is to give a ſanction to the abſurdity of thoſe hereticks who made Cerinthus the author of St. John's goſpel, when it evidently contains a refutation of his principles.

The objections may now be fairly reduced to this dilemma : either the apoſtolical Fathers derived ſeveral paſſages which occur in their remains, from unwritten tradition, or they made uſe of our goſpels.

In caſe the objector ſuppoſed, that if unwritten tradition was the ſource from which the apoſtolical Fathers derived their information, the certainty of the evangelical facts, or the reputation of the evangeliſts would be diminiſhed, he muſt have been intirely ignorant of their works, which manifeſtly eſtabliſh the one, and encreaſe the other.

For let us grant, that ſuch was really the caſe. It may even then be aſſerted upon ſafe grounds, that the apoſtolical Fathers contributed no inconſiderable aſſiſtance to eſtabliſh

the

the credibility of the gofpel hiftory. The leading facts relative to the Author of Chriftianity, and the principal topicks of his inftructions, may be clearly collected from their writings. For in them are recorded the miraculous conception of our Lord, the precife time of his appearance on earth, his inftitutions, his commands, the virtues which he difplayed, and the duties which he recommended, his exercife of miraculous powers, his death, refurrection, and afcenfion, the importance of his miffion, the tranfcendant benefits derived to mankind from his fufferings, and more efpecially a full and pofitive acknowledgment of his divine nature. In confequence of this detail, which, with many other particulars of the fame kind, may be collected from their epiftles, the apoftolical Fathers are to be confidered, as witneffes unacquainted with the writings of the evangelifts, and deriving all their information on religious fubjects, from the perfonal inftructions of the apoftles. The bare fuppofition has the air of an abfurdity, but for the fake of the preceding conceffion, their ignorance, improbable as it is, fhall be allowed. Their remains are even in this cafe undeniable vouchers of apoftolical confiftency, and prove that the inftructions and the writings of the infpired teachers, proceeded

SERMON VII.

ceeded originally from the fame fpirit of divine truth. Thus Clement, Ignatius, and Polycarp become doubly important as they ftand in relation to the tranfactions of our Saviour, and to the records of his biographers. From them is received an independant detail of actions and precepts of the higheft antiquity and refpectability, and their general coincidence with the evangelifts is as ftrong an evidence for the truths of the gofpel, as any atteftation given to the narratives of its writers.

Having thus fhewn that the refult of the conceffion would be far from proving unfavourable to the evangelical hiftory, let us proceed to prove that the apoftolical Fathers quoted our gofpels.

To grant an opponent fome part of his requifition is frequently of fmall advantage to his caufe. We are willing to allow, that the apoftolical Fathers do not exprefs the names of the evangelifts. But does it therefore follow by any fair inference, that they are not quoted, becaufe they are not named? By no means. St. Paul does not name Aratus, Menander, or Epimenides, yet it is unanimoufly allowed that their expreffions may clearly be traced in his epiftles. The antient authors of the letter from the churches of Vienne and Lyons, as well as Juftin Martyr, maintain a profound filence with refpect to the names of the evangelifts, although the identical fentences of fcripture abound in their productions. The authenticity of the larger epiftles of Ignatius, as well as of the apoftolical conftitutions, has been difputed, in confequence of the oftentatious and unneceffary mention of the evangelifts. The objections againft them have proceeded from the violation of a principle, laid down by the criticks, that the omiffion of names is a ftriking characteriftick of the apoftolical times. The conduct of the Fathers under confideration, was confiftent and uniform. Continued pages are cited from the Old, and various paffages from the New Teftament; yet whilft the peculiar fentiments and ftyle indifputably afcertain the refpective writers, their names are equally omitted. Thus the portraits of eminent perfons may ftrike the eye with fuch exact refemblance, that the fpectator fcarcely requires to be informed whofe features they are, which are prefented to his view.

But although the names of the evangelifts do not occur, the traces of their gofpels are very numerous and very evident. Ignatius mentions.

mentions the gofpel, as if written, feveral times, more particularly in his epiftles to the Smyrnæans, and Philadelphians. In his epiftle to the latter, two paffages occur which more pointedly indicate the hiftory of our Lord as recorded by the evangelifts. In the courfe of his cenfures of the Gnofticks, who denied the reality of Chrift's fufferings, he fays, " That " neither the prophecies, the law of Mofes, " nor the gofpel down to the prefent time had " convinced them of their errours." " The " prophets call for attention, but more parti- " cularly the gofpel in which the paffion and " the refurrection are manifefted to us." " Fly " to the gofpel as to the perfon of Chrift, " and to the apoftles as the prefbytery of the " church." By way of illuftration it may be remarked that this mode of expreffion clofely correfponds with the ftyle of the next century, when there could be no doubt as to the pre- cife import of the word gofpel. Tertullian declares " that from the law, the prophets, " the gofpel, and apoftolical writings, we " ought to learn our faith."

From the frequent allufions of the apofto- lical fathers, it feems highly probable that they refer to a collection of thofe books of which there was never any doubt in the church,

church, and which appear to have had an extensive circulation, and to have met with an early and general reception, among all the Christian congregations. We are not however authorized to make a general and unqualified assertion, that the evidence brought in favour of this collection, is always clear and equally strong. Clement makes particular and frequent use of the gospel of St. Matthew, and of St. Luke. He sometimes exhibits passages of the former with such correctness, as to give them a claim to be adopted in preference to the common readings. If his allusions to the latter were distant and vague, they would be rendered in a great degree fixed and determinate, as he has undoubted references to the Acts of the Apostles, which were published some time subsequent to the former treatise addressed to Theophilus.

Ignatius and Polycarp took a wider range of citation, as the gospel of St. John was published before they wrote. They studiously adopted many of his phrases, and followed his train of expression. How far the gospel of St. Mark is cited by any of them, it is very difficult to determine. The shades of distinction between what is quoted from his gospel, and from that of St. Matthew are so slight,

that

SERMON VII.

that they are frequently liable to be confounded by the moſt diſcerning eye. That which is borrowed from the one, may be attributed to the other, without the danger of incurring the charge of a want of critical diſcernment from thoſe who are converſant with the works of Juſtin Martyr. The ſame ambiguity of reference is obſervable in Clement, as well as in the others. The propriety of aſſigning to St. Mark ſome paſſages quoted in Clement's epiſtle, is confirmed by recollecting that St. Mark was a diſciple of St. Peter, as well as Clement, and that his goſpel was written at Rome, of which place Clement was biſhop.

If borrowed ideas be cited by an author, not in identical, but correſpondent terms, the paſſage in which they are found undoubtedly conſtitutes the eſſence of a quotation. This appears to have been the opinion of the ſacred writers, who quote the Old Teſtament from memory, and frequently repreſent the main import of a paſſage, without confining themſelves to literal expreſſions. In the Old Teſtament itſelf, the repetition of texts is far from being perfectly the ſame. The apoſtolical Fathers adopted a practice which was authorized by ſuch venerable examples, as will appear

appear from some very remarkable passages of Clement, Ignatius and Polycarp, in which are respectively contained the substance of a quotation from St. Luke, and the exact words both of St. Matthew, and St. John.

If their opportunities of information be considered, as well as the plain vestiges of the evangelical history, which abound in their works; it seems most reasonable to conclude that the apostolical Fathers made use of our gospels; that they mentioned them under certain general denominations; sometimes adduced passages from them with that vague representation which arises from imperfect recollection, and sometimes cited them with that precision, which indicates a recent and assiduous perusal. That the passages before stated, and many others of the same kind, which so precisely represent the conduct and the sentiments of our Lord were borrowed from tradition, amounts to nothing more than a precipitate conjecture; whereas, the proof of their being derived from our gospels is built upon strong and satisfactory arguments.

The assistance received from the epistles of the sacred writers for the establishment of the faith, and the regulation of practice, is evident

from

SERMON VII.

from the continual use made of them by the primitive writers. The first epistle to the Corinthians is expressly ascribed to St. Paul by Clement. Polycarp makes plain allusions to the Philippians, and Thessalonians; and refers, under the appellation of holy scriptures, to the epistle to the Ephesians, as well as to the other works which at that time composed the apostolical canon. The epistle to the Romans, as may be collected from the testimony of Tertullian, was preserved in the archives of their church, when Clement presided over it. His allusions to it are numerous and clear. So great has been his accuracy in stating some expressions, that an eminent editor of the Greek Testament has been enabled to correct several corrupt readings, which the negligence of transcribers had introduced into many copies of that epistle. His allusions and direct citations are likewise very strong and important proofs of the early notoriety and credit of the epistle to the Hebrews.

From the particular epistles which are expressly named, or clearly referred to, sometimes the train of argument in different words, and sometimes the exact expressions are derived. The practice respecting many others is precisely the same. Many of the other epistles,

though

though lefs clearly referred to, appear notwithstanding to have been imitated by these writers. Numerous passages occur in which the epistolary phrases are accommodated to new subjects, and incorporated with the stile of each writer. In Clement and Ignatius, may more particularly be discerned evident traces of St. Paul. The adoption of his sentiments communicates peculiar animation to their thoughts, and energy to their language. They delight in the amplification of his ideas, and that they expand them with considerable succefs is evident from several passages.

We have seen from the preceding observations, that the disciples of the apostles were well acquainted with the greater part of the sacred writings. Among their immediate descendants, no one was more eminent for zeal in the cause of christianity, or faithful attestation to its records, than Justin Martyr. He speaks of the works of the evangelists, under the general denomination of memoirs and gospels. He follows the example of his predecessors in the omission of names, and cites the precepts of the gospel, as the express injunctions of Christ himself. Of the numerous scriptural passages which occur in his works, many convey general sentiments without an adherence

SERMON VII. 255

adherence to literal expreffions, and many reprefent them with confiderable precifion.

During the age in which this writer flourifhed, the gofpels were publickly recited on the Lord's day in the affemblies of the Chriftians. This curious fact afcertains the high antiquity of a cuftom which has prevailed throughout the univerfal church. It likewife proves the great eftimation and wide diffufion of the gofpels, fo early as the middle of the fecond century.

Irenæus, bifhop of Lyons, the author of an elaborate confutation of the Gnoftick herefies, left an ample account of the New Teftament, which he calls with peculiar propriety of diftinction, the evangelical and apoftolical writings. He affigns many reafons for the gofpels being only four in number, and his citations of them are very copious. He relates the different occafions on which they were compofed, gives diftinct characters of the evangelifts, and proves that their endowments for their undertakings were imparted from on high. It is particularly to be remarked, that he ufually mentions the name of the author from whom he derives his fcriptural authorities; becaufe the practice of this writer fixes

the

the era of formal quotation. The succeeding Fathers of the church followed this example with little variation, and it is much to be regretted that so explicit a mode of reference was not introduced at a more early period, that every circumstance might have concurred to place the attestation of the apostolical Fathers intirely out of the reach of cavil and controversy. The books which Irenæus so particularly describes and so fully quotes, must have been received from his immediate predecessors; from none of whom he is so likely to have received them as from Polycarp, who was his preceptor, and the friend of Ignatius. In these apostolical Fathers we find passages similar to expressions in our gospels. The conclusion therefore is, that they, as well as the persons to whom they afterwards communicated the sacred books, have quoted the New Testament.

Having taken a cursory survey of the evidence given by the most authentick writers of the first and second centuries to the New Testament, it is now proper to draw the line of discrimination between those parts of it, which they cite, and those, which they omit.

SERMON VII.

The allusions to the gospels of St. Matthew, St. Luke, and St. John, even in the apostolical Fathers, are very clear. St. Mark may not be so conspicuous, for reasons already given. By Justin and Irenæus all the four are fully and satisfactorily quoted. Of the Acts of the Apostles, the citations are very full, particularly in the epistle of Clement, the apologies and dialogue of Justin Martyr, and the treatise of Irenæus. The revelation of St. John is accurately described by Justin Martyr, and frequently quoted by Irenæus. All such notices must appear very important and valuable, when we consider with proper attention the integrity of the writers, their high antiquity, and their favourable opportunities of information.

Among the epistles those which are most used are the epistles to the Corinthians. The epistle to the Hebrews was evidently well known to Clement. All the rest are either alluded to, or expressly cited, except the epistles to Titus and Philemon: the epistle of James, the second of Peter, the second and third of John, and the epistle of St. Jude, are omitted by all these writers. For this silence it is not difficult to assign satisfactory reasons. The smallness and private nature of the epistle to Philemon, might prevent it from being cited. The third, if not the second epistle of St. John, was written to a private person, and might remain for some time unknown to the church at large. The remoteness of Crete retarded the circulation of the epistle to Titus, and as the original copies of the catholick epistles belonged to no church in particular, it might not in the infancy of the church be easy to ascertain their authenticity.

How many of the above-mentioned epistles were known to the primitive Fathers, it is difficult to ascertain. It is highly improbable that they were unacquainted with all of them. The curious and minute observer, from the frequent usage of some remarkable words, may contend that Ignatius had read the epistle to Philemon, as well as that addressed to Titus; and from a similarity of thought, he may conclude that Irenæus, when he wrote the passage in his treatise on the Gnostick heresies, relative to the efficacy of good works, recollected the epistle of St. James.

Among other reasons for which we have reason to regret the loss of several works of Justin Martyr; may be mentioned, the important testimony, which they would probably have

SERMON VII.

have afforded to our gofpels and epiftles. If the epiftles of Polycarp had alone efcaped the ravages of time, they would have furnifhed ample, and perhaps fufficient proofs of the early notoriety and credit of the facred writings; fince in his remaining epiftle, fhort as it is, he refers to more than half the productions of which the New Teftament is compofed.

No diftance of time, no remotenefs of place, prevented the unanimous appeal which thefe writers made to the original fcriptures. Their atteftations give and receive mutual confirmation and mutual luftre. Clement flourifhed at Rome, Ignatius at Antioch, Polycarp at Smyrna, Juftin Martyr in Syria and Rome, and Irenæus in Gaul. If circumftances confpired to bring fome of them acquainted with each other, their integrity and piety exclude the flighteft fuppofition that they entertained an unreafonable prejudice in favour of the New Teftament, or united to raife its credit by difhonourable combination. Rejecting all other records, which were invented only to give a plaufible fanction to herefy, they unanimoufly received thofe which were ftamped with the image, and marked with the fuperfcription of truth. One was not a preacher of the gofpel of Ebion, and another an advocate for the theogony of the Gnosticks. *They followed not cunningly devised fables, but built upon the foundation of the apostles, Jesus Christ himself being the chief corner stone.*

The gospels and epistles are never introduced with hesitation or apprehension, lest doubts should arise in the minds of Christians relative to their authority. Appeal is made to them, as to a sacred and immoveable standard of truth, which is established by the consent of all. The language therefore of the early Fathers, is the language of the church. With one voice they proclaim the reception of the scriptures, and with one consent revere them, and them alone, as authentick and sacred.

To confirm these observations it is proper to remark, that the epistle of Clement was written not only with the approbation, but in the name of the whole church of Rome. Polycarp addressed the Philippians in conjunction with all the presbyters of Smyrna. The epistles of Ignatius were written under the inspection of the companions of his painful journey from Antioch to Rome, and of the Christians whom he visited by the way. Justin Martyr in his apologies, makes a publick address

SERMON VII.

addrefs to the emperours in vindication of the whole body of Chriftians. The confutation of the Gnoftick herefy by Irenæus, derives its greateft authority and weight from fuppofing that he fpeaks the prevailing language, and adduces the general arguments of the church.

Of the uniformity of faith which may be obferved in the paftors as well as in their flocks, it is curious to afcertain the caufe. The univerfal reception of the fame facred books, is an obvious and fatisfactory reafon among others. The high regard paid to thefe books was founded on a general perfuafion, that the authors of them wrote under the immediate influence of divine infpiration. " The " Word who was the creator of the univerfe, " who fitteth upon the cherubim, and up- " holdeth all things, even he who was mani- " feft to the world, hath given to us a fourfold " gofpel, which is communicated by the holy " fpirit."

This perfuafion fo fublimely expreffed in the words of Iræneus, which was common to the church at large, was rational and judicious. It arofe partly from the harmony which prevailed between the apoftolical writings, and the apoftolical tradition, which for no incon-

fiderable

fiderable period faithfully reprefented the principles of Chriftianity; and partly from the miraculous powers which were enjoyed by the apoftles on every occafion that was inftantaneoufly or ultimately conducive to the interefts of the gofpel.

They had alfo a *more fure word of prophecy* to eftablifh this conviction, for our Lord kindly anticipating the imminent confternation of his difciples, and gracioufly defiring to fupply his own abfence by adequate comforts; promifed that the holy fpirit fhould *bring all things to their remembrance*. Hence they were armed with courage equal to every outward danger, and endued with knowledge equal to every intellectual difficulty. The holy fpirit revived in their minds the precepts of their Lord, and completed the fcheme of evangelical inftruction. As its affiftance was extended to every branch of the apoftolical miffion, an exact narrative of our Lord's conduct and tranfactions, neceffarily formed a grand and important object of its infallible communications.

The expediency of the divine interference to preferve the writings of the apoftles from inaccuracy and mifreprefentation may ftrike us with greater force, if we examine the nature of

SERMON VII.

of hiftorical evidence to the truth of facts and opinions.

Fidelity of defcription, and accuracy of narrative, are highly neceffary for him who undertakes to record the tranfactions of antient times. Yet of the writers who are eminent for their hiftorical productions, many have been betrayed into inconfiftency and contradiction. The unwearied diligence of Plutarch, the elaborate concifenefs of Tacitus, the extenfive refearches of Dion Caffius and of Jofephus, did not fecure them againft occafional deviations from truth. If their talents, however refpectable, and their erudition, however profound, left them ftill expofed to errour; what caufe lefs than fupernatural can be affigned why men, remarkable for defect of education and flownefs of apprehenfion, as the difciples of Chrift were, fhould be qualified to give a ftatement of facts altogether harmonious and confiftent, and to reach the height of hiftorical excellence which was unattainable by fuperiour minds?

The apoftles have not only avoided errour, with regard to facts, but mifreprefentations, with regard to opinions. To the general conduct of the writers of old, they have furnifhed a ftriking a striking and illustrious exception. Every admirer of antient philosophy laments how often in his search after the characteristic marks of any particular sect, he finds himself bewildered in the labyrinth of uncertainty. The careless writer may blend those tenets, which as they are totally different in their nature, and derived from distinct sources, ought to be kept for ever separate. The neglect of accurate inquiry, may not unfairly be imputed to Plutarch, when he asserts that Plato held the doctrine of a good and an evil principle. The same fault is likewise to be imputed to that sublime philosopher himself, who, hurried away by too great an eagerness to dignify a favourite sentiment with the authority of a celebrated name, afforded grounds for just complaint to Socrates, who accused him of having confounded his tenets with those of preceding sages. Nor can the great Aristotle, notwithstanding the depth of his understanding, and the extent of his knowledge, be freed from a similar charge. He has asserted, that the Deity of Zenophanes was corporeal, although the tenour of his arguments plainly lead to the opposite conclusion. Now, after these deviations from accurate representation in men of the most enlarged and enlightened minds, who could discern the nice distinctions of metaphysical

SERMON VII.

phyſical principles, and feel the neceſſity of ſtating them with exactneſs, how was it poſſible that the illiterate fiſhermen of Galilee could communicate, without ſupernatural aſſiſtance, the preciſe rules of the moſt perfect ethicks, and the ſublime doctrines of the moſt refined theology?

To fix the degree of inſpiration which was imparted to the writers of the New Teſtament, is an object of much greater conſequence than to explain the method in which it was conveyed. That the apoſtles were conſtantly under the divine influence, that ſuch influence extended to ſcrupulous correctneſs in every particular, and rendered them perfectly infallible in the writings they have left us, is an opinion which its advocates will find it difficult to eſtabliſh. Aware of the many objections which may be brought againſt them, it is not for ſuch an hypotheſis that we ought precipitately to contend. There ſeems however nothing repugnant to reaſon, nothing inconſiſtent with the circumſtances of the caſe in ſuppoſing, that the Holy Spirit guarded the ſacred writers from errour in the grand outlines of their narration, in the ſtatement of precepts, and the developement of doctrines.

A divine

A divine affiftance thus favourably imparted, feems to have anfwered the great end of its communication without extending to the revelation of other points. It at once accounts fatisfactorily for thofe flight deviations from exact uniformity which the advocates of infidelity have magnified into apparent importance, and difplayed with oftentatious parade. In the more minute circumftances of facts, the facred writers are left to the refources of their own unaffifted memory and experience, and confequently are reduced to the level of all other credible hiftorians. Upon thofe momentous points which contribute to form an infallible rule and ftandard of faith and practice, they were guided by the hand of divine wifdom into all truth, and foar to a height of credibility which no human writer can attain.

He who perufes the fcriptures with the flighteft degree of attention, muft be ftruck by a radical peculiarity of narrative and fentiment. There is fometimes a greatnefs of thought which furpaffes the conceptions of human genius, and fometimes an unaffected artleffnefs, which attracts by its novelty, and delights by its fweetnefs. Confidered folely as compofitions calculated to pleafe the fancy by lively

lively reprefentations, to fatisfy the judgment by exact probability, and intereft the feelings by affecting reprefentations, they deferve to fhare our attention with the claffical remains of Greece and Rome. In the works of the evangelifts may be found inftances of that captivating fimplicity of narration, which we admire in Xenophon; and in the epiftles of St. Paul, are many examples of that fublime impetuofity of argument, which we applaud in Demofthenes. Here however the fimilarity muft end. One circumftance there is, in which the New Teftament rifes to an elevation, which no other book can reach. Here prefides the majefty of Truth in unadorned but awful ftate, and never turns afide to the blandifhments of Flattery, nor liftens to the whifpers of Defamation. Here alone fhe preferves the fame benign but unchangeable afpect, and points with equal impartiality, to the apoftles at one time, deferting Chrift, and at another, rifquing life by the bold profeffion of his gofpel; to Peter now protefting his unalterable fidelity, and now denying his Lord.

Every fincere chriftian will contemplate this characteriftick with fentiments of veneration and delight, and will think it a prefumptive argument, that when he perufes
scripture,

scripture, *the place whereon he stands is holy ground.* He regards those who deny its celestial origin for the sake of reducing its contents to the low standard of their own degrading opinion, as audacious and deluded innovators, whose temerity excites his astonishment, and whose infatuation awakens his pity. Satisfied with the external as well as internal evidence, he receives with implicit confidence this invaluable treasure, and considers inspiration as the angelick guard placed by heaven around the book of life, to secure it from the attacks of presumptuous and aspiring man.

SERMON VIII.

HEBREWS XII. 1.

Wherefore seeing we are compassed about with so great a Cloud of Witnesses, let us lay aside every Weight, and the Sin which doth so easily beset us; and let us run with Patience the Race that is set before us; looking unto Jesus, the Author and Finisher of our Faith.

IT may be remarked in all political institutions, that laws are never heard with so much attention, nor obeyed with so much alacrity, as immediately after their first promulgation. Their observance is more agreeable to the inclinations of mankind at that, rather than any subsequent period of time, by reason of the comparison made between the advantages which they secure, and the urgent inconveniences which they remove. This observation fervation will be found to hold good not only in political but religious eftablifhments, for Chriftianity itfelf was never embraced with more genuine fincerity, nor adorned with more pure morals, than during the earlieft ages of the church. The perfect freedom of the gofpel became the moft valuable acquifition to thofe who had laboured under the yoke of the Jewifh or Pagan ceremonies; and the dreary profpects of fuperftition were eagerly exchanged for the glorious light of life and immortality.

The view of fociety and manners which ecclefiaftical hiftory prefents during the primitive times, is particularly worthy of attention. We behold the church deriving its eftablifhment from the apoftles, and even from Chrift himfelf, diftinguifhed equally from the Pagans, who were its avowed enemies, and from the hereticks, who were its infidious friends. To the former, in its publick remonftrances it was ingenuous without weaknefs, and prudent without diffimulation; to the latter, in its confutations of their errours, it was condefcending without timidity, and refolute without harfhnefs. Regardlefs of the diftinctions of rank or fortune, it invited all to take refuge from the corruptions of idolatry in its hofpitable afylum, and to participate the

comfort

SERMON VIII.

comfort of prefent tranquillity, and the hope of future happinefs. Its paftors, eminent for virtue and learning, taught with the confidence of full conviction thofe doctrines, which they received from the moft indifputable authority; and made the edification of their flocks the moft important object of their ambition. Their power was exercifed for the moft falutary purpofes, and they laboured with unremitting affiduity for the correction of finners, the reconciliation of enemies, and the converfion of infidels. No variation prevailed in the reftrictions of difcipline, or the confeffion of faith, fince one fyftem of government and one creed were not only adopted by the members of the fame church, but by all the churches difperfed throughout the world.

Such uniformity appears the more extraordinary, when we recollect that it was not promoted by the machinations of human policy, nor enforced by the authority of the civil power: for this was the period, during which Chriftianity was fupported merely by its own native ftrength, and made the moft rapid advances towards a complete eftablifhment amid the threats of legal prohibitions, and the intolerance of polytheifm. The vigorous tree planted by the Son of God flourifhed and caft

its

its grateful shade over the nations; whilst by the strength of its roots and the firmness of its bulk it survived the repeated violence of winds and storms.

The conversion of the Emperour Constantine was eminently favourable to the church; for from that glorious event she dated the origin of her external splendour, and her security. The Christians, however, who had been trained in the rigid school of persecution to the exercise of every distinguished virtue, were succeeded by those who felt the pernicious effects of prosperity. The purity of their morals was gradually stained with licentiousness, their harmony was broken by unedifying disputations, and the vigour of their discipline was relaxed by irresolution.

The clouds of bigotry in the middle ages overspread the world, and the institutions, opinions and ceremonies, which were then by degrees introduced, not only encumbered Christianity with useless appendages, but caused a heavy depression of the powers of the mind. A long night of intellectual darkness prevailed, before mankind were sufficiently roused from the dreams of superstition to accomplish an auspicious reformation.

Whether

SERMON VIII.

Whether we confider the various caufes that gave rife to this event, or the means by which it was accomplifhed; the extenfive field of action which it opened to the underftanding, by the expulfion of fpiritual tyranny, the extraordinary difcoveries which preceded, or the matchlefs exertions of intellect which followed, it may fairly be confidered as one of the greateft occurrences recorded in the annals of time. True fcience derived its origin from this reftoration of true Chriftianity, and learning, which had fhared its corruption and decay, arofe with new vigour on its revival. Their affociation not only afforded mutual fupport, but proved that reafon, when advanced to the higheft ftate of improvement, is moft congenial with revelation, and that the latter never appears to more advantage, than when viewed by the ftrongeft light which the former can impart. The benefits likewife conferred on fociety at large were fimilar to thofe which had been happily experienced during the firft propagation of the gofpel. The facred oracles were laid open to all, and the fulleft opportunities were afforded to the laity as well as the clergy, of becoming acquainted with the pure and uncorrupted principles of duty. Nor was this the only feature of refemblance to the antient times; for the general conformity of

our

our eftablifhment to the primitive church has been celebrated by its own members at home, and its admirers abroad, as its moft illuftrious, and moft diftinguifhing characteriftick.

Prepared by a clofe and ardent perufal of fcripture, and impreffed with due refpect for the authority of the early Fathers, as its moft faithful interpreters, the great Reformers of England came forth to execute their pious tafk. Their judgment was confpicuous both in expunging from the proteftant ritual a long train of unedifying ceremonies, and in retaining the moft decorous ufages of worfhip. We feel a pious fatisfaction in contemplating and enumerating the falutary effects of their labours, more particularly as long experience has afforded ample proofs of their infeparable connexion with the beft and moft exalted interefts of the nation.

The plan of our religious inftitutions was formed by fervent piety, and executed with profound judgment. The fundamental articles of the faith, which they prefcribe, are ftrictly confiftent with fcripture, are recommended by the belief of the antient Fathers, and ratified by the decrees of the moft refpectable councils. The facred edifices, whilft they are divefted

SERMON VIII.

vested of the gawdy decorations, and puerile ornaments of Popery, are furnished with those appendages which give dignity to publick worship, and distinguish the functions of its ministers from ordinary occupations. A code of devotional exercises is established, far superior to all other sacred compositions of human origin for simple energy of language, pure fervour of piety, and evangelical tenour of sentiment. For these distinguishing qualities it is principally indebted to those venerable forms of supplication, which were breathed from the lips of saints and martyrs, and consecrated to the service of the church by holy men of the earliest ages. It gives the most expressive and pathetick utterance to the wants and desires of the devout suppliant, and enables him to fulfil with perfect consistency, the various duties of rational and steady devotion. Engaged in the repetition of our prayers, he avoids the wild rhapsodies of the Methodist, and the cold addresses of the Presbyterian. Thus he is freed from the irregularity and abruptness of extemporaneous effusions, which are unknown until the moment they are uttered, and which as soon as uttered, the judgmen of the critick must always condemn as incoherent, and the conscience of the pious must frequently reject as unscriptural. The hierarchy,

hierarchy, deriving its origin from the apoſtles, is confirmed by primitive uſage, and recommended by the utility of clerical gradations. The political conſtitution of the country, in return for the alliance which it has formed with the church, derives from the aſſociation additional ſecurity for the obſervance of the laws, and the preſervation of order. The unmoleſted profeſſion and free exerciſe of their particular worſhip are allowed to all who diſſent from the eſtabliſhment. The prudent toleration which is allowed, equally avoids the dangerous extremes of cruel perſecution, which breaks the ties of charity; and of that unbounded indulgence, which may convert religion into an engine of ambition. Thus pious in her profeſſions, uncorrupt in her inſtitutions, and judicious in her reſtraints, our church is to the ſectariſt no real ſtumbling-block, and to the ſceptick no more than imaginary fooliſhneſs.

While we ſurvey in our own religious inſtitutions the fundamental articles of belief, and principles of government, which diſtinguiſhed the antient Chriſtians; while we recogniſe in our forms of prayer the traces of their devotion, and practiſe the decent rites which they inſtituted; we declare by our
conformity

SERMON VIII.

conformity the greateſt approbation of their conduct and ſentiments upon ſubjects the moſt important. We are alſo more forcibly impreſſed by the propriety of our reſearches into the means by which they propagated the faith; and we moreover feel a greater ſatisfaction in diſplaying their virtues, and in vindicating them from the miſrepreſentation of prejudiced and uncandid writers.

Attentive to the voice of antiquity, and ſolicitous for the honour of our religion, we have endeavoured to invalidate the objections of *the Hiſtorian of the Decline and Fall of the Roman Empire,* and to rectify his deviations from truth.

The proofs in favour of the continuance of miracles for ſome time after the death of the apoſtles, remain in full force, notwithſtanding the ingenuity which was exerted to ſhake their credibility. They are deſtitute neither of the arguments, nor the authority of modern writers to ſupport them, and if the ſcepticiſm, injudiciouſly imputed to the preſent age, be ſo ſtubborn, and deeply rooted in the minds of Gibbon and of Middleton; from a number of thoſe whoſe opinions are more flexible by the force of evidence, we may ſelect Moſheim and Jortin.

Jortin. These are writers who cannot fairly be accused either of bigotry or credulity; and if any discussion ought to be decided by the sole voice of authority, where can the ecclesiastical student, in the widest extent of his researches, find more candour, deeper learning, or more sound and dispassionate judgment?

The apologies of the primitive Christians have been set in a proper light, and their subjects appear to have been more judiciously chosen, than the blindness of prejudice and the fastidiousness of criticism were inclined to admit. The writers of them deserve to be restored to the rank to which former ages had raised them, and they ought also to be considered as important allies in the service of Christianity.

The primitive Christians are restored to the station so eminently due to their merit, and from the number of their virtues, which we have endeavoured to elucidate, we may fairly conclude, that their motives were more pure than the Historian has represented. Even their avowed enemies have left us ample testimonies of their exemplary conduct, and we cannot venture, without the just imputation of the most unreasonable prejudice, to depreciate

ciate the characters which they have drawn. The candour of the present age might reasonably be called in question if we withheld that tribute to merit, which was chearfully paid by a Lucian and a Julian.

If our representations be conformable to the evidence of antient writers, what becomes of that state of scepticism which the Historian has described as propitious to the diffusion of Christianity? It is found to have existed only among the philosophers, and the small circle to which their opinions were confined; and consequently supplies a very inadequate idea of the general disposition of their contemporaries.

We have developed the various causes of antient persecution, and shown that the magnanimity of the followers of Jesus was tried by the most painful tortures. It has appeared in direct contradiction to the assertions of the Historian, how little Paganism encouraged the advances of Christianity by an indifference to superstitious establishments. We have observed that the heathen assumed a fierce and lowering aspect, and menaced the approach of the believer with outrage and even with death; that Persecution unsheathed her sword, and compelled

compelled the innocent martyr either to offer incense upon the altar of her Gods, or to fall a bleeding victim at her feet.

By a particular discussion of some assertions of this Historian, which materially affect the characters of the early Christians, we have detected the futility of his charges, and as we may infer the general tenour of his unfair representations from those specimens, we may conclude that the fifteenth and sixteenth chapters are altogether unworthy of the rank they hold in his work, and ought to be consigned by every friend of justice and truth to neglect and oblivion.

We have endeavoured not only to mark the first advances of Christianity in the world, but to delineate a picture of its influence on society, and the important alterations, which it effected in publick institutions and private manners; how it removed the inconveniencies and unhappiness of early times, and meliorated the general condition of human life throughout the succeeding ages.

We have brought evidences to prove the early reception of the books of the New Testament; we have ascertained the high esteem

SERMON VIII.

in which they were held, and both stated and confirmed the sentiments of the earliest Christians with respect to the inspiration of the sacred writers.

We have moreover attempted, in our description of the hereticks who destroyed the harmony of the Christian church, to give an accurate statement of the opinions of the Ebionites, with an immediate view to rectify the misrepresentation of the *Historian of the early opinions concerning Christ*. We have seen that their pretensions to the highest antiquity, were ill founded; and that they met with direct opposition from the successive writers of the primitive church.

We have ventured to combat his fundamental principles relative to that most important article of faith, the Divinity of our Lord and Saviour. We have rescued the early Christians from his misrepresentations, and shown that their opinions when fully developed are most favourable to the church of England.

It has appeared to what degree the Ebionites endeavoured to divest our Lord of his divinity, after that the Gnosticks had attempted to explain away his humanity. The

philosophers

philosophers of the present day at once arrogate the refined speculations and comprehensive knowledge of the latter, and model the heresy of the former into a more degrading system of their own. But their labour is as fruitless when soliciting the support of scripture, as their pretensions have been proved to be arrogant and weak, when boasting of the concurrence of the early ages. The evangelists and the apostles, the confessors and martyrs, the pastors and the universal church in the plain language of her original creeds, disavow the errours of Unitarianism, and pronounce with one voice its full condemnation.

But however satisfactory it may be to dispel the mists of prejudice, and give a clear and cloudless prospect of historical truth, the preceding disquisitions are not confined to the arguments of fruitless controversy, or the recital of unedifying facts. On the contrary, they open a wide field of the most profitable speculation, and may excite a more earnest attention to the calls of duty. The fairest and most excellent examples are held up to our inspection, let us view them with deference, and imitate them with fidelity; let us be followers of the primitive Christians, even as they were of the apostles and of Christ.

In

SERMON VIII.

In the ardour of their zeal and the livelinefs of their faith, the firft Chriftians appear to have excelled all the generations which fucceeded them. Many Chriftians of the prefent times, however they may believe all that the apoftles have fpoken, are too liable to the imputation of remiffnefs, by not adding virtue to their faith. To the evidences of revelation they give only that languid affent of the underftanding, which is deftitute of the warm and invigorating approbation of the heart. If all embraced with cordial affection the gofpel of Chrift as the deareft pledge of divine love, we fhould then behold in the conduct of every one that ardent piety to God, that univerfal charity to man, that meek endurance of infults and injuries, that ftrict temperance, perfect content and unruffled tranquility, that firmnefs of principle and refignation of will which the Saviour of the world recommended in his difcourfes, and exemplified in his conduct. But the diligence of labour and the ardour of hope which ought to be fhown in the exercife of thefe virtues, are directed to unworthy objects. For they too often affift ambition to climb the giddy heights of power, diffipation to feek the flowery paths of pleafure, avarice to amafs her wealth, and the paffions to overleap the bounds of duty. Let the

the alacrity of mankind, which is so apparent in all these pursuits, be transferred to religion, and its injunctions will appear the most engaging incitements to goodness. The difficulties of religious practice will be alleviated, and we shall enjoy the full relish of its pure and sublime gratifications. When employed in executing the commands of God, we shall never drag the heavy chain of reluctant compliance, but shall tread the path of duty with delight, and glory in the perfect freedom of the gospel.

We have in the preceding discourses remarked the profound humility, which was the most striking ornament of the primitive church. This virtue distinguishes Christianity from all other religions, more than any duty which it recommends. Duly influenced by this we are convinced that the brightest faculties of mind, the greatest attainments of learning, the fairest gifts of nature, the highest rank of honour, or the most profuse bounty of fortune, afford no grounds for pride or presumption. They are all primarily derived from the goodness of God, and are to be ultimately dedicated to his honour and service. Our various wants and infirmities contribute likewise to convince us of the expediency of
this

SERMON VIII.

this duty, and hourly to suggest to us our constant dependance upon the Supreme Being. Our Saviour himself, by every action of his life inculcated its observance, and furnished the most persuasive arguments to *learn of him who was meek and lowly*.

But more particularly the humility which is so strongly recommended in the gospel is calculated to subdue the pride of the intellectual powers, and check the sallies of ambitious reason. We ought therefore to bring to the severest test of examination the plausible arguments of those pretenders to superiour knowledge who affect to contemn, or attempt to mutilate the revelations of the divine will. We ought to meet their prophane sarcasms with contempt, and reject their subtle insinuations with disdain. For we may be well assured that the cavils, which are wantonly thrown out at the articles of our holy faith, result only from the pride and self-sufficiency of the human understanding. The caviller makes his own limited capacity the measure of his creed, and reasons upon the most weak of all principles, for he will not believe what he cannot comprehend. Instigated by presumptuous eagerness to reject the mysteries relative to the divine Essence, he confounds

the

the proofs of an article of belief with the nature of it. All however who have the judgment to discern and the ingenuousness to acknowledge the imperfections of the intellectual powers, will readily assent to the truth of many things, although they are incompetent to the solution of the difficulties which attend them.

We believe that there is a God who is an eternal Being endued with every perfection that the mind of man can conceive; but in what manner this Almighty Being exists, how his prescience can be fully reconciled with the free agency of man, how the high and lofty One who reigns in heaven above, can at the same point of time be universally present in every part of the creation, and yet be unextended, is a labyrinth of perplexity to our minds, for which our conceptions can furnish us with no clue. The mathematician informs us that a line may be supposed to approach perpetually towards another, without a possibility of ever reaching it. The ignorant may treat the assertion with ridicule as absurd, but certain it is, that the problem is capable of demonstration. The discovery of the circulation of the blood gave new and surprizing insight into the internal fabrick of the human frame;

SERMON VIII.

frame; but where is the acute chemift who after his moft laborious decompofitions of this vital fluid, can tell what caufe produces its firft motion, or for what reafon its action is lefs voluntary than that of the lungs?

Let the Philofopher therefore fufpend awhile his operations againft Chriftianity, let him direct the acutenefs of his difcernment and the toil of his application to develope the obfcurities of metaphyfical, mathematical, and natural truth, before he fcornfully rejects the myfteries of faith becaufe they are not reducible to the ftandard of his faculties, and becaufe the limit which terminates his profpect is not the boundary of the univerfe.

Wifdom has never been more fully juftified by her children, and her true intereft has never been more fuccefsfully purfued, than when they have afcertained with precifion their own powers of mind, applied them to acceffible objects, and confeffed the immeafurable diftance between things human and divine. Unlike the vaunting fciolifts of the prefent day, they prefumed not to tear the veil of the fanctuary and rufh into the holy of holies, but firmly confiding in the evidence of divine revelation, at due diftance adored its awful myfteries.

mysteries. The great, the wise, and the learned of the present times ought to think it no degradation to be meek and lowly of heart, when a perfect submission of the understanding to divine truth was the characteristick of the most sublime poet, the most profound philosopher, the most devout physiologist, and the most correct moralist who have adorned the circle of modern literature. All ought surely to bend with awe before the throne of the divine Majesty, and acquiesce in the scriptural representations of the divine essence, when they consider the sound and unshaken principles of Milton, of Bacon, of Boyle and of Johnson.

From pursuing a course far different from these teachers of truth and masters of solid erudition, the antient hereticks adopted all those errours which degraded them from the rank of sound reasoners, and rendered them unworthy of communion with orthodox Christians. They exalted the tenets of their darling philosophy to excessive consequence, incorporated them with the principles of Christianity, and adopted only that part of the creed, which could be accommodated to their own hypothesis. They corrupted those doctrines which they could not comprehend, and placed the

visionary

SERMON VIII.

visionary refinements of the human intellect upon the same level with the revelations of divine truth.

By a similar abuse of the powers of an enlightened understanding, *the Historian of the Early Opinions concerning Christ*, under pretence of reforming abuses, darkens the glorious picture of the gospel; under pretence of obliterating the stains, which its doctrines have contracted by the injuries of time, he mutilates the features of the most august personage whom the sacred writers hold up to our view. He gives an idea of the Saviour of the world no less inadequate and imperfect than might be formed of the bright luminary of day when divested of his beams, and deprived of his lustre by the temporary obscurity of a total eclipse.

The Historian of the Decline and Fall of the Roman Empire may be charged with a similar perversion of his talents. Eager to cavil where he cannot confute, and to insinuate that, which he dares not to avow, he is regardless of the consequences which might ensue from the success of his endeavours to depreciate Christianity. For if there be still so much wickedness in the world, notwithstanding the general knowledge of revelation that is disseminated

minated among us, how deplorable would the state of society become, if its glorious light were totally extinguished? What obstacles would then stop the torrent of vice, which, although opposed by the firm bulwark of religion, now swells with impetuosity and rage? If the unbeliever would turn his attention to the inestimable benefits which Christianity confers on mankind, if he would duly consider the aid it affords to the political institutions of his country, its salutary influence upon the conduct where laws cannot reach the commission of sin, its genial effects on the habits and relations of social life, its direct and obvious tendency to make men happy in themselves and useful to others, he could not seriously desire its debasement. Nor can he wish to see his countrymen disengaged from the ties of a pious education, and totally abandoned to licentiousness and libertinism, unless he has forfeited his right to the character of a good citizen, and is so much influenced by the malignity of a misanthropist as to rejoice in the ignorance and wretchedness of mankind.

Upon a fair estimate of the benevolent spirit of antiquity as well as of that which marks the present times, we maintain with satisfaction as well as with justice, that in the most
conspicuous

conspicuous and splendid acts of charity the modern Christian has no reason to retire with apprehensions of inferiority from a comparison with the antient believer. The example, which was held out by a Roman matron, who erected a fabrick for the cure of diseases, has been very frequently followed, and variously improved upon. The ample and costly edifices, consecrated to health in every part of this kingdom, are as salutary to the poor whom they supply with that relief, which they could not otherwise procure; as they are honourable to the rich, who could not by the adoption of any other expedient, render their bounty so extensively beneficial. The humane of the present age listen with eagerness to the various and remote cries of distress, extend their concern to mental as well as corporeal diseases, and combine in their plans of benevolence the immediate comfort of individuals with the best interest of society. A benevolent zeal for the spiritual welfare of the youthful poor has gone forth, and multitudes of them are taught to devote that sacred day to the duties of piety and the acquirement of useful learning, which was formerly wasted in idleness and vice. By an institution not less novel in its plan, than excellent in its consequences, the offspring of the condemned criminal and destitute mendicant are rescued from the corruptions of their wretched parents, and receive the bounty of subsistence with the light of education. The children of the bleak provinces and barren isles of North Britain are taught the elements of learning and religion, and thus are enabled to repel the force of popular superstitions with new vigour of mind, and acquire new patience to reconcile them to the severity of their climate. Of the various measures, which have been pursued in the metropolis of the empire, to alleviate and remove the distresses of mankind, several have been adopted by the country at large. Thus the tide of riches possessed in such superiour abundance by many inhabitants of this country, are taught to flow through various channels for the relief of the indigent. Every supply which they afford may be considered as an important advantage to society, because the most helpless are relieved, the most useful part of the community are restored to their ordinary occupations, and by the general effects of munificence, the quantity of human misery is lessened. Still, however, the triumph of the present age, as well as the great and important work of Christian charity, is incomplete, unless liberality be a blessing to him who gives, as well as to him who receives. This it cannot be

SERMON VIII. 293

be in its fulleft and moft defirable fenfe, if the principle which roufes him to action be not the love of God, and the defire of obtaining his favour. This motive was the glory of the primitive church, and rendered it a pattern peculiarly worthy of the imitation of pofterity. Whilft oftentation courts the publick notice, and gives with ready hand, that applaufe may follow its fteps; whilft profufion fcatters her ftores thoughtlefsly and without diftinction; whilft fenfibility feels only a momentary impulfe of compaffion when the object of diftrefs is at hand; the humanity of the gofpel is calculated to fupply all deficiencies, and to extend its impartial and ready affiftance to all cafes of wretchednefs, want and calamity, without reftraint or diftinction. The enlarged and liberal fpirit of the evangelical promifes is moft abundantly fhown, as well by giving to every one the power of fharing its advantages, as by holding forth a fure recompence for the flighteft exercife of Chriftian kindnefs, fince *whofoever giveth even a cup of cold water in the name of Chrift, fhall in no wife lofe his reward.*

When we contemplate the perilous fituation of the Chriftians of the firft ages of the church, we ought to pour forth the moft ardent

dent expreffions of gratitude to heaven, that we live in an age when the profeffion of our religion does not involve us in perfonal danger, nor fubject us to the confifcation of property, and the lofs of life. We ftand on the peaceful fhore, and view in the remote profpect of antient times the ftorms which agitated the primitive converts upon the fea of perfecution. Compared with fuch circumftances of diftrefs and difficulty we are blefied with perfect tranquillity, true comfort and folid happinefs. Still however it is not a ftate of floth, and inactivity. We have duties to perform, lefs rigorous and painful indeed, but not lefs obligatory, or lefs connected with our eternal intereft. Our warfare is not the warfare of the primitive Chriftians. They faw the authority of the magiftrate and the turbulence of the multitude leagued againft them in the moft formidable confederacy. *The heathen furioufly raged, and the rulers took counfel againft the Lord and againft his followers:* we on the contrary are protected by the laws of our country, and enjoy the bleffings of a liberal eftablifhment. They went forth, to attack the powers of darknefs, to fubvert the empire of fuperftition, and fubdue the world to the dominion of Chrift. It is our tafk to check the progrefs of infidelity, to oppofe the torrent of licen-

tioufnefs

SERMON VIII.

tioufnefs and errour, and fhow the foundnefs of our principles by the integrity of our conduct.

Thofe who thus follow the example of the great and good, who have gone before them, will, as they advance in virtue, advance likewife in wifdom. They will improve in the comprehenfivenefs of their views and the clearnefs of their underftandings. They will feel a growing conviction that an adherence to Chriftianity is juft and rational, efpecially when they remark that far from yielding to other religious inftitutions, its value is never more apparent than when it is weighed in the balance againft them.

Let therefore the learned and the inquifitive explore all the treafures of human wifdom, and all the repofitories of religious inftruction; let them revolve the philofophical productions of Greece and Rome, the koran of Mahomet, the laws of Confucius and the inftitutes of Brama, and after a careful inveftigation of their excellence, let them confefs with juftice and with gratitude, that they fall as low in comparifon with the gofpel of Chrift, as the character and the nature of their authors were inferiour to the Saviour of the world. For where, we may confidently afk, in the wideft extent of their researches, will they find the founder of a religion foretold by a long and splendid train of prophecies, and recommended to universal reception by such an astonishing display of miracles? Where will they find a religion so rapidly and so widely spreading itself in a short period after its first promulgation, and subduing all opposition by the irresistible loveliness of truth? Where, in short, if not in the gospel, will they find a plan so perfectly and wonderfully adapted to enlighten ignorance, to correct the errours of reason, to purify the affections, to excite the most ardent aspirations of hope, to exalt the happiness of man to the highest pitch of rational gratification, and to diffuse the glory of God through the whole extent of the universe.

As we thus enjoy the advantages of a religious institution so far superiour to all others, what manner of men ought we to be in all holiness and godly conversation? Let the important truths which shine with such unrivalled lustre, and of which we have such satisfactory evidence, influence our general conduct. Let our adherence to them supersede every earthly consideration, and let the love of God triumph over every attachment to the occupations and the pleasures of the world.

Let

SERMON VIII.

Let charity by indiſſoluble ties unite us to all mankind, and not only warm our hearts with the moſt benevolent ſentiments, but ſtimulate us to the performance of every generous action. Let the precepts of the goſpel ſo ſhine in our conduct, that the infidel and the gainſayer may be led to confeſs the divine origin of our religion by its viſible effect on the actions of its profeſſors.

Finally—Let us exalt our minds to thoſe ſublime proſpects which are open to the eye of faith, and which are eminently capable of encouraging the exerciſe of our virtues, and of ſecuring our final perſeverance. Let us always be mindful that while we fill up the meaſure of our reſpective duties, and encreaſe our reliſh for the pure gratifications of religion, we become gradually leſs unworthy to be admitted into the glorious ſociety of heaven; and that in proportion as we adhere to the faith which was once delivered unto the ſaints, and produce its genuine fruits; in proportion as we imitate that ſacred band of primitive Chriſtians who ſtood forth as the guardians of their religion againſt all oppoſition; in proportion as we concur with them in copying the bright example of our common Lord and Maſter, we encreaſe our holy hope of divine favour and

our

our pious confidence in the divine mercy; we diminish our apprehensions of the awful day of retribution, and are better prepared to unite with the blessed assembly of just men made perfect, in ascribing glory and honour, and power to Him that sitteth upon the throne for ever and ever.

THE END.

NOTES

AND

AUTHORITIES.

IT has been obferved, and the obfervation was made without the leaft intention of detracting from the merit of thofe refpectable Writers who have preceded me, that the line which I marked out for myfelf in thefe Lectures, was peculiarly conformable to the directions of Mr. Bampton. Some of the principal fubjects mentioned in his Will, however apparently different from each other, are combined in one Plan.

Page 8. l. 22. *Sharing the imperfections of other Writers, they fairly claim the fame indulgence*] Reverentia, quam Patribus debemus, hoc unum a nobis poftulat, ut iis hallucinantibus ignofcamus, utque bonâ fide et imprudentiâ eos erâffe et loquutos effe putemus. Clerici Eccl. Hift. p. 601.

Nam et labuntur aliquando et oneri cedunt, et indulgent ingeniorum fuorum voluptati, nec femper intendunt animum, et nonnunquam fatigantur: cum Ciceroni dormitare interim Demofthenes, Horatio etiam Homerus videatur. Quintilianus, lib. 10. c. 1.

P. 11. l. 24. *The general principles and particular fentiments of Chryfoftom and Bafil*] Waterland's Importance of the Doctrine of the Trinity, p. 428. Grotius de Jure Belli et Pacis in Prefatione.

P. 12. l. 6. *They abound in ftrong and folid proofs of the fundamental principles of Chriftianity*] Daillé on the right ufe of the Fathers. Eng. Tranflation, B. ii. p. 184. Waterland's Importance of the Trinity, p. 426.

P. 17. l. 6. *The frugality of the venerable Bafil, the noble moderation of Gregory of Nazianzum, the benevolent condefcenfion of the Emprefs Pulcheria, and the mildnefs of the amiable and learned Pamphilus*] Theodoreti Hift. Eccl. lib. 5. c. 3. Cave's Primitive Chriftianity, p. 3. c. 3. Lardner has collected the detached paffages of Eufebius and of Jerom, which relate to Pamphilus. He has concluded his lift, with a character of that incomparable Chriftian, drawn with his ufual fimplicity of language, and accuracy of obfervation. Credibility, Vol. 7. p. 304, 335.

Lardner's Account may be farther illuftrated by the elegant Quotation from Simeon Motaphraftes in the Notes of Valefius. Annotationes in Eufeb. p. 180.

P. 20. l. 23. *In the foremoft rank of Chriftians ftand the Apoftles*] Potteri Prælectiones, Vol. 2. p. 234.

234. Beveregii Codex Canonum vind. in Prooemio. Grotius de Jure B. et P. in proleg.

P. 22. l. 8. *The works of those whose names have been recited*] Many of these Works are so voluminous, that the attention of the Ecclesiastical Student must of course be confined to particular parts of them. The following selection would, perhaps, give no very inadequate idea of the general merits of their authors. The apology of Tertullian, the Dialogue of Minucius Felix, the Commentaries of Origen, and his books against Celsus, the Epistles of Cyprian, the Institutions of Lactantius, the Ecclesiastical History and Evangelical Preparation of Eusebius, the Homilies of Basil, the Orations of Gregory of Nazianzum, the Commentaries and Epistles of Jerom, the City of God by Austin, the Duty of the Priesthood by Chrysostom, the Commentaries and Homilies of Theodoret, and the Ecclesiastical Histories of Socrates and Sozomen.

P. 23. l. 18. *Ignatius, Polycarp and Justin sealed the truth with their blood*] Eusebii Ecc. Hist. lib. 3. c. 36. lib. 4. c. 15, 16. Ruinarti Acta Sancti Ignatii, p. 9. Epistola Ecclesiæ Smyrnensis, p. 28. Acta Sancti Justini, p. 43. Clerici Eccl. Hist. p. 693, 726.

P. 36. l. 21. *The degrading description which the Historian has given of the Jewish Nation*] Jews Letters to Voltaire, p. 5. &c. Dictionnaire Philosophique, Articles Christianisme, Histoire des Rois Juifs, et Moise, &c. &c.

P. 34. l. 5. *That miraculous powers were exercised after the death of the Apostles upon certain occasions, is a fact supported by the unanimous and succeffive testimony of the Fathers, down to the reign of the Emperor Julian]* The following are the moſt important teſtimonies which have occurred in the courſe of my inveſtigation of this curious and intereſting ſubject.—Clementis Romani Epiſt. ad Corinth. cap. 2 et 48. Ignatii Epiſt. ad Smyrn. in Salutatione. Epiſt. ad Philadelph. Epiſt. ad Trallian. S. 5. Juſtini Mart. Dialogus, p. 247, 302. Irenæi, lib. 2. c. 56, 57. Tertulliani Apol. c. 23. Ejuſdem ad Scapulam, c. 2, 4. Euſebii Eccl. Hiſt. lib. 3. c. 37. 39. lib. 5. cap. 3, 7. Ejuſdem Demonſtratio Evan. lib. 3. Origenes contra Celſum, lib. 1, 2, 3 et 7. Chryſoſtomi Opera, tom. 3. p. 65. Edit. Benedict. Arnobius contra Gentes, lib. 1. Fabricii lux Evangelii, p. 169, 199. Waterland's Importance of the Trinity, p. 382, 383. Clerici Hiſt. Eccl. p. 533.

I feel inclined to adopt the ſentiments of Tillemont upon this ſubject. Nous aimerions mieux, tant qu'on n'aura point de preuve claire et convaincante de la fauſſeté de cette opinion, nous tromper avec les ecrevains qui precedent, que d'être obligé d'accuſer d'une credulité indiſcrete un grande nombre des plus illuſtres Maitres de l'Egliſe. Tillemont. Hiſt. Eccleſ. tom. 1. p. 178.

P. 38. l. 19. *It is objected that the Apoſtolical Fathers are ſilent relative to the continuance of miraculous powers]* Middleton's Inquiry, vol. 1. p. 121. Jortin's Remarks on Eccl. Hiſt. vol. 2. p. 43, 46, 49, &c. Clementis Epiſtola, Sect. 2.

P. 41. l. 7. *Juſtin Martyr, Irenæus, and Athenagoras are ſaid to have been unanimous in embracing frivolous*

frivolous doctrines, &c.] Middleton's Inquiry, vol. 1. p. 189, 190.

P. 44. l. 6. *How are we to account for the infenfibility of Chriſtians to the ceſſation of miracles?*] Gibbon, vol. 1. p. 477. Chryſoſtomi Op. tom. 3. p. 65.

Σημεια δε τε άγιε πνευματος και' αρχας μεν της Ιησε διδασκαλιας, μεία δε την αναληψιν αυΐε πλειονα εδεικνυτο, υςερον δε ελατ]ονα· πλην δε νυν ετι ιχνη αυτε παρ' ολιγες. Origen. contra Celſum, lib. 7.

Poſſum quidem dicere neceſſaria prius fuiſſe miracula, quam crederet mundus, ad hoc, ut crederet mundus. Quiſquis adhuc prodigia, ut credat, inquirit, magnum eſt ipſe prodigium, qui, mundo, credente, non credit. Auguſt. de Civit. Dei, l. 22. c. 8.

P. 46. l. 14. *The Emperor Julian determined to rebuild the Temple at Jeruſalem*] Warburton's Julian. Gibbon, vol. 2, p. 388.

P. 51. l. 15. *The elegant Author of the Inquiry into the miraculous Powers, at the concluſion of his controverſy*] Compare vol. 1. Introductory Diſcourſe, with vol. 2. p. 251. Moſheim, Sæculum 2^{dum}. p. 221, 222, &c.

P. 55. l. 28. *The diligence of Euſebius has reſcued their names and ſome fragments of their works from oblivion*] Eccl. Hiſt. lib. 4. c. 3, 26.

P. 56. l. 22. *The Apologiſts expoſe with ſuperfluous wit and eloquence the extravagance of Polytheiſm.*] Gibbon, vol. 1. p. 517. For proofs of the attachment which even the Philoſophers ſhowed to the eſtabliſhed Religion of their country, ſee Hume's Eſſays, vol. 2. p. 464. Philoſophi quamvis philoſophando

sophando Deos negarent, attamen in cultu externo religionis, non secus ac Plebecula, se gerebant; nec ullos novos Deos quos aliter colerent, inducebant. Clerici Hist. Eccl. p. 547.

P. 58. l. 14. *The Apologists insist much more strongly on the predictions which announced, than on the miracles which accompanied the appearance of the Messiah.*] Gibbon, vol. 1. p. 517. Justini Martyris Apol. 1ma. p. 55, 61, 71. Eusebii Ecc. Hist. lib. 4. c. 3. Justini Martyris Apol. 1. p. 48. Irenæus, lib. 2. c. 57. Lactantius, lib. 5. c. 3. Watson's Apology, p. 242.

P. 61. l. 19. *The eagerness of the Romans to explore the events of futurity, may be collected from the invectives of their Satyrists, the censures of their Philosophers, and the narratives of their Historians.*] Juvenalis, Sat. 3. ver. 42. Sat. 6. ver. 550. Cicero de Naturâ Deorum, lib. 3. Idem, De divinatione lib. 1. et 2. Taciti Annales, lib. 4 et 6. Aulus Gellius, lib. 14. c. 1.

Nullo tempore vaticiniorum insanius fuit studium quam sub extrema Reipublicæ Romanæ tempora, primosque Imperatores: cum bellorum civilium calamitates hominum animos terroribus omnis generis agitatos ad varia portentorum, prodigiorum & vaticiniorum ludibria convertissent.

Heyne in Virgil: Tom. 1. p. 66.

P. 62. l. 5. *The most celebrated of their Poets anticipated the happiness ordained to succeed the approaching Birth of the Son of Jupiter*] I am fully aware that it is a point undetermined by the Criticks, to what person the fourth Eclogue may most properly be applied.

By

AUTHORITIES.

By some we are assured that Drusus was intended; others say Saloninus, or his Brother Asinius Gallus, the Sons of Pollio. As the question is left undecided, I thought it best to adopt the language of Virgil himself, and call the predicted Infant the Son of Jupiter. The Emperor Constantine hesitated not to apply this Eclogue immediately to the Messiah, and paraphrased it in a loose Greek version, as if he considered it of almost equal authority with the prophesies of the Old Testament. Constant. Orat. ad Sanctos, C. 19 & 20. Valesii Annotationes in eadem. We are the less surprized at his looking upon Virgil as a Prophet, when we recollect that Chronology is not unfavourable to the supposition of his having been so; for the Poem in question was written near forty years before the Birth of Christ. Considering the eagerness of Constantine to press classical poetry into the service of Christianity, we cannot wonder that he saw, or fancied he saw the Virgin Mary, the fall of the Serpent, the Birth of Christ, and the effects of his advent very clearly represented in such expressive and beautiful lines as these—

Jam redit & *Virgo*, redeunt Saturnia regna,
Te duce, si qua manent sceleris vestigia nostri,
Jurita perpetuâ solvent formidine terras.
Ille deûm vitam adcipiet, divisque videbit
Permixtos heroas, & ipse videbitur illis.
Pacatumque reget patriis vertutibus orbem.
Occidet & *Serpens*, & fallax herba veneni
Occidet; *Assyrium* vulgò nascetur amomum.
Eclog. 4. l. 6, &c.

The lofty ftile in which Virgil fpeaks of the Infant about to be born, the elevated rank in which he is placed, and the fplendid train of Metaphor with which he is introduced, are furely unlike that fpecies of Imagery and Sentiment which occur in his other Poems. To judge properly of this, compare the account of the Birth of this Child, with the Birth of Marcellus, to whom the Poet was certainly defirous of paying every compliment that could exalt his character, and foothe the grief of his parents for his untimely death. His encomium reaches no farther than to celebrate him as a youth who fhould fill his family with the moft fanguine expectations of his Valour and Renown. Thefe qualities are reprefented by fuch fpecifick and appropriate Imagery as give a diftinct Portrait of a Roman Hero trampling on his proftrate Foes. Æneid, lib. 6. V. 878. But the Perfonage who is the fubject of the Eclogue is of far more elevated rank, and even foars above the nobleft of the mortal Race. He is the offspring of the Supreme God, and the effect of his coming into the world is not limited to a fingle country or people. His influence is not felt by fpreading the ravages of war, but by conferring on mankind the bleffings of peace. He was deftined to reform a degenerate world, and to govern it with the virtues of his Father, whilft the wonderful changes made in the face of Nature were to atteft the return of the golden Age. Such a train of defcription as this is unufually lofty and dignified, and the Poet was raifed above the general tenour of his correct and elegant fentiments. Perhaps the comparifon I have attempted to make between

AUTHORITIES.

between the character of the Son of Jupiter and the Son of Augustus may strengthen the arguments of those who maintain that Virgil was conversant with the Writings of the Old Testament. Or supposing only that he drew his ideas from the predictions of the Sibylls, there might be many oriental descriptions and images contained in them which were derived from that source.

P. 65. l. 3. *We are informed by the most authentick evidence of Ecclesiastical History*] Euseb. Ecc. Hist. lib. 3. c. 37. Mosheim de Rebus ante Constant. Sæc. 2. p. 224.

See the curious Catalogue of 142 authors, Greek, Latin, French, English and German, who have commented upon the Travels of the Apostles. Fabricii Lux Evangelii, p. 73.

P. 67. l. 6. *In the primitive Missionary we may contemplate the greatest firmness of resolution*] The admirer of Horace will recollect the similar situation of Regulus—

    Fertur pudicæ conjugis osculum
    Parvosque natos———
    Ab se removisse, et virilem
    Torvus humi posuisse vultum,
    Interque mœrentes amicos
    Egregius properaret exul.
    Atqui sciebat quæ sibi barbarus
    Tortor pararet.——— Hor. Od. 5. l. 3.

P. 69. l. 7. *There is no subject which seems to have inspired the early Fathers with such exultation, or which they describe with more lively powers of eloquence, than the general diffusion of the Gospel*] Irenæus, lib. L. c. 10.

c. 10. Tertullianus adversus Judæos, c. 7. Idem in Apologetico, c. 37. Origenes contra Celsum, lib. 1. p. 6, 7, 23. Idem, περι αρχων, lib. 4. c. 1. Chrysostomi Homilia in Rom. 15, 18. Eusebii Præparatio Evang. c. 3. p. 8. Ουρανιω δυναμει και συνεργεια αθροως οια τις ηλια βολη την συμπασαν οικαμενην ο σωτηριος καἶνυγαζι λογος. Euscb. Ecc. Hist. lib. 2. c. 3.

P. 70. l. 1. *The Historian labours with much solicitude to confine primitive Christianity within the narrowest limits*] Chap. 15. passim. Compare p. 509 with 512. vol. 1.

P. 77. l. 20. *The first persecution raged in the sanguinary reign of Nero*] Mr. Gibbon imagines that this persecution might arise, from the Christians being confounded with the lawless Banditti of Judas the Gaulonite. It is curious to observe that this conjecture, if it be only a conjecture, may be found in Dodwell, Dissert. Cyprian. xii. 2.

P. 77. l. 26.] *For the imputed Conflagration of Rome, of which he was himself the insidious and unfeeling Author*] In the Translation of the remarkable Passage of Tacitus, in which this fact is recorded, Mr. Gibbon is certainly right, and the Correspondent of Bishop Watson is as certainly wrong. Gibbon, C. 16. P. 533, 534. Watson's Apology, p. 288, &c. The Passage alluded to is this. Igitur primò correpti qui fatebantur ; deinde indicio eorum multitudo ingens, haud perinde in crimine incendii, *quam odio humani generis* convicti sunt. That the words printed in Italicks ought to be translated *for their hatred to human kind*, and not that the Christians *were hated by all mankind*, is very evident. They were confounded

AUTHORITIES. xi

with the Jews, who, as Tacitus says in another place, exercised *adversus omnes alios hostile odium.* It is remarkable that this is the exact character which St. Paul gives them. Ιȣδαιων πασιν ανθρωποις εναν]ιων. 1 Theffal. c. 2. v. 15. I am happy to confirm my opinion by the Remarks of Le Clerc upon the passage in question. Quibus verbis Christianos Tacitus absolvit incendii, sed damnat odii in reliquum humanum genus concepti, quod eos non satis secerneret a Judæis. Hist. Eccles. p. 427.

P. 78. l. 8. *The boasted harmony of the antient world respecting religious worship must be understood to have existed only under certain restrictions*] Gibbon, vol. 1. c. 2. Davis's Vindication, p. 96. Phileleuth. Lipsiensis, p. 159. Athenagoræ Apol. p. 1. Tertulliani Apol. p. 5. Euseb. Ecc. Hist. lib. 2. c. 2. Justini Mart. Apol. p. 36. Mosheim de rebus ante Constant. p. 6.

P. 80. l. 22. *In the celebration of the Bacchanalian Rites*] S. Consult. Marcianum. Taylor's Roman Law, p. 547.

P. 82. l. 7. *The calumnies which were industriously reported probably took their rise from the superficial remarks of those who had been present at the celebration of the Sacraments*] Justin. Martyr. Apol. 2. p. 128. The Servants of the Martyrs of Lyons, desirous of saving their lives at the expence of truth, confessed, when put to the torture, that their masters feasted upon human flesh. Euseb. Eccl. Hist. lib. 5. c. 1.

P. 85. l. 21. *The interval of Persecution, far from becoming a state of tranquillity, was a season of awful expectation and anxious fear*] The situation of the

U 2 Christians

Chriftians at fuch a time, naturally reminds us of the defcription of Galba, when Otho was advancing againft him. Agebatur huc illuc Galba, vario turbæ fluctuantis impulfu, completis undique bafilicis et templis, lugubri profpectu. Neque populi aut plebis ulla vox: fed attoniti vultus, et converfæ ad omnia aures. Non tumultus non quies, fed quale magni metûs, et magnæ iræ filentium eft. Taciti Hift. lib. 1. Sect. 40.

P. 85. l. 26. *The Church was kept in a continual ftate of alarm.*] Huc adverti debet, de publicis, gravioribus, et notioribus perfecutionibus loqui qui decies Chriftianos vexatos effe dicunt. In provinciis enim paffim, perpetuo fere vim Chriftianis a Præfidibus et Plebe al... n effe, certiffimis conftat teftimoniis. Mofheim. Inftitut. c. 5. p. 61.

P. 89. l. 18. *In the Epiftles of Ignatius are found mere ardent effufions of zeal, which to the Hiftorian of the Roman Empire appear unnatural and cenfurable.*] Ignatii Epiftola ad Romanos, Sect. 5. We may apply to Mr. Gibbon, on this occafion, fome of the judicious arguments of Le Clerc, which he employs to vindicate the Martyrs from the afperfions of Marcus Aurelius. Si qui, quod interdum factum negare nolim, crudelitate fuppliciorum, propinquitate mortis, fpeque proximæ beatitatis, extra fe rapti quædam proferebant quæ fupra vulgi Ethnici captum erant, an tribuenda hæc funt παραλαξει, obftinationi, vel perturbationi? Imò eo aut vitio aut adfectu vel maxime laborabant, qui innocentes excarnificatos occidebant, quod facere nollent, quæ illicita, et a Deo

Deo improbari pro certo ſtatuebant. Clerici Hiſt. Ecc. p. 694.

P. 92. l. 13. *Amidſt the multitude of ſimilar inſtances, with which later monuments of eccleſiaſtical antiquity abound*] Cotelerii Notæ in Ignatii Epiſt. ad Romanos, p. 26. Pearſoni Vindiciæ Ignat. lib. 2. c. 9.

P. 93. l. 9. *As no traces are to be found of ſuch expectations in the works of the earlieſt Fathers*] Tertulliani Apol. ad finem. Euſeb. Eccl. Hiſt. lib. 6. c. 42. Wake's Apoſtolical Fathers, p. 126. Middleton's Works, vol. 1. p. 333, 334.

P. 96. l. 15. *The conduct of Blandina, among the Martyrs of Lyons and Vienne, was as conſpicuous and as exemplary as that of the venerable Pothinus*] Jortin's Remarks, vol. 2. p. 135.

Every reader of ſenſibility will be inclined to apply the obſervation of Scaliger on the Acts of the Martyrs in general, to the Epiſtle of the Churches of Lyons and Vienne in particular. Eorum lectione piorum animus ita afficitur, ut nunquam ſatur inde recedat: quod quidem ita eſſe, unuſquiſque pro captu ſuo et conſcientiæ modo ſentire poſſit. Certe ego nihil unquam in Hiſtoriâ Eccleſiaſticâ vidi, a cujus lectione commotior recedam, ut non amplius meus eſſe videar. Animad. in Euſebium.

P. 101. l. 1. *The Church reſembled the fruitful vine.*]
Ὁποῖον, εαν αμπελε τις εκτιμη τα καρποφορησανḷα μερη, εις το αναϐλαςησαι ετερες κλαδες και ευθαλεῖς και καρποφορες αναδιδωσι· τον αυτον τροπον και εφ' ἡμῶν γινεται. Juſtin. Martyr. Dial. p. 372.

Nec quicquam proficit exquiſitior quæque crudelitas veſtra, illecebra eſt magis Sectæ. Plures efficimur

mur quoties metimur a vobis. Semen eſt ſanguis Chriſtianorum. Tertullianus in Apol.

P. 101. l. 6. *From the patience of the ſuffering Chriſtians, the more contemplative and rational Pagans inferred the innocence of their lives, and the purity of their characters.*] Και γαρ αυτος εγω τοις Πλατωνος χαιρων διδαγμασι διαβαλλομενες ακεων Χριςιανες, ορων δε αφοβες προς θανατον, και παντα τα νομιζομενα φοβερα, ενενοεν αδυνατον ειναι εκ κακιᾳ και φιληδονιᾳ ὑπαρχειν αυτες. Juſtin. Martyr. Apol. p. 51.

Lactantius declaims with great ſpirit and elegance upon this ſubject. De Juſtitia, lib. 5. c. 13.

P. 113. l. 24. *The Hiſtorian of the Decline and Fall has made an omiſſion with reſpect to the Gnoſticks.*] Gibbon, vol. 1. p. 459. Epiphanius, vol. 1. p. 88, &c. Irenæus, lib. 1. c. 23, 24. Euſeb. Ecc. Hiſt. lib. 3. c. 28, 29. Moſheim, vol. 1. p. 65.

P. 116. l. 1. *The derivation of the Ebionites is involved in ſome obſcurity.*] Euſeb. lib. 3. c. 27. Epiphanius Hær. 30. Hieronymus in Epiſt. ad Auguſtinum. Whilſt ſo many writers, both antient and modern, are advocates for the exiſtence of Ebion, I cannot cooperate with Mr. Gibbon, and Dr. Prieſtley, in his annihilation. Compare the authorities cited by Waterland, in his Importance of the Trinity, p. 276, with Early Opinions, p. 177. vol. 3. and Gibbon, Note 22. c. 15. vol. 1. Theodoretus apud Pearſoni Vindicias, p. 2. c. 2. Grabii Notæ in Irenæum, lib. 1. c. 26. Fabricii Lux Evangelii, p. 49, Tertullianus de Præſcrip. adverſus Hæreſ. c. 33.

P. 116. l. 10. *The two Sects of Nazarenes and Ebionites have been very improperly confounded*] Early Opinions,

AUTHORITIES.

Opinions, vol. 3. c. 8, &c. Horſley's Letters, p. 130, 378. Horſley's Charge, p. 33, 34. Howes's Obſervations, No. 9. Moſhemii Inſtitutione, c. 5. p. 130, 131. Moſheim de Rebus ante Conſtantinum, 172, S. 58. The conjunction, or rather the confuſion, of the Nazarenes and the Ebionites, is the corner-ſtone of Unitarianiſm. It was firſt laid by Epiſcopius, and overturned by Biſhop Bull. The reader is referred to his Judicium Eccleſiæ Catholicæ, c. 2. for complete ſatisfaction upon this ſubject. The arguments and authorities brought againſt Epiſcopius will apply moſt exactly to Dr. Prieſtley. If Biſhop Bull, the great Champion of the Nicene Faith, was now living, he would exclaim in the words of Æneas,

>Suggere tela mihi (non ullum dextera fruſtrà
>Torſerit in Rutulos ſteterunt quæ in corpore Graiûm
>Iliacis campis.—— ÆN. lib. 10. 333.

P. 117. l. 11. *From a ſpurious Hiſtory of Chriſt, the Ebionites drew their opinions*] This ſeems to have been a characteriſtick diſtinction between them and the Nazarenes. Moſheim de Rebus ante Conſt. Sæc. 2. p. 328, 329, 330, 331. Epiphanius Hær. 30. Irenæus, lib. 3. c. 2.

P. 118. l. 18. *Jeſus Chriſt, our inſeparable Life, is ſent by the Will of the Father*] For a variety of paſſages to the ſame purpoſe, ſee Ignatii Epiſt. ad Epheſ. c. 6, 18. ad Magneſ. Sect. 6, 9, 10, 11. ad Philadelph. Sect. 6, 8, 9. ad Smyrn. Sect. 1. Pearſoni Vindic. Ignat. p. 2. c. 5.

P. 119. l. 23. *The cenſures of Juſtin Martyr are directed againſt the ſame Hereticks*] Dr. Prieſtley himſelf

acknow-

acknowledges that "Juftin Martyr makes no men-
"tion of Ebionites, but fpeaks of the Jewifh Chrif-
"tians, which has been proved to be a fynonimous
"expreffion."   Early Opinions, V. 3. c. 10.

My reprefentation is chiefly drawn from the remarkable paffage, Dialogus cum Tryphone, p. 234,
which has been fo much the fubject of difpute. Although ἀπο τοῦ ἡμετέρȣ γενȣς ufurps a place in the
Text, yet there can be no doubt but that the legitimate reading is ὑμετέρȣ. This is the opinion of Waterland, Thirlby, Bull, and Horfley; and this muft
be the opinion of every candid and impartial critick.
The interpretation of the paffage by Dr. Prieftley is
fo extremely ftrained, that it preferves fcarcely a
fhadow of fenfe. In addition to the paffages cited
by Thirlby to fupport the various reading, may be
mentioned ἐν τῷ γενει ὑμων, p. 241. ἀπο τȣ γενȣς τȣ
ὑμετέρȣ, p. 274. The expreffion, p. 231. of ὑμετέρȣ
γενȣς is applied to the fame perfons, and fully efta-
blifhes the various reading. See Bulli Defenfio, c. 7.
fect. 7. If the prefent reading be allowed to ftand,
I fuppofe the ἡμετερȣ to have been ufed merely to
point out the common extraction of Trypho and of
Juftin Martyr. Trypho was a Jew, and Juftin was
a Samaritan. I fubmit this conjecture to the learned
reader, with the utmoft deference to his judgment,
and the utmoft diffidence of my own. The kind and
tolerant manner in which Juftin Martyr mentions
the Ebionites is moft ably and fatisfactorily accounted
for by Thirlby, Juftin Mart. p. 234. ad Notas.

P. 120. l. 13. *Irenæus, in his elaborate work in which
he confutes the various Sectaries of the fecond century*]
Lib.

Lib. 5. c. 1. The Ebionites are particularly cenfured in not lefs than ten different paffages, fo that Dr. Prieftley cannot prefume much on the flight mention made of them by Irenæus. He confutes their leading tenet when writing againft Carpocrates and Cerinthus. Lib. 1. c. 25, 26. lib. 3. c. 21. ad Notas. Dr. Prieftley feems to miftake the temper of Irenæus, and the genius of his age. It was not the practice of the mild and candid Bifhop of Lyons to ftigmatize Hereticks with opprobrious epithets. So far otherwife, that he fpeaks in the moft liberal manner of them all, and profeffes a truly chriftian regard for them, lib. 3. ad finem.

P. 128. l. 14. *Ariftodemus declared to the celebrated Sage of Athens*] Xenophon. Memorabilia, lib. 1. c. 4, 15. Platonis Apologia Socratis. Cicero Tufc. Quæft. vol. 7. Clerici Hift. Ecc. c. 7. fect. 11, 12, 13.

P. 131. l. 20. *In the firft rank of primitive virtues ftood humility*] Clementis Epift. fect. 2. Eufeb. Ecc. Hift. lib. 5. c. 24. Tertullian ad Uxorem, lib. 2. c. 4. Ignatii Epift. ad Ephef. fect. 12. Ejufdem ad Trallian. fect. 3. Ejufdem ad Roman. fect. 3, 4. Barnabæ Epift. fect. 1, 4, 9, 17, 21. Clerici Hift. Ecclef. p. 467.

P. 134. l. 3. *The primitive Chriftians were equally remarkable for the exercife of charity in its moft enlarged and proper fenfe*] Irenæus, lib. 3. c. 46. Juftini Dialogus cum Tryphone, p. 236, 254, & 323. Edit. Parif. Cave's Primitive Chriftianity, p. 328, &c. &c.

P. 134. l. 22. *The faireft fruit of this comprehenfive virtue was beneficence*] Clement. Epift. fect. 2. Juftini Martyris, Apol. 1. p. 98. Eufeb. Ecc. Hift. lib. 4.

c. 29. Juliani Epistola ad Arsacium, 49. Clerici Ecc. Hist. p. 630, 698.

P. 135. l. 23. *Many rescued their fellow Christians from captivity by voluntarily occupying their places.*] Επισαμεθα πολλως εν ημιν παρεδεδωκοτας εαυτως εις δεσμα, οπως ετερως λυτρωσονται. Πολλοι εαυτως παρεδωκαν εις δουλειαν, και λαβοντες τας τιμας αυτων, ετερως εψωμισαν. Clement. Epist. sect. 55. To this passage Cotelerius has subjoined a very curious note, in which he enumerates various instances of this romantick philanthropy.

P. 136. l. 22. *The sarcastick Satyrist of the Philosophers*] Watson's Tracts, vol. 5. p. 201, 229. Julian in Fragment. Orationis. Clerici Ecc. Hist. p. 518. ad Notas.

P. 137. l. 17. *Their firm attachment to the established Government*] Τινες γαρ δε δικαιοτεροι ων δεονται τυχειν, η οιτινες περι μεν της αρχης της υμετερας ευχομεθα, ινα παις μεν παρα πατρος κατα το δικαιοτατον διαδηχησθε την βασιλειαν, αυξιν δε και επιδοσιν και η αρχη υμων παντων επιχειριων γιγνομενων λαμβανη; τουτο δ' εςι και προς υμων, οπως ηρεμον και ησυχιον βιον διαγειμεν, (forsan melius διαγοιτε) αυτοι δε παντα τα κεκελευσμενα προθυμως υπηρετοιμεν. Athenagoræ Legatio ad finem. Justini Martyris Apol. Prima, p. 26. Fabricii Lux Evangelii, p. 194. c. 10. Theophilus ad Autolychum, lib. 1.

P. 138. l. 22. *In the christian character the opposite extremes of torpid apathy and boundless gratification were avoided.*] The morality of the Fathers, however strict, was certainly of a milder and more amiable cast than Mr. Gibbon represents it to have been. They condemned

demned without doubt the excesses of Pleasure and Luxury in the strongest terms. But whilst we agree that the representation of the Historian is so far just, we must take care that he does not lead us to mistake the ardour of their declamation for a recital of facts. He says that " our devout Predecessors, vainly aspi-
" ring to imitate the perfection of angels, disdained,
" or affected to disdain, every earthly and corporeal
" delight." C. 15. p. 321. Now, we are to take for granted that this account is drawn from Lactantius. But Lactantius does not affirm that he or any other Christian had ever reached such a height of mental mortification, as this fine period expresses them to have done. Lactantius does not aspire to the rank of an Historian, but only lays down the precepts of christian piety and morality in the more humble character of a Teacher. He does not state a fact, but delivers an admonition. This is plain from his own words. Venio nunc ad id quod est summum operis hujus & maximum, ut *doceam* quo ritu Deum coli oporteat. Lib. 6. c. 1.

P. 141. l. 15. *The triumph of Christianity was completed partly by the subversion of the most antient and most popular superstitions.*] Justini Apol. p. 61. Eusebii Præp. Evang. lib. 1. c. 4. Fabricii Lux Evangelii, p. 278.

P. 142. l. 16. *The parents who formerly exposed their infant offspring, awoke to the exquisite feelings of Nature*] Justini Apol. p. 44. Clerici Hist. Ecc. p. 57.

P. 142. l. 26. *The bloody combats of the gladiators, which had long been the favourite spectacles of the polite as well as the vulgar*] Eusebii Vita Constantini, lib.

lib. 4. c. 21, 25. Plutarchus in Cæfare. Ciceronis Tufc. Quæft. lib. 2.

P. 143. l. 7. *The horrid barbarity of human facrifices*] Livius, lib. 22, 53. Lactantius, lib. 1. c. 2. Clerici Hift. Ecc. p. 52.

P. 143. l. 14. *As foon as divine honours were paid to Chrift, the Heathen acknowledged the weaknefs of their gods*] Νυνι δε θαυμαζυσιν, ει τοσουτων ετων κατειληφε την Πολιν η νοσος, Ασκληπις μεν επιδεμιας και των αλλων θεων μηκετ' εσης, Ιησε γαρ τιμωμενε, εδεμιας τις θεων δημοσιας ωφελειας ησθετο. Porphyrius apud Eufebium. Præp. Evang. lib. 5. c. 1. An Oracle of Apollo Delphicus was given to the Emperour Julian, and is preferved by Cedrenus.

Ειπαίε τῳ βασιληϊ, χαμαι πεσε δαιδαλος αυλα;
Ουκέζι Φοιβος εχει καλυβαν, ε μανίιδα δαφνην
Ου παγαν λαλιεσαν, απεσβέζο καν λαλον ὑδωρ.

The elegant Jortin has happily applied his critical talents to the emendation of thefe curious lines. By their affiftance, he was enabled to illuftrate the beautiful paffage in the Epiftle of Ignatius to the Romans, Sect. 7. Jortin's Remarks, vol. 1. p. 356, 359.

P. 143, l. 19. *Whilft broken arches and proftrate columns fpread the floors of the deferted temples, the numerous edifices of Chriftian devotion were erected*] Λελυσθαι μεν και καθηρησθαι αυτοις ναοις και ξοανοις τα πεπαλαιωμενα της των εθνων απανλων πλανης ιδρυματα· ιερα δε ουτως σεμνα και ευσεβεας διδασκαλεια τω Παμβασιλει και Δημιεργῳ των ολων εν μεσαις πολεσι τε και κωμαις ανεγηγερθαι. Eufeb. Præp. Evang. l. 3. c. 4. Idem de Vitâ Conftantini, lib. 3.

AUTHORITIES. xxi

P. 144. l. 11. *The barriers of national enmity and inveterate prejudice were broken down,* &c. Juſtini Mart. Apol. 1. p. 20. Apol. 2. p. 61.

P. 145. l. 6. *The Parthian and Perſian Tribes inſtituted the decent rites of ſepulture*] Euſeb. Evang. p. 11. c. 4. Τι δ' εραμεν περι της των Χριςιανων αιρεσεως, ης ημεις οι δοξασαι πολλοι οντες και εν διαφοροις ανεςημεν κλιμασιν, εν παντι ηθνει και κλιματι, οιτινες πολλοι οντες ενι ονοματι κεκλημεθα. Και ουτε οι εν Παρθια Χριςιανοι πολυγαμϗσι, Παρθοι υπαρχοντες, ουδ' οι εν Μηδια κυσι παραβαλλϗσι τϗς νεκρϗς, ϗχ οι εν Περσιδι γαμϗσι τας θυγατερας αυτων, Περσαι οντες, &c. Bardeſanes Syrus apud Euſeb. Præp. Evang. lib. 6. c. 10. p. 279.

P. 145. l. 10. *The warlike inhabitants of Scythia, of Germany, of Spain, of Pannonia, of Britain, forſook their gloomy ſuperſtition*] Moſheim de Rebus ante Conſtant. Sæc. 2. c. 2, 3. Sæc. 3. c. 1, 2, 3.

P. 148. l. 3. *The Providence of the Almighty was not only active in cooperating with the votaries of Chriſtianity, but likewiſe in preparing the way for its reception*] Εξ αναγκης αναιρεχειν εκβιαζομαι επι την τϗ αιτιϗ ζητησιν, και συνομολγειν μη αλλως αυτϗς κεκρατηκεναι τϗ τολμηματος η θειοτερα και υπερ ανθρωπον δυναμει και συνεργια τϗ φησαντος αυτοις Μαθητευσατε παντα τα εθνη εν τῃ ονοματι μϗ. Euſeb. Demon. Evangel. lib. 3. p. 139.

P. 163. l. 24. *The firſt inſtance of the miſrepreſentations of the Hiſtorian of the Decline and Fall conſiſts in aſſigning a viſionary cauſe for the propagation of Chriſtianity*] See Gibbon, vol. 1. p. 472. and compare the firſt and ſecond Editions. Origenis Philocalia, c. 26. Photii Bibliotheca Cod. 232. Juſtini Mart. Dialog. 311. Irenæus, lib. 5. c. 31, 32, 33, 35.
Euſeb.

Eufeb. Ecc. Hift. lib. 3. c. 39. lib. 7. c. 24. Epiphan. Hæref. 77. Hieronymus in Ezech. c. 36. Mofheimii Sæc. 3. p. 270. Perhaps all the Hiftorian's information upon this fubject was borrowed from Middleton; evident traces of it may certainly be found in the Inquiry into the Miraculous Powers, vol. 1. p. 153.

P. 169. l. 21. *The second instance consists in an attempt to invalidate the truth of Prophecy*] Gibbon, vol. 1. p. 472. Epift. Peter 2. c. 3. v. 3. c. 4. v. 7. 12, 13, 14. Gibbon, v. 1. c. 15. Note 61. Compare 1 Theff. 4, 17, with 2 Theff. 2. 2. 2 Timothy 4. 6. Philip. 3. 11. 2 Corinth. 4. 14. Whitby's Paraphrafe, vol. 2. p. 385.

P. 173. l. 4. *The number, for which no authority is produced, is most probably that of Theophilus Bishop of Antioch.*] Theophilus ad Autolychum, l. 3. p. 135. Petavius de Doctrinâ Temporum, vol. 2. p. 267.

Even Clemens Alexandrinus, whofe computations include the greateft number of years, of all the Ante-Nicene Fathers, reckons not more than 5620 years from the Creation to the Birth of Chrift. He reckons about ten years lefs than the Septuagint of Riccioli.

P. 173. l. 21. *Lactantius expressly asserts that six thousand years from the Creation of the World were not completed in his time*] Sciant igitur Philofophi, qui ab exordio mundi feculorum millia enumerant, nondum fextum millefimum annum effe conclufum. Lactantius, lib. 7. c. 14.

P. 175. l. 1. *The third instance of misrepresentation consists in an unwarrantable charge of uncharitableness against the primitive Christians*] Gibbon, vol. 1. p. 473, 474.

AUTHORITIES. xxiii

474. Davis's Examination, p. 29. Cafauboni Exercitatio 1ma. in Baronii Annales. Juftini Apol. 1. p. 48, 69, 70. Tertullianus de Spectaculis, c. 30. Hermæ Paftoris, lib. 3. c. 14. Notæ Cotelerii in eundem locum. 1 Peter 3. 19. Prideaux's Prælectiones, p. 112. Clementis Alexand. Strom. 2. p. 379.
P. 178. l. 3. and P. 183. l. 18. *The fourth inflance of misreprefentation confifts in drawing wrong conclufions from facts; and the fifth confifts in felecting paffages manifeftly inconclufive, and fuppreffing others of the fame writers more decifive, and equally connected with the fubject*] Gibbon, vol. 1. p. 530, 540. Plinii Epift. 97. lib. 10. Ruinarti Acta fincera Martyrum, p. 11. Tertulliani Apol. c. 12. Eufeb. Ecc. Hift. lib. 3. c. 32. Eufeb. lib. 5. c. 1. Athenagoras in Legat. c. 1. Mofheim. Sæc. primum, c. 83. p. 106. Clerici Ecc. Hift. p. 702. Cave Hift. Ecc. p. 159.

To the Paffages of the Decline and Fall of the Roman Empire, which I have examined in my 5th Lecture, I muft here make an addition. Mr. G. infinuates, or feems to infinuate, that the Evidence of the Evangelifts is not fufficient to eftablifh the truth of Facts, unlefs it is fupported by the concurrent Teftimony of their pagan Contemporary Writers. His obfervations at the clofe of his fifteenth Chapter, are thefe.

" Under the Reign of Tiberius the *whole Earth*,
" or at leaft a *celebrated* Province of the Roman
" Empire, was involved in a preternatural darknefs
" of three hours. Even this miraculous event,
" which ought to have excited the wonder, the curi-
" ofity, and the devotion of mankind, *paffed without*
X " *notice*

" *notice* in an age of Science and History. It hap-
" pened during the life time of Seneca and the Elder
" Pliny, *who must have experienced the immediate*
" *effects, or received the earliest Intelligence of the Pro-*
" *digy.* Each of these Philosophers in a laborious
" work has recorded *all the great Phenomena of Na-*
" *ture, Earthquakes, Meteors, Comets and Eclipses,*
" *which his indefatigable industry could collect.* Both
" the one and the other have omitted to mention the
" greatest Phenomenon to which the mortal Eye
" has been witness, since the Creation of the Globe.
" *A distinct Chapter of Pliny is devoted to Eclipses of*
" *an extraordinary nature, and unusual duration,* but
" he contents himself with describing the singular
" defect of light, which followed the murder of
" Cæsar, when during the greatest part of the year,
" the Orb of the Sun appeared pale and without
" splendour, V. 1. P. 518.

Now, I shall preface my strictures upon this specious and sophistical passage by a remark, which however bold, may still be found to be just, that there is
scarcely a single sentence, or even a member of a sentence, which is accurately stated. Every part of it
either offends the judgment of the candid Reader
by weakness of remark, or insults his understanding
by deficiency of argument. In order to prove these
points more fully, I shall throw my detached objections into the form of Notes, and subjoin to them
some general reflections.

The whole Earth] This Clause is evidently designed
to raise our surprize at the silence of the Pagan
Writers to the greatest degree. But the original
language

language of the Gospels cannot consistently be so understood, as to allow such a latitude of interpretation. It is very clear that many of the supernatural events that happened at the time of the Crucifixion were confined to Jerusalem and its Environs. This has been particularly understood by the most learned Criticks and Expositors with respect to the darkness which then happened. Origen, Vossius, Beza, and many others, are decidedly of this opinion. Our Translators have taken the words of Matthew and Mark in the same limited sense by rendering την γην *the Land*. In St. Luke, indeed, I acknowledge that the word is translated the *Earth*, but in opposition to that expression, may be placed the five Versions cited in Wilson's Testament, in which την γην is rightly and uniformly rendered the land. The usage of the term in this sense is agreeable to the similar usage of other terms, which are nearly synonymous. Lardner has very satisfactorily proved that by πασαν την οικυ-μενην, Luke c. 2. v. 1. is intended only the *land of Judæa*. Lardner's Cred. V. 3. p. 574. But a stronger, and indeed a decisive argument in favour of the sense we contend for, is furnished by Luke c. 4. v. 25. where the same term, πασαν την γην, cannot possibly be otherwise understood. This is surely sufficient to decide the question with respect to the extent of the darkness, and to expose the artifice of the Historian in introducing this clause of the sentence.

A celebrated *Province of the Roman Empire*] The Epithet *celebrated* is surely misapplied upon this occasion, but the design for which it is introduced is sufficiently obvious. Tacitus, whom our Author so frequently follows in his praise and his censure, might have given him another idea, if it had suited his purpose to have adopted it. Tacitus, when he speaks of the Jews in his most handsome manner, calls them sometimes " despectissima pars servientium," and sometimes " teterrimam Gentem." Hist. lib. 5. c. 9. They are ridiculed by the Satyrists for their Poverty, Credulity and Superstition, nor does their Country seem to have stood very high in the estimation of their Conquerors. What Roman Poet has sung its Praises, or what Historian has ranked it among the Places renowned in antient Story? Sicily was famous for its fertility in corn, but if Judæa was ever mentioned in the detail of the Geographer, he could expatiate only upon its barrenness. Ουκ' επιφθονον ου το χωριον, ουδ' υπερ ου αν τις εσπεδασμενως μαχεσαιlο, ιsι γαρ πιlρωδες. Strabo, p. 1104. lib. 10. Edit. Casaub.

It passed without notice in an Age of Science and History.] In other words it was not recorded by any prophane Author. If Origen, Tertullian and Eusebius are to be credited, it was circumstantially mentioned by Phlegon, a Pagan Chronologist, who flourished in the Reign of the Emperor Hadrian. Origen Tract. 35. In Matthæum. Tertull. Apol. C. 21. Euseb. Chron. Anno MMXL. If Julius Africanus, a Writer of great eminence and probity, who flourished at the beginning of the third Century is to be believed, an Eclipse which corresponds with the time of the Passion, was recorded by Thallus. Lardner, V. 5. p. 167. We are fully aware that doubts have been started respecting these testimonies, but Mr. G.

Mr. G. has much exaggerated thefe doubts by roundly afferting, that the teftimony of Phlegon is given up. The learned are certainly at variance upon the fubject, but unlefs it can be proved that the citations in Eufebius and Julius Africanus never exifted in the original Works of Phlegon and Thallus, we are furely juftified in thinking them worthy of credit.

Seneca and Pliny muft have experienced the immediate effects] By no means, as the Eclipfe was confined to Judæa. Has the Hiftorian any authority for fuppofing that Seneca and Pliny were upon the Spot?

Or received the earlieft Intelligence] To eftablifh this affertion it is neceffary to fhow, that thefe Naturalifts had immediate Information from all parts of the Globe, as foon as any extraordinary Phenomenon had taken place. Mr. G. furely forgets the times of which he is writing, and expreffes himfelf as if the intercourfe between Rome and her diftant Provinces was as common and as eafy as it is at prefent between the different Counties of England and the Metropolis.

Each of thefe Philofophers, in a laborious work, has recorded all the great Phenomena of Nature, Earthquakes, Meteors, Comets and Eclipfes, which his indefatigable Induftry could collect.] That this is a magnificent fentence, and worked up in Mr. G's. beft manner, we pretend not to deny. All the extraordinary wonders of Heaven above, and Earth beneath, are called together to make it ftriking, and the indefatigable diligence of Pliny and Seneca is artfully introduced to heighten the general effect of furprize at the filence of the Pagan Writers relative to the point in question. The learned World would surely be much obliged to Mr. G. to announce where he has discovered such works of Pliny and Seneca as come up to his pompous description. *The natural Questions* of Seneca are referred to in the Notes on the Decline and Fall; but in the places cited we find no mention whatever of Eclipses. He speaks indeed of Earthquakes; but he treats that subject in a very cursory manner, and does not instance more than four or five, because his object was plainly not to write a History of them, but to investigate their symptoms, causes and prognosticks. The same remark applies exactly to Pliny with respect to Earthquakes. They are mentioned only to introduce philosophical observations and inquiries. The Historian therefore has but very feeble props to support his assertion. We may reasonably imagine that if Pliny and Seneca have recorded all the great Phenomena of Nature, they must of course have explored the Grecian and Roman Histories, which were immediately open to their inquiries. Now let us try an experiment as to what they have derived from those sources with regard to Eclipses. Do they mention the total Eclipse of the Sun, when the celebrated Plague happened at Athens in the first Year of the Peloponnesian War? Do they mention the solar Eclipse on the day when the Foundations of Rome were laid. Do they mention the Eclipse foretold by Thales, by which a Peace was effected between the Medes and the Lydians? It would be too tedious and useless to ask for many others which might be mentioned without

any

AUTHORITIES.

any fear of our queftions being anfwered in the Affirmative.

A diſtinct Chapter of Pliny is devoted to Eclipſes of an extraordinary Nature, and unuſual Duration, &c. &c.] This Sentence prefents us with a perfect Specimen of the Anticlimax: it begins with ftating a general fubject made up of numerous particulars, and then dwindles down to a folitary example.

—————— —————— Amphora cœpit,
Inſtitui, currente rotâ cur urceus exit?

One would naturally fuppofe from fo promifing an exordium, that Pliny had exhaufted the topick of Eclipfes by his full and elaborate detail. The whole Chapter however is literally no more than this, Circulus rubri coloris. L. Julio P. Rutilio Confulibus fiunt prodigiofi & longiores folis defectus, qualis occifo Dictatore Cæfare, & Antoniano bello, totius penè anni pallore continuo. Plin. Nat. Hift. lib. 1. C. 30. Ed. 1669.

But let us now clofe the fkirmifh of objections to particular expreffions, which might be eafily prolonged, and come to the conteft of clofe Argument. Suppofing we allow the faftidious Hiftorian the liberty of rejecting or admitting the evidence of Thallus and Phlegon as he pleafes, what will the credibility of the Evangelifts lofe by the conceffion? The Hiftorian cannot fuppofe that filence is conclufive againft exprefs and pofitive Teftimony. If fo, he will difannul the facts which he relates himfelf, and prove by negative authorities that thofe whofe actions he relates had no actual exiftence. He fays that the Chriftians are totally unnoticed by Seneca, Pliny the Elder

Elder and Plutarch, c. 15. N. 189. But he defcribes the Chriftians, at that very period, as compofing a very numerous body, and attracting the general notice of mankind, by their peculiar eftablifhments.

Again, the Hiftorian it feems was at a lofs for teftimony that was independant of ecclefiaftical Writers, and fuch as was wholly unbiaffed. We are to fuppofe then, that if fuch could have been found, he would have been fatisfied, and all his fcruples would have vanifhed. But we deceive ourfelves by fo flattering a hope, if we may judge by a fimilar cafe. For to that wonderful interference of Providence which took place when Julian attempted to rebuild the Temple of Jerufalem, there is fuch an independant teftimony given by Ammianus Marcellinus, and yet the Hiftorian difcovers ftrong fymptoms of doubt and difbelief as we have already remarked, Lect. 2. p. 47.

Many good and folid reafons may be affigned for the darknefs at the Crucifixion, being made no mention of by the prophane Writers. The moft obvious is, that they might have no fufficient information of it. The Provinces of the Roman Empire were very extenfive, and we find in general that the attention of Writers was chiefly confined to thofe which were neareft to the Metropolis. The antient Hiftorians and Biographers are remarkably concife, and feldom ftop to mention occurrences, which although they may have happened during the times of which they write, have no relation whatever to their main fubject. This was their general Rule, and there is no reafon for which it fhould be violated merely to indulge

dulge the caprice of the captious, or satisfy the scruples of the petulant. There is no more reason in the nature of the thing itself why the testimony of the prophane writers should be called for to support the sacred, than the sacred should be called for to support the prophane. We may then retort the Argument, and ask Mr. G. in our turn, how he can credit the accounts given by Paterculus, Pliny the Elder, V. Maximus and Seneca, when Matthew, Mark, Luke and John take not the least notice of them? Supposing that the Roman Writers had received information of the fact in question, would it have been consistent with their principles as Heathens to have mentioned it? They must plainly have foreseen what great advantage would have been given to Christianity by it. Their Readers would naturally have been led to inquire into the character of the extraordinary Person, at whose death the laws of nature were infringed, and this inquiry, as it opened a more complete view of the new dispensation, must have led to their conversion.

Hence we collect a very satisfactory reason for their silence. Supposing that they knew the fact, and from motives of policy suppressed it, their silence furnishes as strong a proof of its truth, as their express testimony could possibly have done.

Upon the whole, we may venture boldly to assert, that if even this Fact be destitute of support from the prophane writers, it is a deficiency which may easily be dispensed with. We believe many things upon the evidence of one credible witness. But in the case before us, we have no less than three, whose knowledge of the fact was never denied, whose veracity is indisputable, and integrity not to be impeached. So plainly are the characters of truth marked upon their writings, that every Person of common discernment must see them, and he who is not satisfied as to the certainty of what they relate, must give up all pretensions to a sound Judgment, and be abandoned to the incurable obstinacy of his own forlorn scepticism.

P. 184. l. 13. *— reckons only ten men and seven women*] Mr. G. with his usual indulgence to the frailties of the primitive Christians, says that one of these men was accused of robbery. Note 74. C. 16. Now Dionysius not only says in express terms, that this was a false accusation, but particularly relates, that even the officer who took the unfortunate sufferer into custody, was convinced of his perfect innocence by the clearest proofs. Εσυκοφανΐηθη μεν, ώς δε συνοικος λησων. απεδυσαμενος δε ταυΐην παρα τω εκαΐονΐαρχω την αλλοΐριωΐαΐην καΐ' αυΐα διαβολην κ:ε δεσμωΐης σπι τον ηγουμενον. Euseb. Ecc. Hist. lib. 6. c. 41.

P. 194. l. 6. *That the Apostolical Fathers held the simple Humanity of Christ*] Early Opinions, vol. 1. p. 92.

P. 194. *That Justin Martyr corrupted the primitive Faith by the adoption of the Logos of Plato*] Early Opinions, vol. 1. 92. vol. 2. p. 23, 42, 53, &c.

Cicero may not improperly be considered as a faithful Interpreter of Plato, and of course be appealed to as conveying his opinions with considerable accuracy. Yet it is very remarkable, that in his statement of the metaphysical tenets of his Master, there

there is nothing that refembles the doctrine of a Logos. There are many paffages in his Philofophical Works, particularly de Naturâ Deorum, lib. 1. p. 198, 200. where that topick would naturally have been mentioned, had fuch been the explicit dogma of Plato; but fo far is Cicero from introducing it, that he was at a lofs in what manner to make the Opinions of Plato confiftent with themfelves. Juftin Martyr and Cicero found this tafk equally arduous, and their labour in performing it equally unfuccefsful. Jam de Platonis inconftantiâ longum eft dicere, qui in Timæo, patrem hujus mundi nominari negat poffe, in Legum autem libris, quid fit omnino Deus, inquiri oportere non cenfet. P. 200. l. 10. Fol. Lutel. 1565.

Ει δε τις ακριβως τα καθ' αυτες σκοπειν εθελοι, ουδε ταις εαυῖων δοξαις εμμενειν προηρηνῖαι· ὁ γουν Πλαῖων ποῖε μεν τρεις αρχας τε παντος ειναι λεγει, ποῖε δε τεσσαρας. Juftin. Martyr. Cohort. p. 8, 19, 21. Fol. 1615.

P. 194. *That the Paftors of the Church maintained a corrupted Faith, whilft the illiterate Chriftian continued to maintain the fimple Humanity of Chrift*] Early Opinions, vol. 1. p. 244, 286. vol. 3. p. 7, 235, vol. 4. p. 311, &c.

P. 197, l. 16. *The Author of the Early Opinions firft appeals to the authority of thefe writings, then refufes to acquiefce in the plaineft fenfe of paffages, which prefs him with infuperable difficulties; and afterwards affirms that they are greatly corrupted, or intirely fpurious*] Early Opinions, vol. 1. p. 91. Prieftley's Letters to Horfley, p. 13. Horfley's Reply, p. 118. Prieftley's Doctrine

trine of the Atonement, Sect. 5. Horsley's Reply, p. 166, &c.

P. 199. l. 17. *The sceptre of the majesty of God*] Clementis Epist. Sect. 16. Early Opinions, vol. 1. p. 95, 96.

P. 202. l. 24. *The objection made to the Epistles, because Eusebius does not mention the name of Ignatius,* &c.] Early Opinions, vol. 1. p. 108. Euseb. Ecc. Hist. lib. 5. c. 28.

P. 204. l. 14. *The smaller Epistles of Ignatius are proved to be genuine by many eminent scholars of the last and present century*] These Epistles are some of the most curious and valuable remains of apostolical antiquity. It is no wonder that the Socinian is eager to overthrow their authority, when not only every page, but almost every sentence must convince him of his erroneous opinions. Dr. Priestley in his eagerness to depreciate the testimony of Lardner, and to pronounce his own infallible ipse dixit of condemnation, omits intirely the decisions of Cave, Brucker, Huetius, Petavius, Fabricius, Ittigius, Du Pin, Fleury, Tillemont, Cotelerius, Le Clerc, Grotius, Berriman, Waterland, and Bull. " Quid feli-
" cissimos eruditissimi Primatis Armachani conatus,
" quid conspirantem originalis Græci Codicis a
" doctissimo Vossio peropportunè procuratam editi-
" onem, quid Hammondi viri optimi consummatissi-
" mique lucubrationes commemmorem ?" But his silence with respect to Pearson is the most unaccountable and extraordinary. Must Dr. Priestley be reminded at this late period of the controversy, that the honour of a complete triumph over the opponents
of

of the authentick Epiftles of Ignatius, was referved for that great and illuftrious Prelate? He entered into a fyftematical difcuffion of the inconfiftent cavils and bold affertions of the learned and ingenious Dallæus, who had attempted to prove that the Epiftles were fpurious. It is rather the fpontaneous tribute of juftice, than the conftrained language of panegyrick to affert, that the " Vindiciæ Ignatianæ" is a work which may claim one of the firft places among critical difquifitions, either of antient or modern times. I except not the profound criticifms of Bentley, nor the ingenious Remarks of Warton on the Poems of Chatterton.

The author of the Vindiciæ difplays that happy verfatility of attention, which can eafily accommodate every literary acquifition to the prefent purpofe, and exerts that refiftlefs power of argument to which the artifices of fophiftry, however fubtle, and the attachments of prejudice, however rooted, muft neceffarily give way. We find not in any part of his Work either the faftidioufnefs of the pedant, or the pofitivenefs of the dogmatift; but found reafon without affectation, and folid learning without parade. It breathes that uniform fpirit of candour and moderation, which is peculiarly adapted to liberal controverfy. In a cool and difpaffionate manner, every fubject is difcuffed with that exact degree of attention which it deferves. Its author, on all occafions ingenuous and impartial, never lays on the falfe colours of mifreprefentation, never brings forward perfonalities, when he ought to bring proofs; and never attempts to bear down his opponents with rafh and empty

empty affertion. The encomium which he has fo judicioufly given to Eufebius, may with the utmoft propriety be applied to himfelf. Ego vero Eufebium tantâ diligentiâ tantoque judicio in examinandis Chriftianorum primævæ antiquitatis fcriptis, fuiffe contendo, ut nemo unquam de ejus fide aut de fcriptis, quæ ille pro indubitatis habuit, poftea dubitaverit. Vind. Ignat. Par. 1. c. 8.

Until Dr. Prieftley fhall confute the arguments contained in this work, vain will be his attempts to deftroy the credit of the Epiftles. When that glorious era of light and found criticifm fhall arrive, it will then, and not fooner, be neceffary for the admirers of the Epiftles to allege fome new arguments in their fupport.

If I were called upon to give an idea of the ftile of Ignatius, I could not perhaps convey a more proper one, than by adopting the remark of certain criticks upon the language of Cicero. " Homines " inceffere âudent, ut tumidiorem, et Afianum, et " redundantem, et in repetitionibus nimium, et in " compofitione fra&tum." Quint. lib. 12. c. 10. See Jortin's Remarks, vol. 1. p. 355.

The circumftances under which thefe Epiftles were written, are calculated to render them extremely interefting. An eminent Bifhop of the Primitive Church, venerable for his piety and extreme age, was conducted through the chief cities of the empire to fuffer for the faith in the publick amphitheatre at Rome. His courage was unbroken by the fatigues of his tedious journey, notwithftanding the cruelty of his guards, which he endeavoured by every folicitation

citation to soften. He employed the scanty intervals of repose which they allowed him, in writing Letters to various Societies of Christians, to whom he gave the last and most endearing pledges of his affection, and omitted no argument that could animate their hopes and inspire them with constancy equal to his own.

Socrates and Ignatius were both condemned by an unjust and cruel sentence, and were perhaps equally ardent in their attachments to their friends. But there was an immense disparity as well between the grounds of their own hopes, as the nature of those consolations, which they imparted for their loss. Socrates, whilst hovering over the dark abyss of eternity, was dubious how far to trust the faint glimmerings of reason. As his imperfect conjectures, relative to a future state, had no sufficient evidence for their support, he could impart no conviction as to its certainty to the minds of others. Ignatius, with all the authority of Revelation to assist him, recommended the faith, which raised him above his own sufferings, as the only anchor which could secure his friends against the storms of life. Here then was fully shown the triumph of Christianity over Natural Religion. Dim and gloomy were the views of the Heathen Philosopher, but clear was the prospect presented to the Christian of the Crown of Immortality and joy.

P. 207. l. 4. *Polycarp refers the Philippians to the Epistle not long before written to them by St. Paul*] Epist. Sect. 3, 11.

P. 211.

P. 211. l. 8. *Ariſtotle and Plato differed ſo much in explaining the nature of earthly things*, &c. &c.] Juſtin. Martyr. Cohort. ad Græcos, p. 2, 7, 8, 21, 22. Apol. 2. Dialog. p. 143, 152.

P. 215. l. 21. *After raiſing our expectations to ſuppoſe that Juſtin Martyr will be detected*, &c.] Early Opinions, vol. 1. p. 320. vol. 2. p. 25, 28, 29, 30, 36, &c.

P. 215. l. 23. *He inſinuates that he adopted the Logos from Philo*] Early Opinions, vol. 2. p. 15, 18, 19.

P. 216. l. 8. *Philo, an eminent Jew of Alexandria*] Euſeb. Ecc. Hiſt. lib. 2. c. 5. Cave Script. Ecc. vol. 1. p. 21. Philonis Op. Edit. Colon. p. 3, 5, 71. 552, &c. &c.

P. 217. l. 20. *A tradition has prevailed in the Church*] Photii Bibliotheca, Cod. 105. p. 278.

P. 219. l. 20. *If Juſtin Martyr had corrupted the doctrines of Chriſtianity*, &c.] Baltus ſur la Platoniſme des Peres, paſſim. Irenæus, lib. 1. c. 31.

P. 224. l. 12. *We do not derive the opinions which we maintain from others*, &c.] Juſtini Apol. p. 143. Irenæus, lib. 1. c. 3. Tertullian. De Præſcrip. Hær. p. 238, 243. Idem, adverſus Marcion. l. 4. c. 5. Euſebius contra Hieroclem, p. 540.

P. 227. l. 24. *In order to render Tertullian conſiſtent with himſelf*] Tertullianus adv. Praxeam, p. 634, 635. Cave Scriptores Ecc. p. 93. Prieſtley's Early Opinions, vol. 3. p. 265, 266, 267, &c.

P. 231. l. 22. *Pliny in his Epiſtle, Lucian in his Hiſtory of the Death of Peregrinus, and his Dialogue intitled Philopatris*] Lucianus de Morte Peregrini. Ejuſdem

Ejufdem Philopatris, Sect. 12. Plinii Epift. lib. 10. Epift. 97.

P. 233. l. 3. *And here we might multiply the number of our proofs.*] Sulpitii Severi Hift. lib. 2. c. 31. Julianus apud Eufeb. lib. 4. c. 15. Cyril, l. 10. p. 327. Eufebii Præparatio Evang. lib. 1. c. 5.

Dr. Prieftley is much difpleafed at Mofheim, for relating that the Chriftian Converts of Paleftine deferted the Laws of Mofes, in confequence of the Edicts of Hadrian, whilft they ftill retained the Orthodox Faith. But furely the reprefentation made by Mofheim is warranted by the words of Sulpicius. " Maxima Chriftianorum in Paleftinâ degentium pars " a lege Mofis cui antea paruerat defcifcebat." Mofheim Sæculum fecundum, p. 324. The " maxima " Chriftianorum pars, are the pœne omnes qui Chrif- " tum Deum fub legis obfervatione credebant" exprefsly mentioned by Sulpicius. The remaining part of Mofheim's fentence may be inferred from the general reprefentation of Sulpicius, and more particularly from this remark, " Nimirum id Domino " ordinante difpofitum, ut legis Servitus a libertate " Fidei atque Ecclefiæ tolleretur." After a clofe comparifon of the two writers, furely no one will be inclined to agree with Dr. P. that Sulpicius Severus is not *favourable* to the account of Mofheim.

Mofheim's willingnefs to find Orthodox Chriftians *fomewhere*, which Dr. P. is fo complaifant as to impute to him, would never have led that candid and judicious writer to affert what he knew to be unfounded. I am difpofed to give him full credit for his affertion, when he declares, " Neque enim quæ

Y " ex

" ex aliorum opinione, fed quæ reipsâ, fi veteres non
" fallunt fcriptores, inter Chriftianos, gefta effent,
" referre *volui.*"

Præfat. in Res geftas ante Conftant.

P. 239. l. 21. *They were not addreffed to individuals, in whofe poffeffion they continued in concealment*] Coloff. 4. 15, 16. Potteri Prælect. vol. 2. p. 31.

P. 240. l. 25. *The Works of Matthew, Mark, and Luke, which had been for fome time well known*] Eufeb. Ecc. Hift. lib. 3. c. 24. lib. 6. c. 14. Photii Bibliotheca, No. 254. p. 1403.

P. 243. l. 3. *The noble Author of the Letters on Hiftory.*] Bolingbroke's Letters, 5. p. 143. Octavo.

P. 246. l. 2. *The leading facts relative to the Author of Chriftianity, and the leading topicks of his inftructions may be collected from the writings of the Apoftolical Fathers.*] Clementis Epift. Sect. 7, 16, 21, 35, 36, 38, 42, 46, 48, 49, 58. Polycarpi Epift. Sect. 1, 2, 5, 6, 8, 12. Ignatius ad Ephef. Sect. 1, 3, 4, 18, 19, 20. Ad Magnef. Sect. 7, 8, 9, 11, 13. Ad Trallian. Sect. 9, 10. Ad Roman. Sect. 3, 6. Ad Philadelph. Sect. 4, 8, 9, 10. Ad Smyrn. 1, 2, 3.

P. 248. l. 5. *The authenticity of the larger Epiftles of Ignatius and of the Apoftolical Conftitutions has been difputed,* &c.] Jortin's Remarks, vol. 1. p. 62. Dupin on the Canon, vol. 2. p. 148. Pearfoni Vindiciæ, p. 1. c. 4. Lardner's Credibility, vol. 10. p. 319. Ed. 1.

P. 251. l. 10. *If borrowed ideas be cited by an author not in identical but correfpondent terms,* &c.] Owen's Mode of Quotation, p. 11. Clerici Differt. 3. p. 542.

P. 252. l. 1. *Some very remarkable paffages, in which are refpectively contained the fubftance of a quotation from*

St.

AUTHORITIES.

St. Luke, and the exact words both of St. Matthew and of St. John] Compare Clementis Epift. Sect. 46. with Luke c. 6. v. 36. Ejufdem Sect. 13. with Matt. c. 7. v. 1. Ignatii Epift. ad Magnef. Sect. 8. with John c. 8. v. 29. and John c. 1. v. 1. Ejufdem Epift. ad Polycarpum, Sect. 2. with Matthew, c. 10. v. 16. Polycarpi Epift. Sect. 7. with Matthew, c. 26. v. 41.

P. 253. l. 2. *The firft Epiftle to the Corinthians is exprefsly afcribed to St. Paul by Clement*] Lardner's Credibility, v. 2. p. 63, 85, 201, 202, 220. Millii Prolegomena, p. 17.

P. 254. l. 11. *That Clement, Ignatius and Polycarp frequently expand the ideas of St. Paul with confiderable fuccefs, is evident from feveral paffages*] Compare Clement. Epift. Sect. 49. with 1 Corinth. c. 13. v. 7, &c. Ignatii Epift. ad Polycarp. Sect. 6. with Ephef. c. 6. v. 13. Clementis Epift. Sect. 36 and 55, with Hebrews, c. 1. v. 3. and c. 12. v. 1, &c. Polycarpi Epift. Sect. 4. with Hebrews, c. 4. v. 12.

P. 254. l. 19. *No one was more eminent for faithful atteftation to the records of Chriftianity than Juftin Martyr*] Lardner, vol. 2. p. 254. Thirlby in Juftin, p. 21. Apologia prima, p. 98. It is rather doubtful how far Juftin Martyr alludes to St. Mark. Jones, Lardner and Thirlby fuppofe that he cites his Gofpel in a few inftances. Compare Mark 3. 16. with Juftin. Mart. p. 20. Mark 8. 31. with Apol. p. 327. Mark 12. 30. with Apol. p. 25.

P. 255. l. 12. *Irenæus, Bifhop of Lyons, left an ample account of the New Teftament*] Irenæus, lib. 1. c. 3. lib. 3. c. 1, 10, 11, 14, 15. Lardner, v. 2. p. 343, &c.

P. 258. l. 15. *The curious and minute observer, from the frequent usage of some remarkable words, may contend that Ignatius had read the Epistle to Philemon, as well as that addressed to Titus*] Lardner, vol. 2. p. 173, 174. Irenæus, lib. 5. c. 1. James, c. 2. v. 23.

P. 261. l. 21. *This persuasion, so sublimely expressed in the words of Irenæus, which was common to the Church at large, was rational and judicious*] Irenæus, lib. 2. c. 46, 47, &c. lib. 3. c. 1, 11, 18, 21. Clement. Epist. c. 42, 44, 47. Polycarp. c. 7. Justini Apol. p. 97. Potteri Prælectiones, vol. 2. p. 114. Dupin's Canon, vol. 2. p. 12.

P. 263. l. 9. *The unwearied diligence of Plutarch, the elaborate concisness of Tacitus, the extensive researches of Dion Cassius, and of Josephus, did not secure them against occasional deviations from truth.*] Stradæ Prolusiones, Sect. 2. lib. 1. Warburton on Prodigies, p. 98. Jortin's Critical Remarks, vol. 2. p. 74.

P. 264. l. 9. *The neglect of accurate inquiry may not unfairly be imputed to Plutarch, when he asserts that Plato held the doctrine of a good and of an evil principle.*] Cudworth's Intellectual System, p. 218, 378. Brucker's Philosophia Critica, vol. 1. p. 632.

P. 274. l. 2. *The general conformity of our Establishment has been celebrated by its own members at home, and its admirers abroad, as its most illustrious and most distinguishing characteristick*] Cave Hist. Ecc. in Dedicatione. Qui Ecclesiam habeas in tuo Regno, partim jam olim ita institutam, ut ad florentis quondam Ecclesiæ formam, nulla hodie propius accedat, quam tua, inter vel excessu vel defectu peccantes mediam viam secuta. Isaaci Casauboni

Cafauboni Præfat. in Animad. in Baronii Annales: Grotius de Veritate, p. 312.

P. 282. l. 23. *The faireſt and moſt excellent examples are held up to our imitation*] Operæ pretium eſt ſicut in precepta vitæ a Chriſto et Apoſtolis tradita tanquam in normam, ita in mores et fanctimoniam primorum Chriſtianorum tanquam in exemplum intueri; quod non fine fructu et voluptate, facturas mihi perfuadeo candidas et Chriſtum amantes animas. Fabricii Lux Evangelii, p. 195.

If it were neceſſary, at the cloſe of my work, to apologize to the publick for having purſued a train of Study with a view to polemical difcuſſions; I think I could not juſtify my conduct in terms more appoſite, or ſentiments more rational, than by citing the remarks of the learned Fabricius.

Apoſtoli quidem et horum inſiſtentes veſtigiis alii præclari viri ſubinde aucto adverſariorum numero non dubitarunt pro aſſerendâ, quam profiterentur, religione, vocem adhibere et calamum, ne ulterius tacere diffidentiæ ſignum eſſet, et ut ignari de fundamento ſpei noſtræ docerentur, dubii confirmarentur, nec inimici in objectionum ſuarum argutiis exultarent, falsâque earum ſpecie poſſent incautos decipere. Imprimis vero hoc debere ſe exiſtimarunt Deo et Salvatori ſuo, ut quam ipſe tribuerat vocem ac facultatem eam pro illius gloriâ et veritate vindicandâ impenderent libenter. Non mirum porro eſt hoc veniſſe multis in mentem; quid enim eſſet in quo

quo libentius verfaretur Chriftiani hominis meditatio et ftylus, quam in explicandâ et tuendâ ab objectionibus fanctiffimâ religione, five ad animum fuum confirmandum, five ad alios erudiendos aut ftabiliendos, five ad inimicorum retudendos impetus et cauffationes removendas. Nec tamen ideo quifquam neget veriffima effe certiffimaque, quæ toties a tot præclaris ingeniis de integro demonftranda fumuntur. Religionis Chriftianæ Veritas, p. 30.

FINIS.

www.ingramcontent.com/pod-product-compliance
Lightning Source LLC
Chambersburg PA
CBHW030304240426
43673CB00040B/1058